INFINITUM
Written and Illustrated by
G.M.B. Chomichuk

Infinitum *is dedicated to*
my mother and father,
whatever their souls are made of
                    it's the same.

Thank you:

Tara Cole-McCaffrey, Lief and Finnley, for sharing all the good stuff.

Michael Sanders and Leanne Veale, for being good creative supporters, good allies
and good friends.

Ariel Gordon, Jonathan Ball, James Gillespie, Dan Bohemier first among readers.

Special thank you to the staff and owners of The Cornerstone restaurant in Osborne
Village who let me write and illustrate most of the first draft between helpings of
chicken dumplings.

PREFACE.

When Words Collide.

That's why you are holding this book.

The When Words Collide literary festival was host of the Auroras, and as a nominee I was happy to attend. I met Randy McCharles, we shook hands and spoke about how the convention had grown and why he was architect of such a thing. "Look, people make books. These people." When Words Collide was there to celebrate that and to bring creative people together.

ChiZine, ChiGraphic's surly parent, had a big spread of scary books. I was taken by the true talent of their main cover artist Erik Mohr, so I started gushing a bit to the fellow behind the table. Turns out that was Brett Savory, co-publisher. We talked books, we talked graphic novels. *The Imagination Manifesto* didn't win an Aurora and after a busy few days I went home to Winnipeg. People who understand conventions know that you never go home from one with nothing. Sure your suit-cases are full of new books, but that isn't what I mean. A good convention sends you home full of possibilities. I had made new friends and new connections and right then I knew something had happened. The way you *know*.

That year a documentary crew for the film *Artists By Night* had been following me around. The director, Kelly Reiss, filmed me as I balanced work and family and made things in my studio late into the night. Along the way I put together two pitches for ChiZine. I had hoped one of them would be right for them. Kelly took some delight, I think, in watching me try to figure out which pitch would do the trick. Kelly and Thomas Bartlett stayed late filming at the Secret Headquarters while I made, then picked, my pages to send off.

Brett Savory and Sandra Kasturi have carved out a strange territory in Canadian genre with ChiZine; it's a place filled with monsters and odd sorts and I feel quite at home here. As for the pitches, ChiGraphic accepted both books. *Midnight City* will be out next year from Chi-Graphic but you can peek at some work from it in the back of this very volume.

I'll admit that making books is not for the feint hearted or those fear-ful of monsters. But I love it all the same. Making *Infinitum* was not without its share of difficult moments but none of them had to do with the book itself. You can read what I mean about that in the Afterword, but it sort of spoils the plot so leave it to the end.

Infinitum is noir. *Infinitum* is a love story. *Infinitum* is piled on the bones of great time travel stories and is my attempt to break the rules as I saw them.

A book itself is a time machine. You can go back to any point you like and see it again, it comes from the past and is always heading toward the future. Everyone a book encounters is changed by its passing. When you turn the pages you force the characters ahead into their uncertain future. That future is already written for them, yet godlike, it is up to you to reveal it.

We all get ideas for books. Ideas are easy. Making books requires that many things and many people all line up just so, just right. A chain of events to change a collection of pages in the studio into something more. For me it was the right people, in the right place, at the right time. When it works you *know* it. To get it right more often may require a time machine.

Maybe you've got an idea for a book. I hope so. I hope you take it with you out into the word. I hope you take all your hard work and show it to people and that it grows into the thing you want. Maybe I'll see you at When Words Collide, and you can show me *your* book. When Words Collide is not the only fine genre convention out there, but it is the reason you are holding this book this way. If you're reading a physical copy, bring it over and I'll draw you something on the inside cover. It's the least I could do. It's you, after all, that powers this little machine.

G.M.B. Chomichuk
Just after midnight.

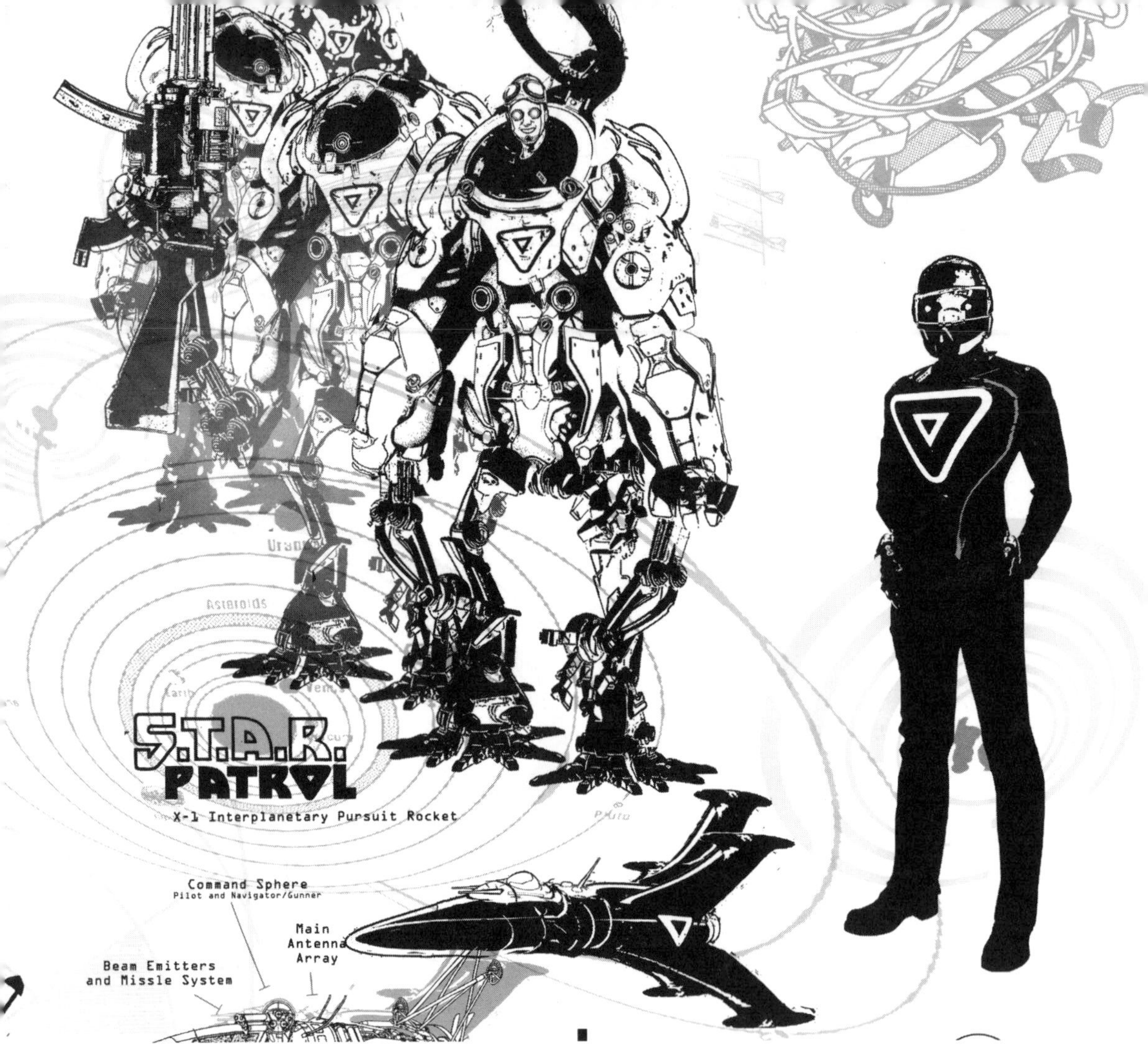
S.T.A.R.
PATROL
X-1 Interplanetary Pursuit Rocket
Command Sphere
Pilot and Navigator/Gunner
Main Antenna Array
Beam Emitters and Missle System

"He's more myself than I am. Whatever our souls are made of, his and mine are the same."

Emily Bronte

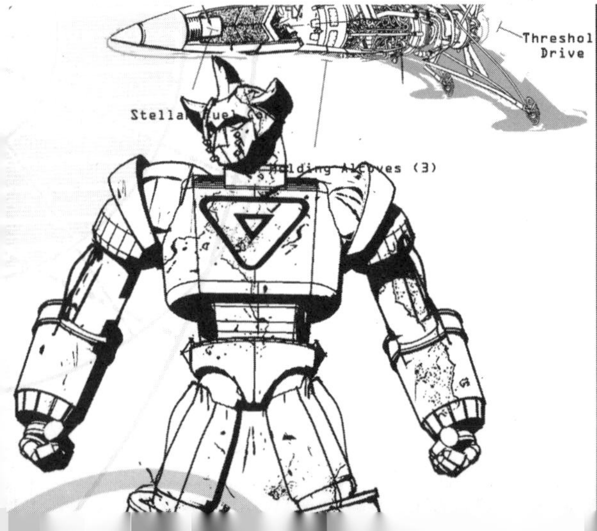
Threshol
Drive

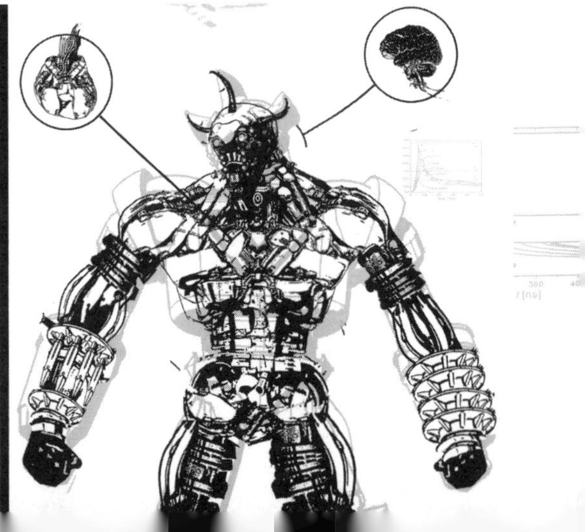

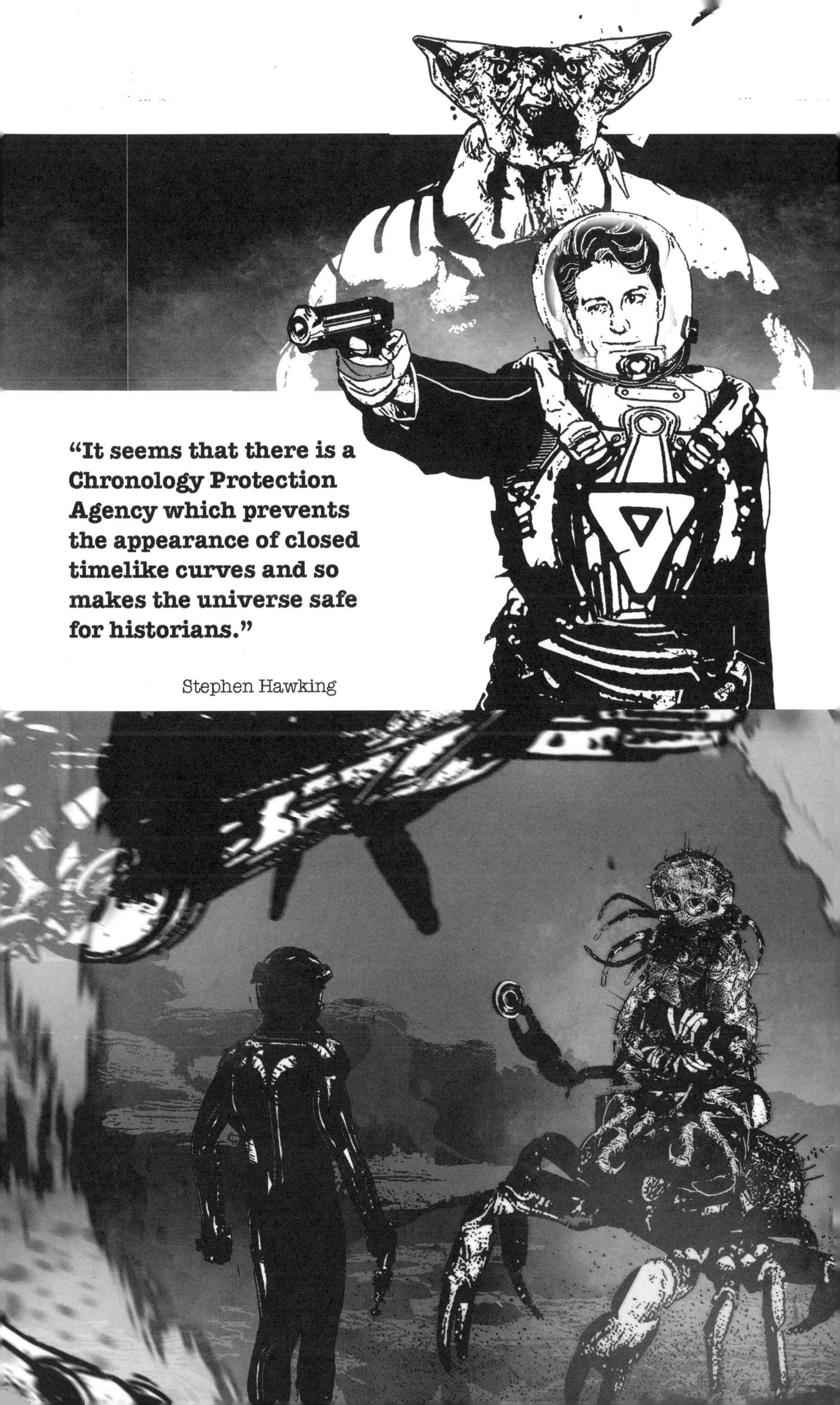

"It seems that there is a Chronology Protection Agency which prevents the appearance of closed timelike curves and so makes the universe safe for historians."

Stephen Hawking

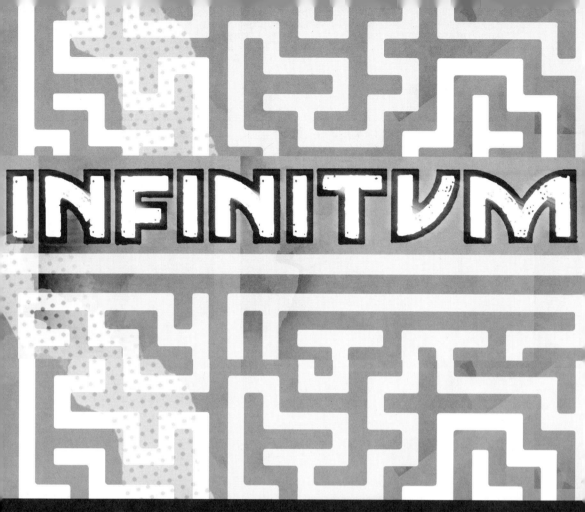

INFINITUM

You're back. Here again. A new beginning.

Will things be different this time?

Only time will tell.

Do you ever feel like things are moving too fast? Have you ever felt the pace of life is just getting away from you?

Of course. Everyone feels that way sometimes. That's just progress, I guess.

No. That's the Infinitum. Time running out.
That's the future being fed to the past.

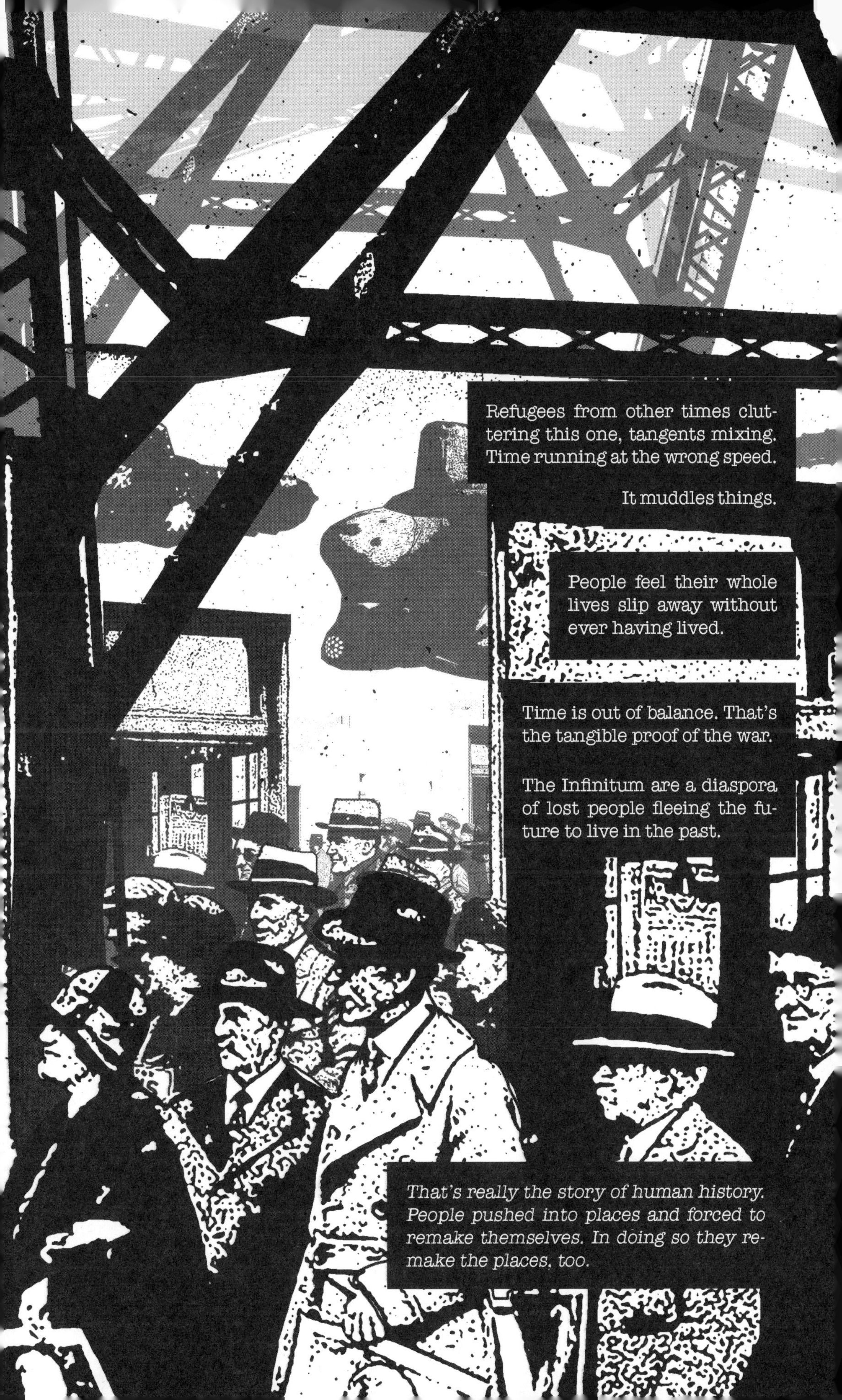

Refugees from other times cluttering this one, tangents mixing. Time running at the wrong speed.
It muddles things.
People feel their whole lives slip away without ever having lived.
Time is out of balance. That's the tangible proof of the war.
The Infinitum are a diaspora of lost people fleeing the future to live in the past.
That's really the story of human history. People pushed into places and forced to remake themselves. In doing so they remake the places, too.

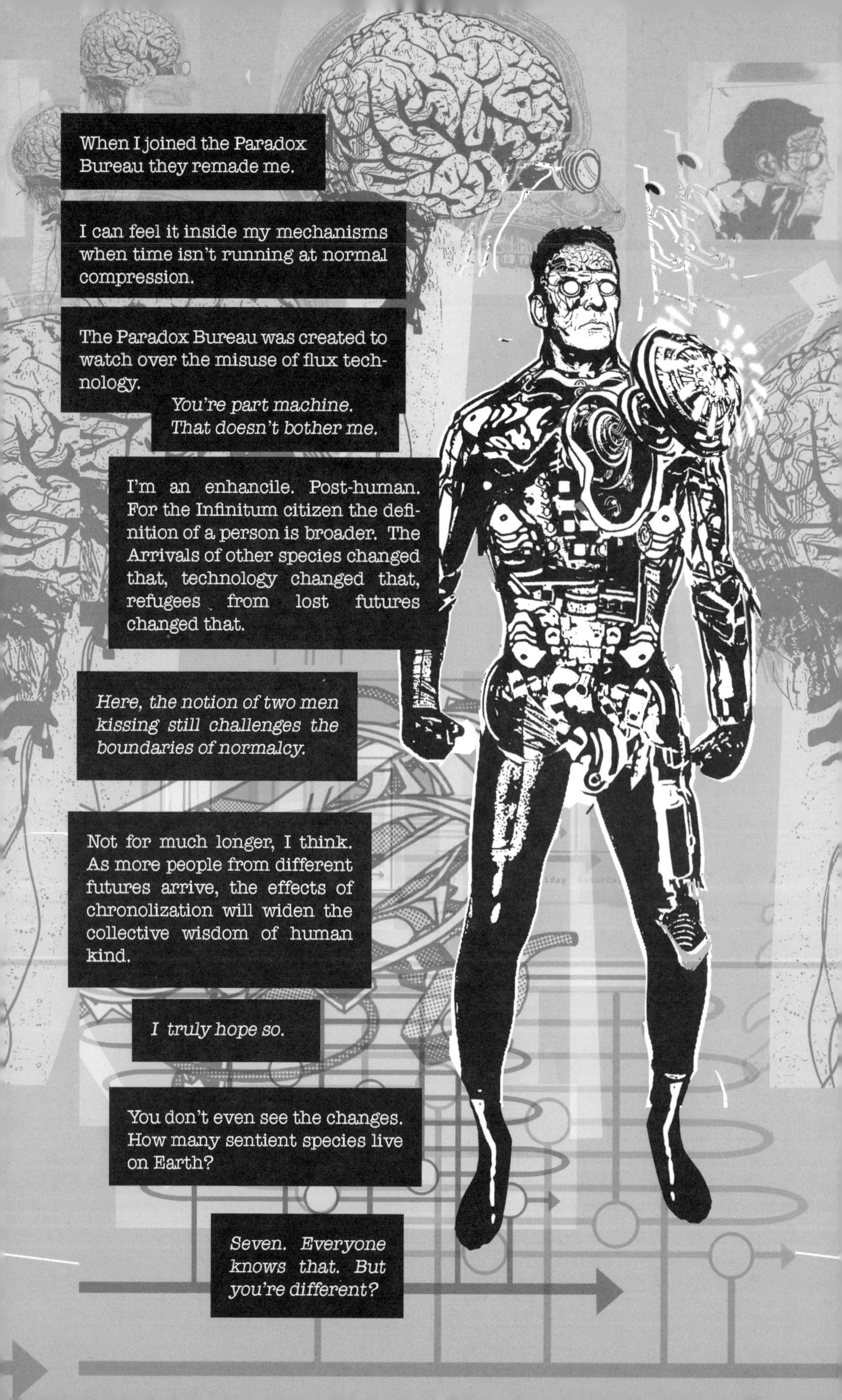

When I joined the Paradox Bureau they remade me.
I can feel it inside my mechanisms when time isn't running at normal compression.
The Paradox Bureau was created to watch over the misuse of flux technology.
You're part machine. That doesn't bother me.
I'm an enhancile. Post-human. For the Infinitum citizen the definition of a person is broader. The Arrivals of other species changed that, technology changed that, refugees from lost futures changed that.
Here, the notion of two men kissing still challenges the boundaries of normalcy.
Not for much longer, I think. As more people from different futures arrive, the effects of chronolization will widen the collective wisdom of human kind.
I truly hope so.
You don't even see the changes. How many sentient species live on Earth?
Seven. Everyone knows that. But you're different?

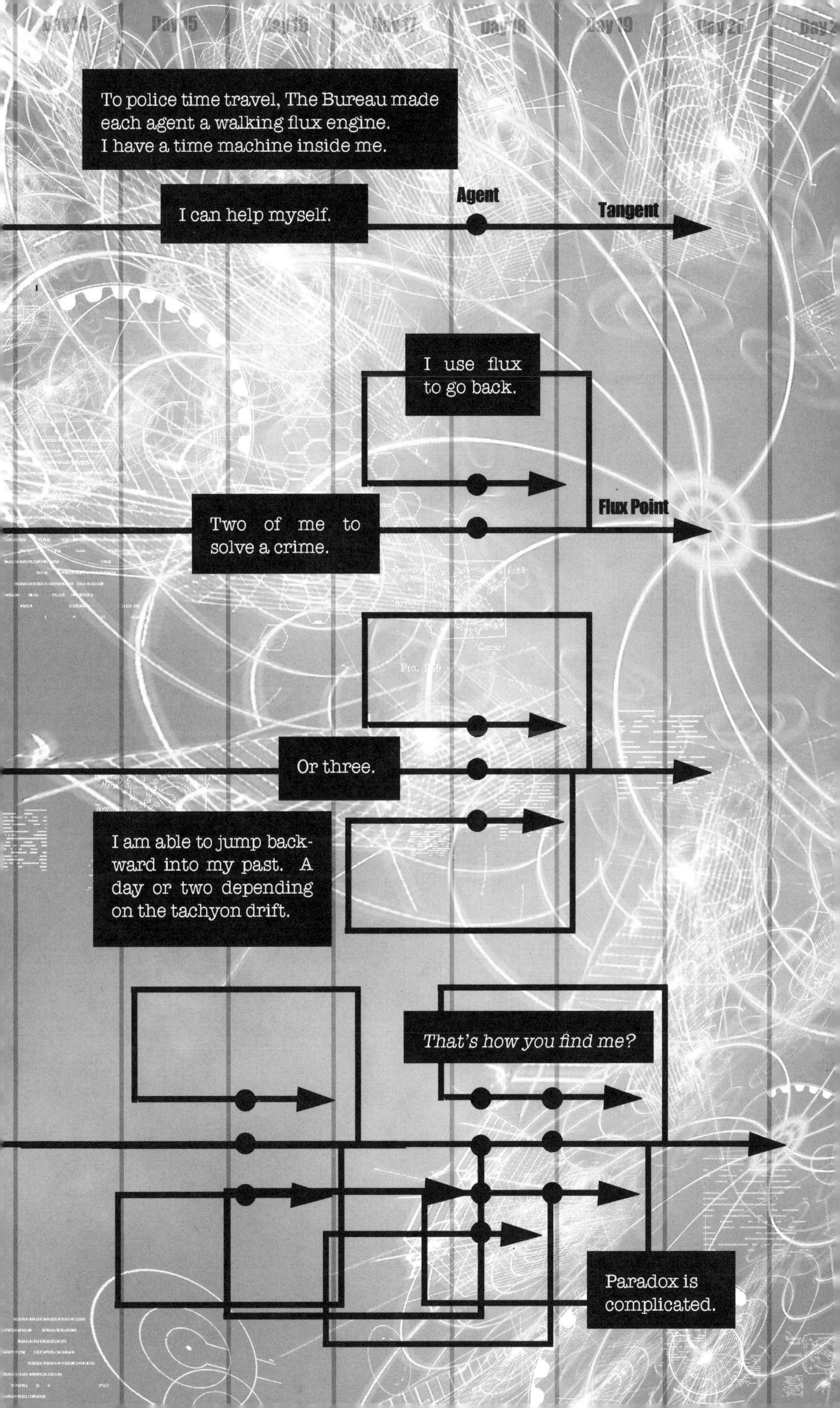

Day 15
Day 19
To police time travel, The Bureau made each agent a walking flux engine. I have a time machine inside me.
Agent
I can help myself.
Tangent
I use flux to go back.
Flux Point
Two of me to solve a crime.
Or three.
I am able to jump backward into my past. A day or two depending on the tachyon drift.
That's how you find me?
Paradox is complicated.

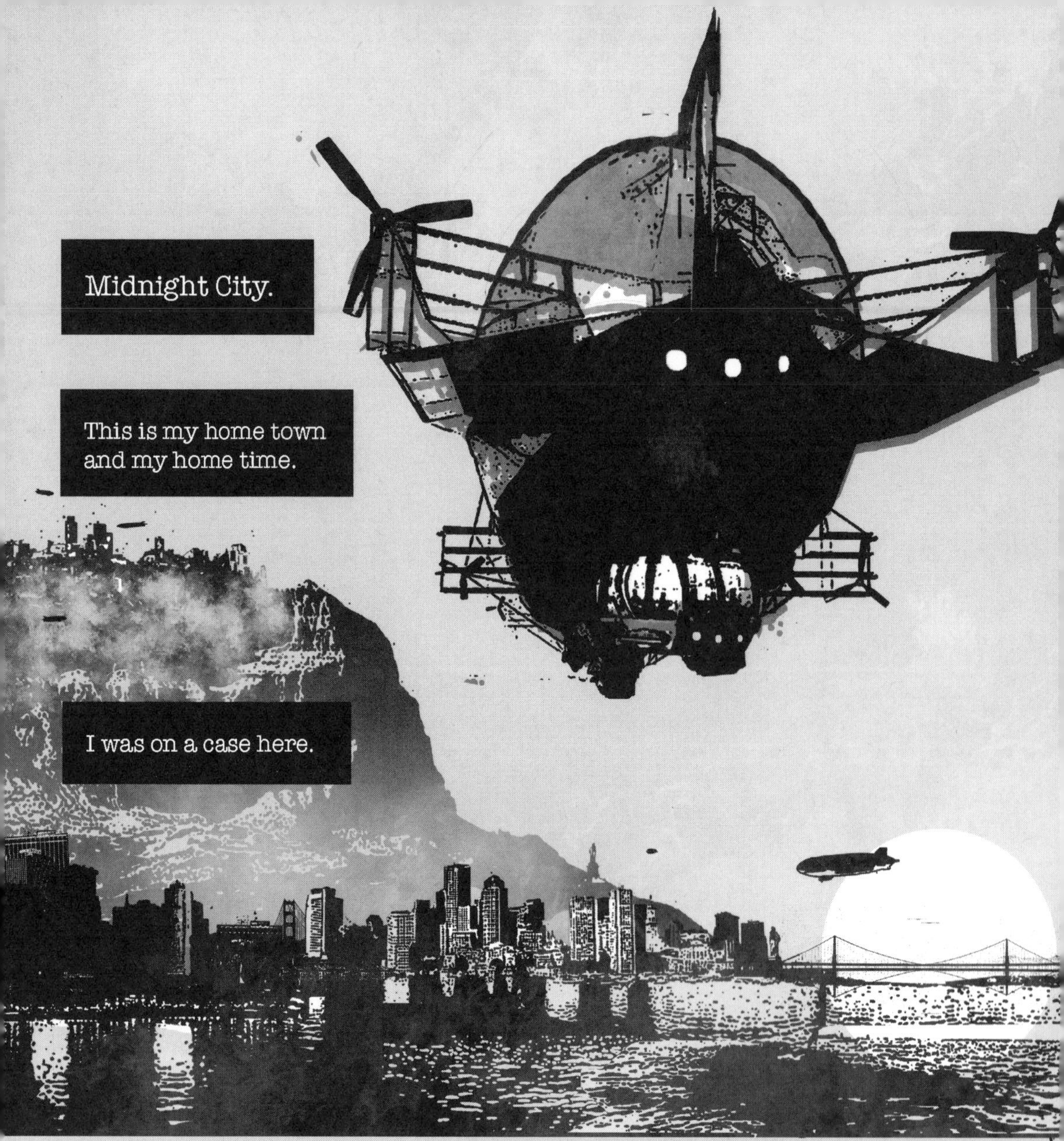

Midnight City.
This is my home town and my home time.
I was on a case here.

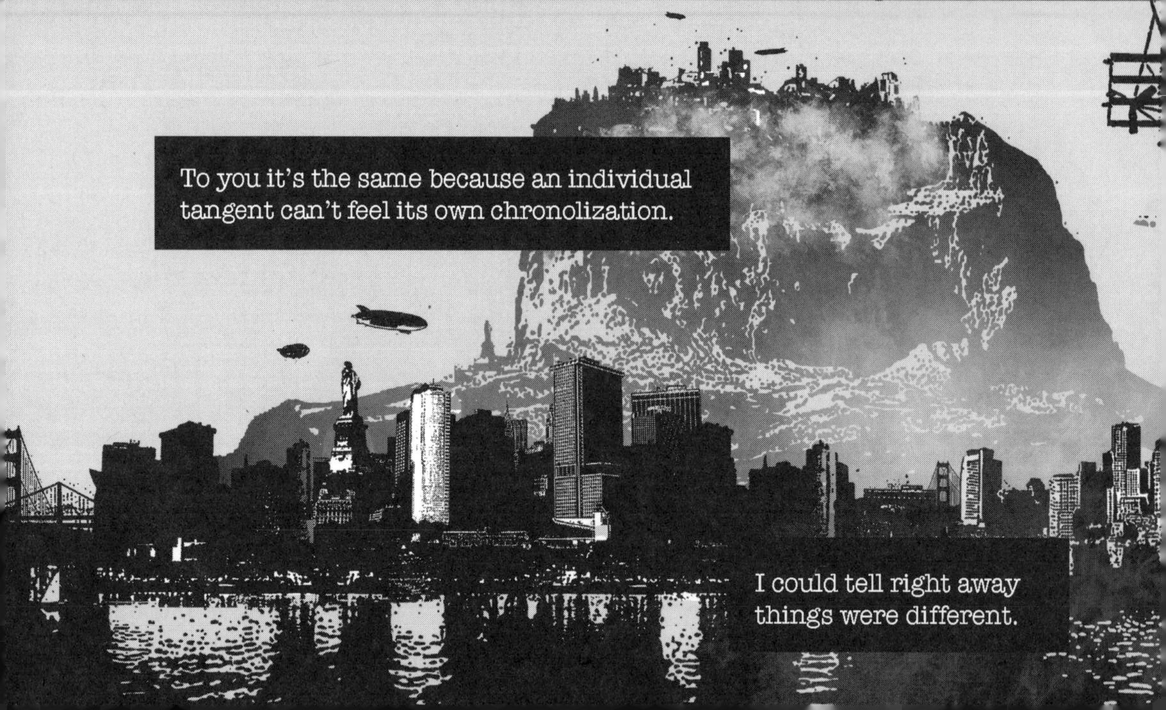

To you it's the same because an individual tangent can't feel its own chronolization.
I could tell right away things were different.

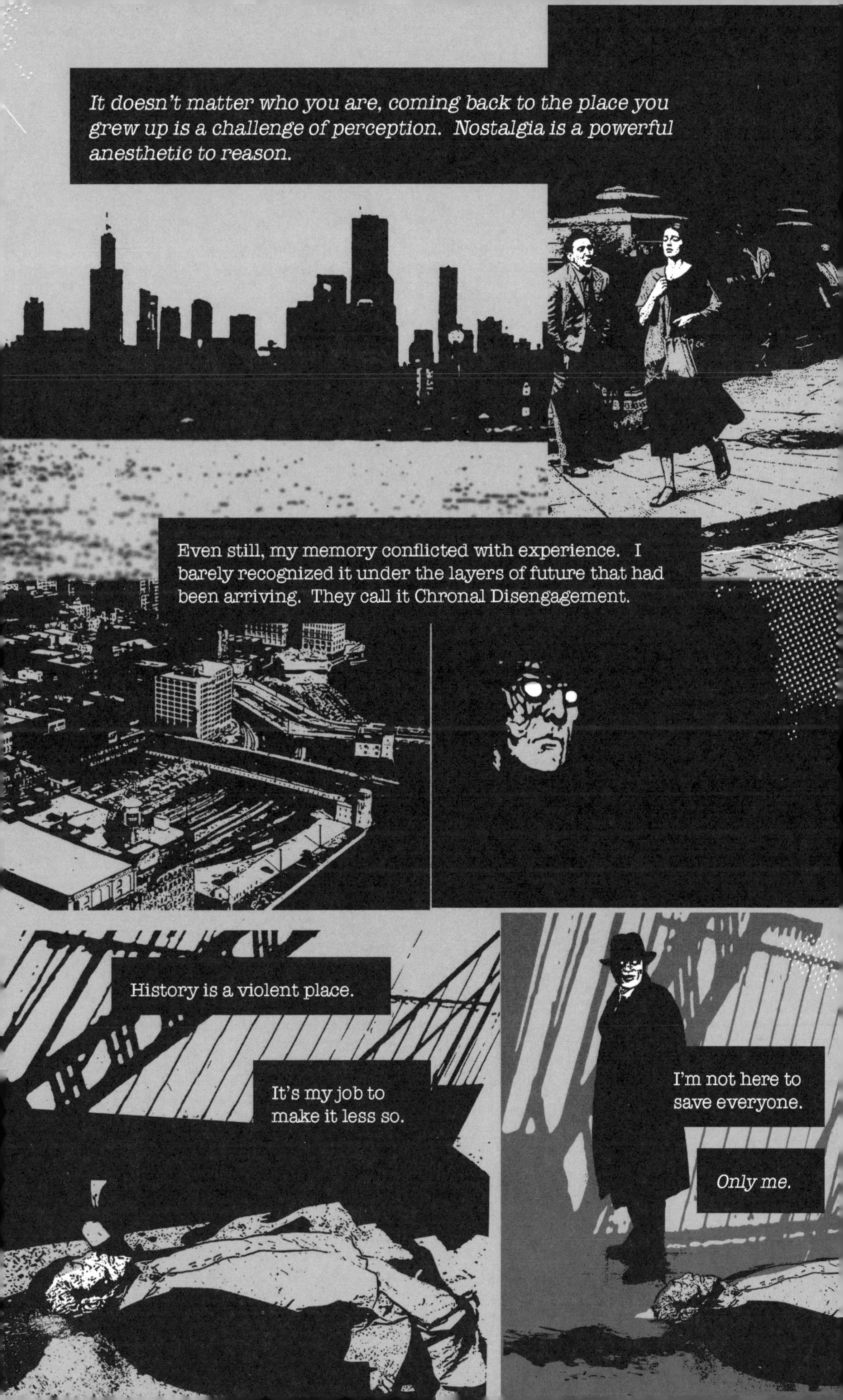
It doesn't matter who you are, coming back to the place you grew up is a challenge of perception. Nostalgia is a powerful anesthetic to reason.
Even still, my memory conflicted with experience. I barely recognized it under the layers of future that had been arriving. They call it Chronal Disengagement.
History is a violent place.
It's my job to make it less so.
I'm not here to save everyone.
Only me.

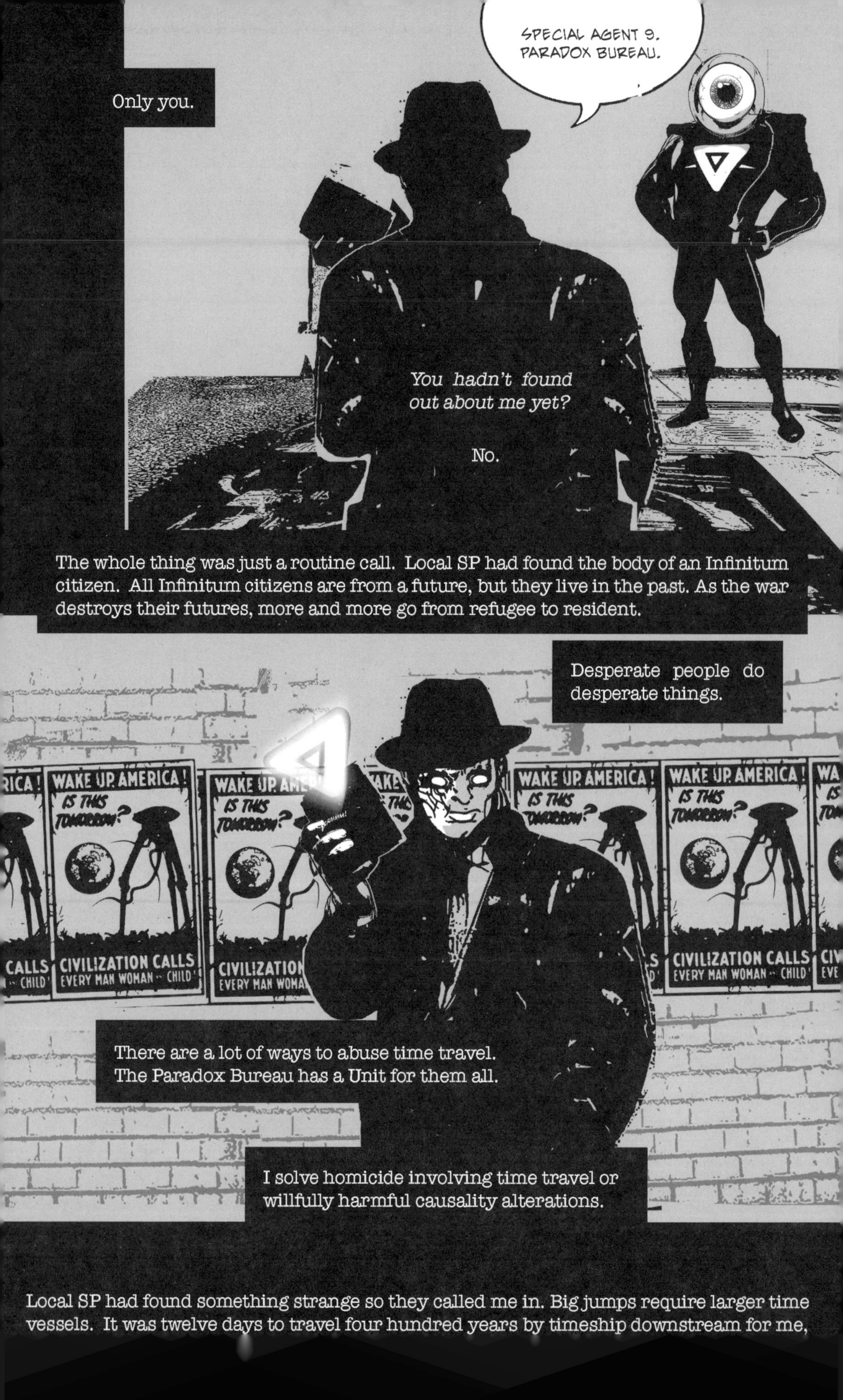

SPECIAL AGENT 9.
PARADOX BUREAU.
Only you.
You hadn't found out about me yet?
No.
The whole thing was just a routine call. Local SP had found the body of an Infinitum citizen. All Infinitum citizens are from a future, but they live in the past. As the war destroys their futures, more and more go from refugee to resident.
Desperate people do desperate things.
WAKE UP AMERICA!
IS THIS TOMORROW?
CIVILIZATION CALLS
EVERY MAN WOMAN - CHILD
There are a lot of ways to abuse time travel. The Paradox Bureau has a Unit for them all.
I solve homicide involving time travel or willfully harmful causality alterations.
Local SP had found something strange so they called me in. Big jumps require larger time vessels. It was twelve days to travel four hundred years by timeship downstream for me,

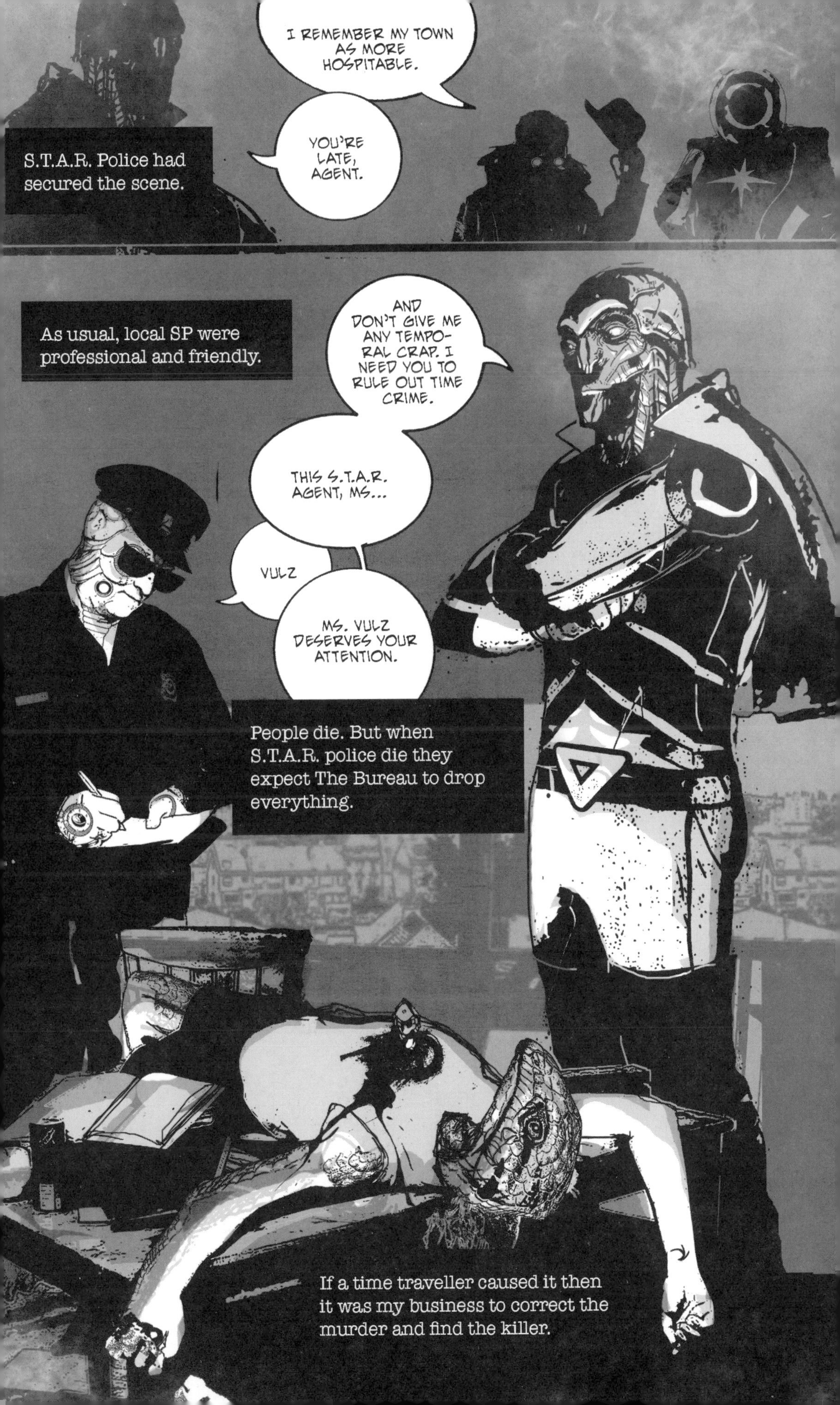
I REMEMBER MY TOWN AS MORE HOSPITABLE.
YOU'RE LATE, AGENT.
S.T.A.R. Police had secured the scene.
As usual, local SP were professional and friendly.
AND DON'T GIVE ME ANY TEMPORAL CRAP. I NEED YOU TO RULE OUT TIME CRIME.
THIS S.T.A.R. AGENT, MS...
VULZ
MS. VULZ DESERVES YOUR ATTENTION.
People die. But when S.T.A.R. police die they expect The Bureau to drop everything.
If a time traveller caused it then it was my business to correct the murder and find the killer.

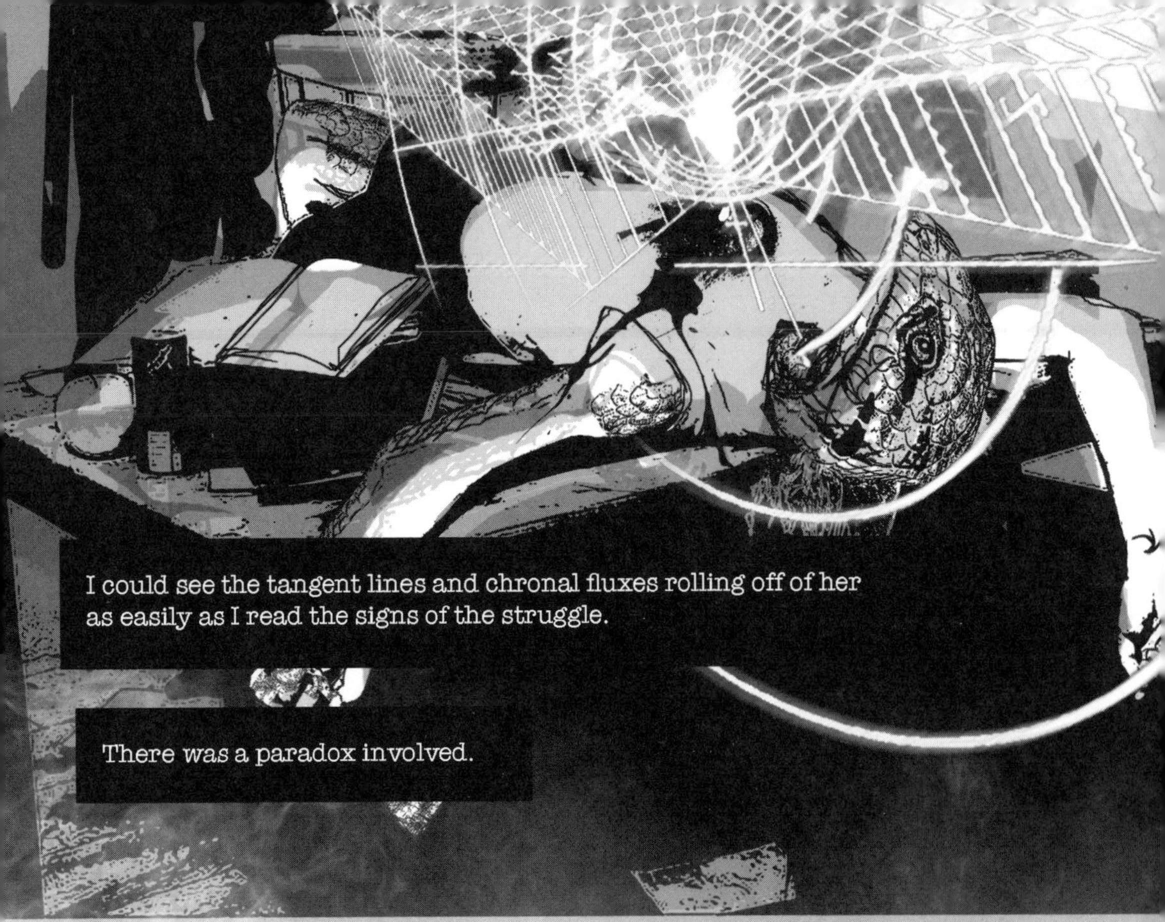

I could see the tangent lines and chronal fluxes rolling off of her as easily as I read the signs of the struggle.
There was a paradox involved.

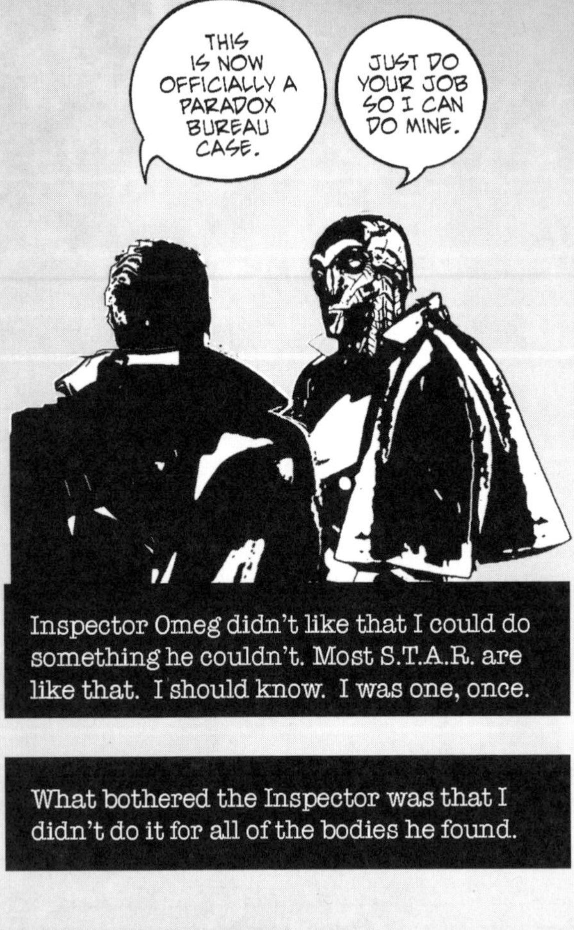

THIS IS NOW OFFICIALLY A PARADOX BUREAU CASE.
JUST DO YOUR JOB SO I CAN DO MINE.
Inspector Omeg didn't like that I could do something he couldn't. Most S.T.A.R. are like that. I should know. I was one, once.
What bothered the Inspector was that I didn't do it for all of the bodies he found.

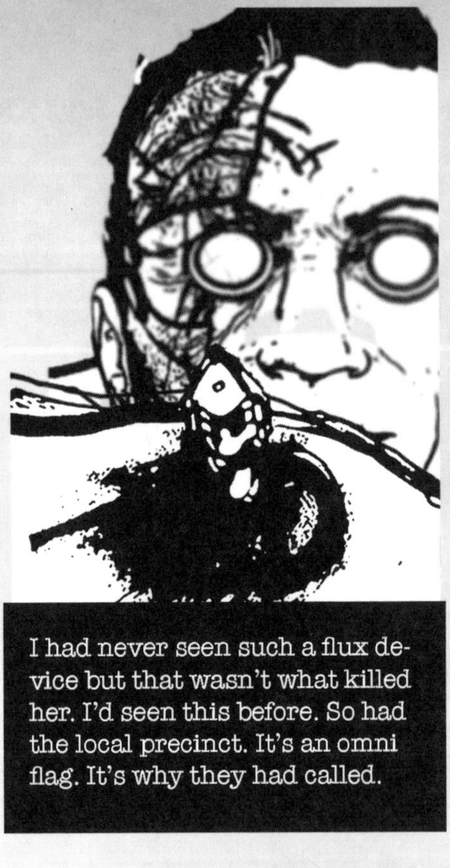

I had never seen such a flux device but that wasn't what killed her. I'd seen this before. So had the local precinct. It's an omni flag. It's why they had called.

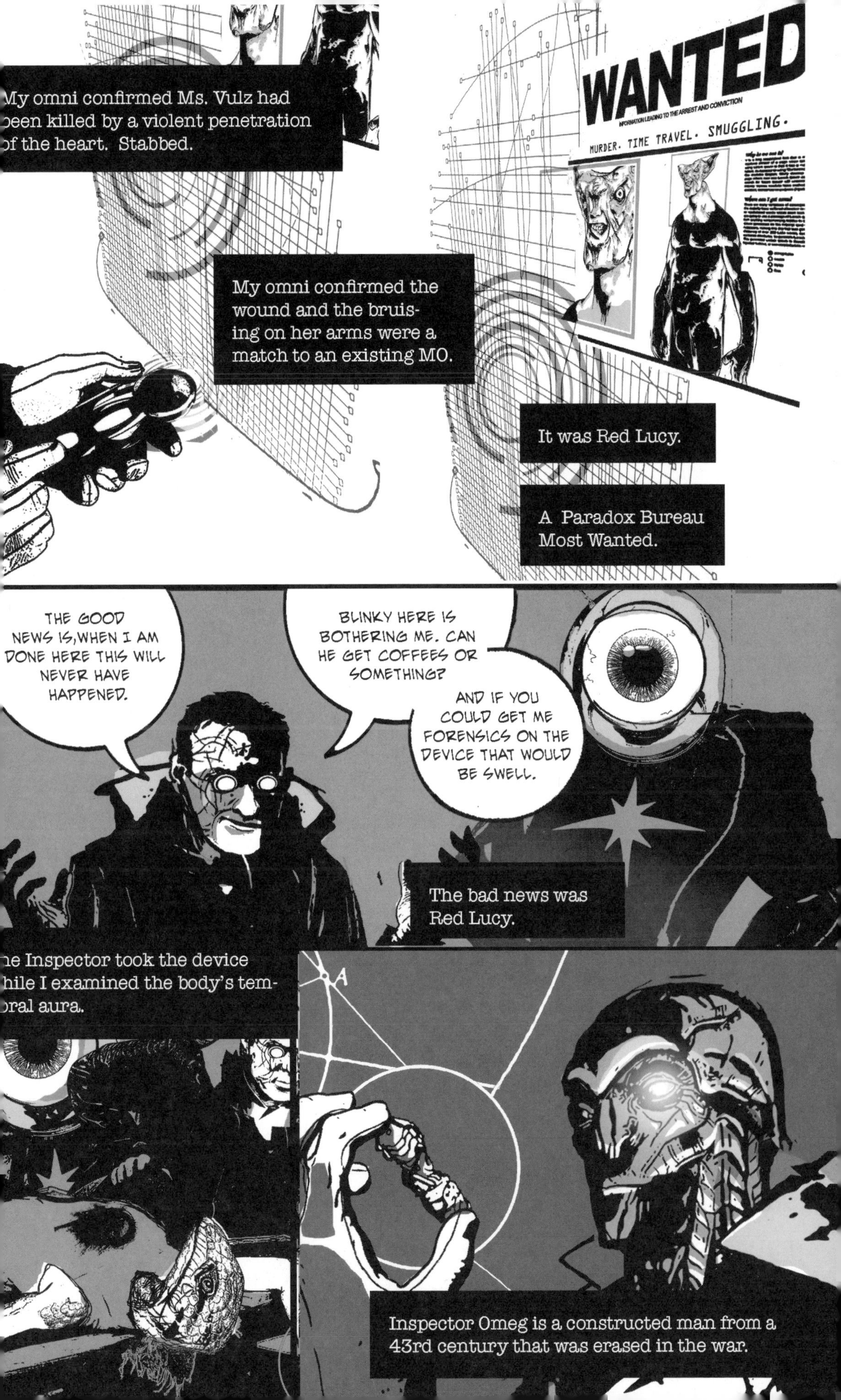
My omni confirmed Ms. Vulz had been killed by a violent penetration of the heart. Stabbed.
WANTED
INFORMATION LEADING TO THE ARREST AND CONVICTION
MURDER. TIME TRAVEL. SMUGGLING.
My omni confirmed the wound and the bruis-ing on her arms were a match to an existing MO.
It was Red Lucy.
A Paradox Bureau Most Wanted.
THE GOOD NEWS IS, WHEN I AM DONE HERE THIS WILL NEVER HAVE HAPPENED.
BLINKY HERE IS BOTHERING ME. CAN HE GET COFFEES OR SOMETHING?
AND IF YOU COULD GET ME FORENSICS ON THE DEVICE THAT WOULD BE SWELL.
The bad news was Red Lucy.
he Inspector took the device hile I examined the body's tem-oral aura.
Inspector Omeg is a constructed man from a 43rd century that was erased in the war.

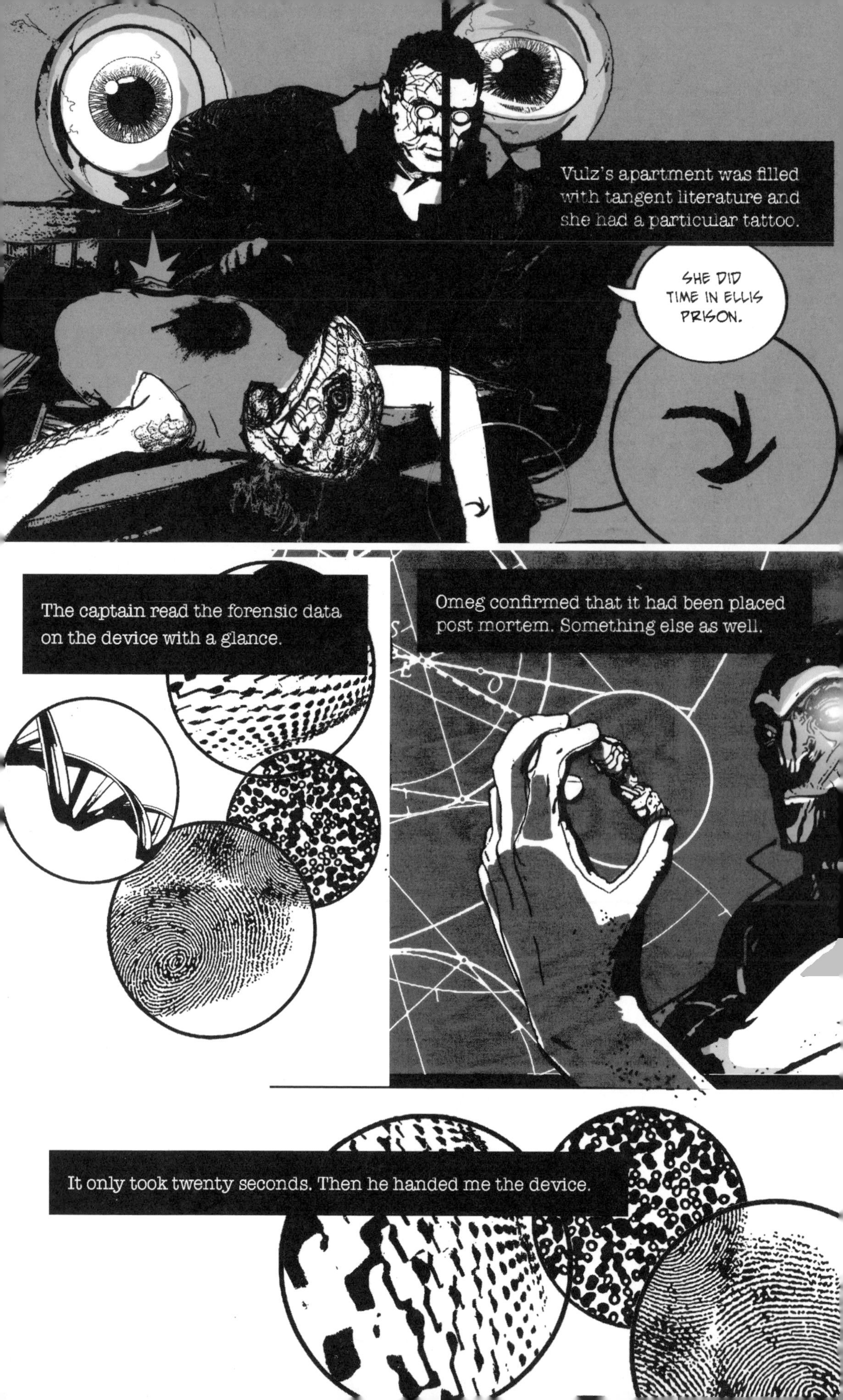
Vulz's apartment was filled with tangent literature and she had a particular tattoo.
SHE DID TIME IN ELLIS PRISON.
The captain read the forensic data on the device with a glance.
Omeg confirmed that it had been placed post mortem. Something else as well.
It only took twenty seconds. Then he handed me the device.

He pointed his finger and uploaded the file directly to my omni.

Fingerprints. DNA. Temporal Decay Signature. Cell analysis.

The inspector confirmed I had put the device there.

Somewhen I had gotten very close to Red Lucy. It had already happened in chronological order, but not yet to me.

WANTED

INFORMATION LEADING

MURDER. TIME TRAVEL. HIJACK

Red Lucy is a known terrorist and co-founder of the Tangent Separatists. She had personally murdered hundreds of Infinitum citizens in an attempt to achieve their goal.

How could she be against the Infinitum? Wasn't she a refugee, too? Wasn't what she was doing the same?

The separatists want to stop the flow of future to the past. Stop chronolization.

XENO CLASS EPSILON

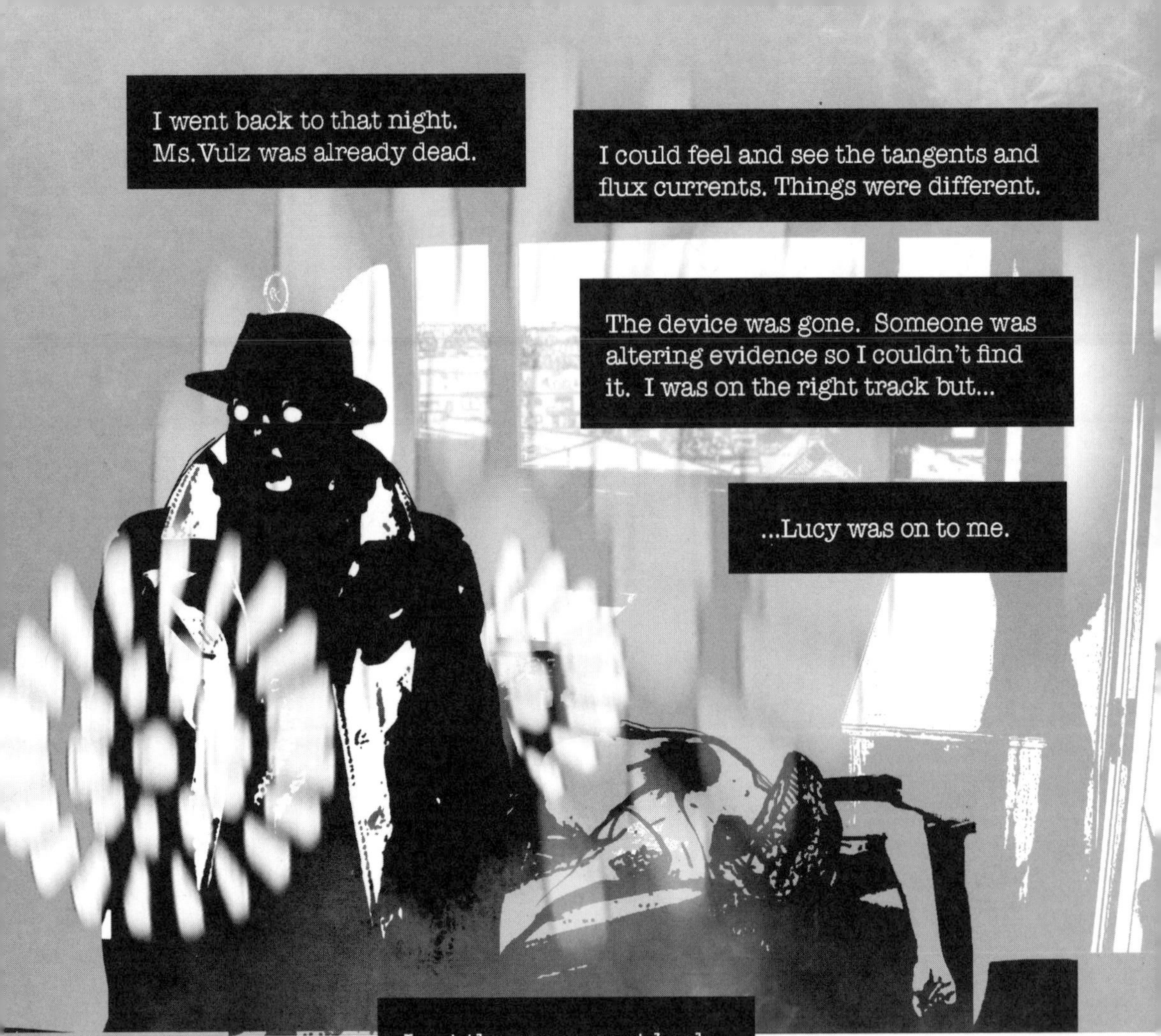
I went back to that night.
Ms. Vulz was already dead.
I could feel and see the tangents and flux currents. Things were different.
The device was gone. Someone was altering evidence so I couldn't find it. I was on the right track but...
...Lucy was on to me.

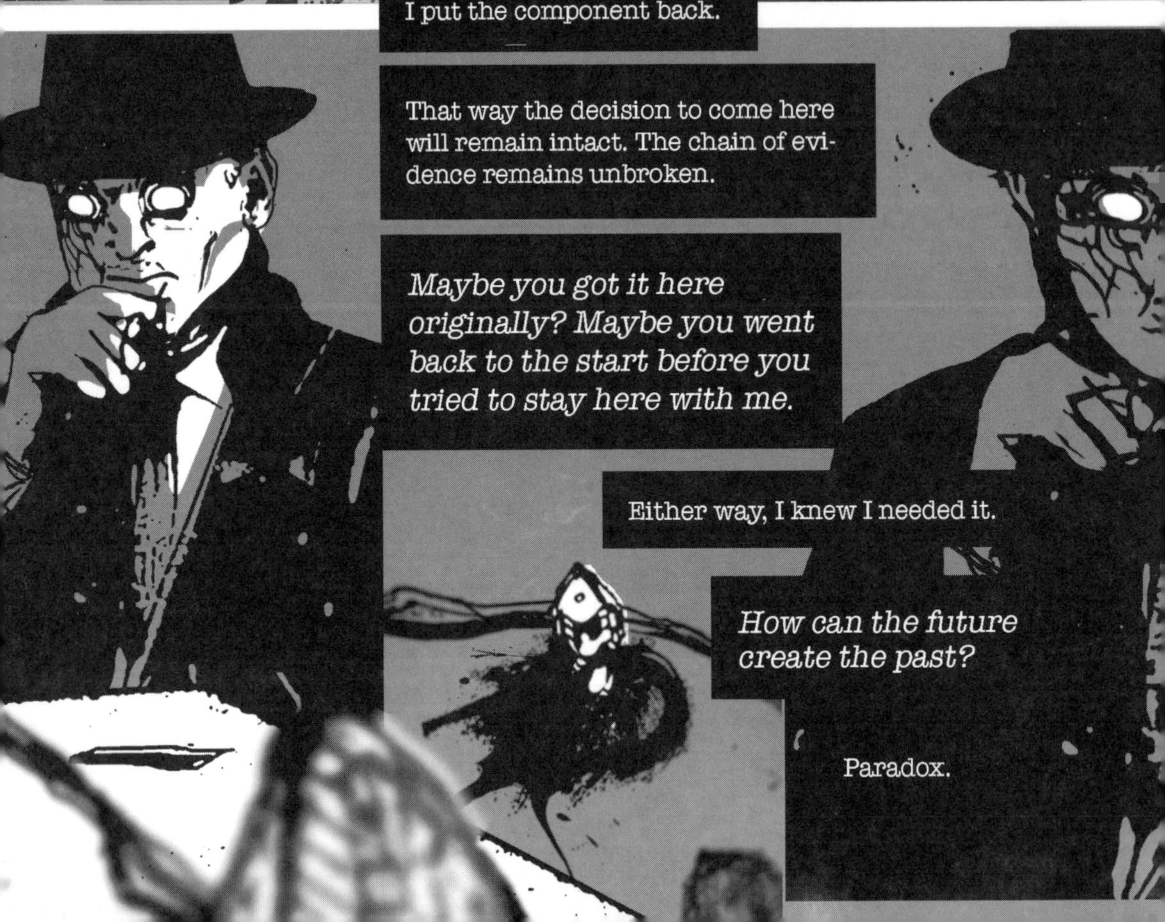
I put the component back.
That way the decision to come here will remain intact. The chain of evidence remains unbroken.
Maybe you got it here originally? Maybe you went back to the start before you tried to stay here with me.
Either way, I knew I needed it.
How can the future create the past?
Paradox.

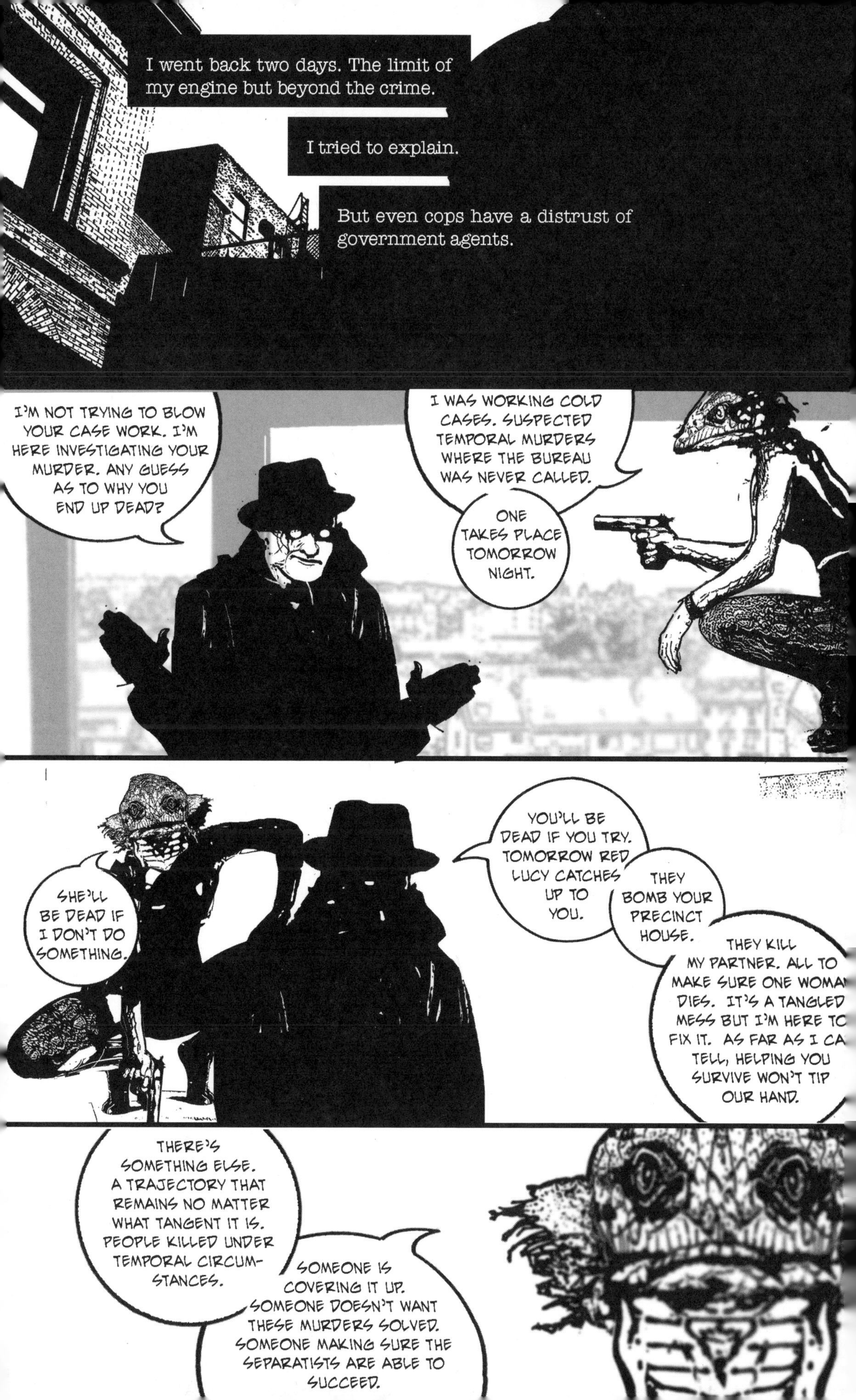
I went back two days. The limit of my engine but beyond the crime.
I tried to explain.
But even cops have a distrust of government agents.
I'M NOT TRYING TO BLOW YOUR CASE WORK. I'M HERE INVESTIGATING YOUR MURDER. ANY GUESS AS TO WHY YOU END UP DEAD?
I WAS WORKING COLD CASES. SUSPECTED TEMPORAL MURDERS WHERE THE BUREAU WAS NEVER CALLED.
ONE TAKES PLACE TOMORROW NIGHT.
SHE'LL BE DEAD IF I DON'T DO SOMETHING.
YOU'LL BE DEAD IF YOU TRY. TOMORROW RED LUCY CATCHES UP TO YOU.
THEY BOMB YOUR PRECINCT HOUSE.
THEY KILL MY PARTNER. ALL TO MAKE SURE ONE WOMAN DIES. IT'S A TANGLED MESS BUT I'M HERE TO FIX IT. AS FAR AS I CAN TELL, HELPING YOU SURVIVE WON'T TIP OUR HAND.
THERE'S SOMETHING ELSE. A TRAJECTORY THAT REMAINS NO MATTER WHAT TANGENT IT IS. PEOPLE KILLED UNDER TEMPORAL CIRCUM-STANCES.
SOMEONE IS COVERING IT UP. SOMEONE DOESN'T WANT THESE MURDERS SOLVED. SOMEONE MAKING SURE THE SEPARATISTS ARE ABLE TO SUCCEED.

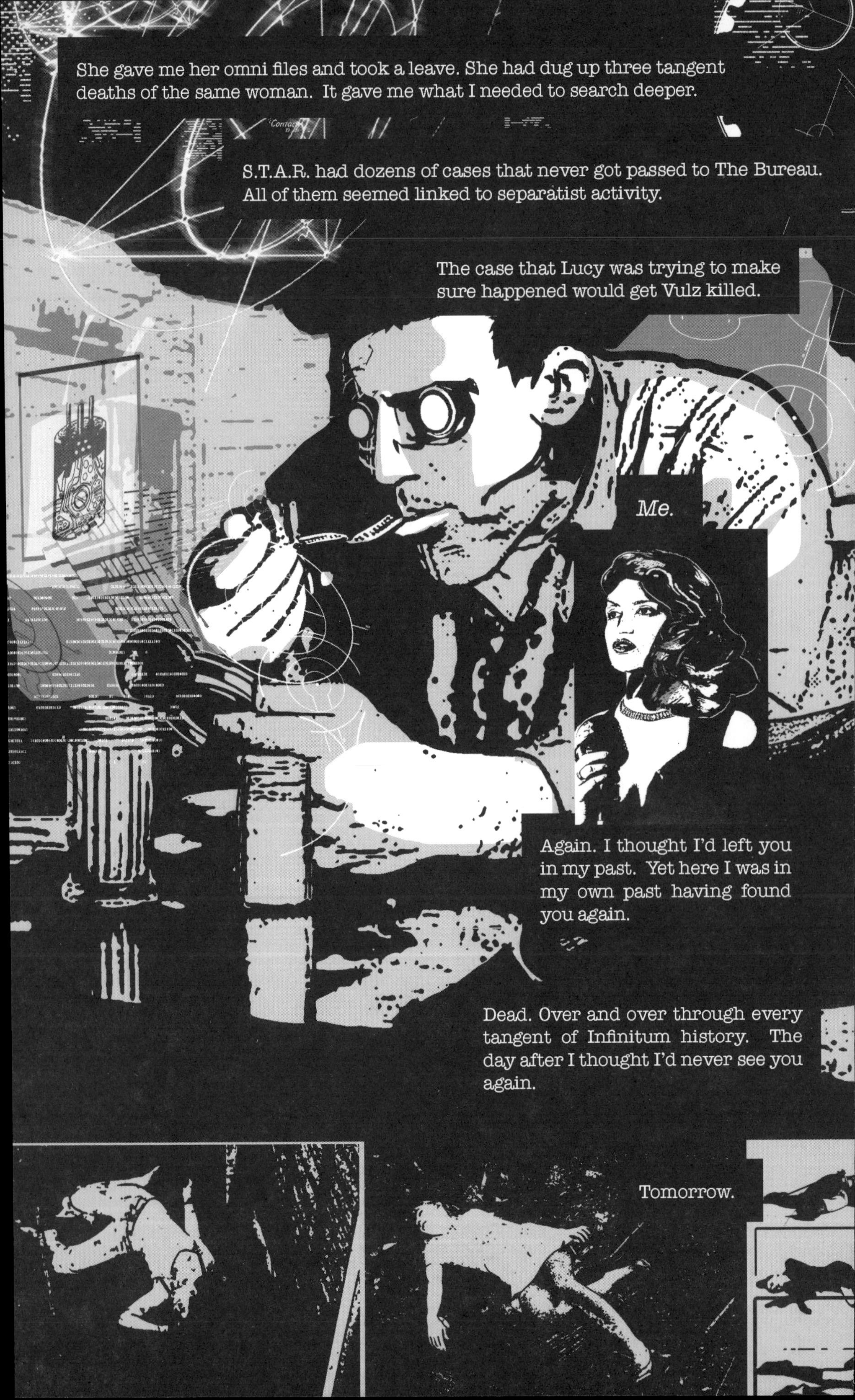
She gave me her omni files and took a leave. She had dug up three tangent deaths of the same woman. It gave me what I needed to search deeper.
S.T.A.R. had dozens of cases that never got passed to The Bureau. All of them seemed linked to separatist activity.
The case that Lucy was trying to make sure happened would get Vulz killed.
Me.
Again. I thought I'd left you in my past. Yet here I was in my own past having found you again.
Dead. Over and over through every tangent of Infinitum history. The day after I thought I'd never see you again.
Tomorrow.

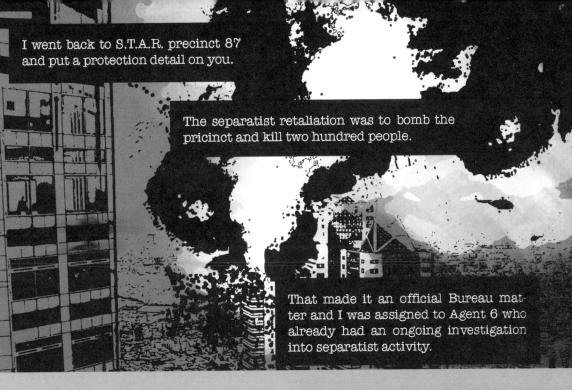

I went back to S.T.A.R. precinct 87 and put a protection detail on you.

The separatist retaliation was to bomb the pricinct and kill two hundred people.

That made it an official Bureau matter and I was assigned to Agent 6 who already had an ongoing investigation into separatist activity.

The previous day we held a briefing on a mobile Infinitum Precinct.

"THIS MAN IS DREXAL DREEN. LEADER OF THE SEPARATISTS. HE IS THE REASON WE CALLED YOU ALL HERE."

"YOUR TEAM IS GOING TO ASSIST US IN THE APPREHENSION OF THIS KNOWN CHRONOLOGICAL FELON AND HUSBAND OF RED LUCY. DREXAL IS THE BRAINS AND LUCY IS THE MUSCLE FOR THE SEPARATISTS. THEY ARE RESPONSIBLE FOR HUNDREDS OF TANGENT MURDERS AND FIFTY THAT ARE CURRENTLY FIXED."

"I KNOW YOU AREN'T ALL FAMILIAR WITH THE PARADOX BUREAU, THOUGH AGENT 9 AND I HAVE HAD THIS BRIEFING WITH YOU A NUMBER OF TIMES. TOMORROW ALL OF YOU WILL BE KILLED BY A BOMB IN YOUR PRECINCT HOUSE. WE HAVE JURISDICTION OVER THE RED LUCY CASE AS OF 18:34 TOMORROW. MYSELF AND AGENT 9 ARE HERE FROM TOMORROW TO ASSIST OURSELVES IN THE ONGOING INVESTIGATION."

WANTED

INFORMATION LEADING TO THE ARREST AND CONVICTION

MURDER. TERRORISM. TIME TRAVEL. SMUGGLING.

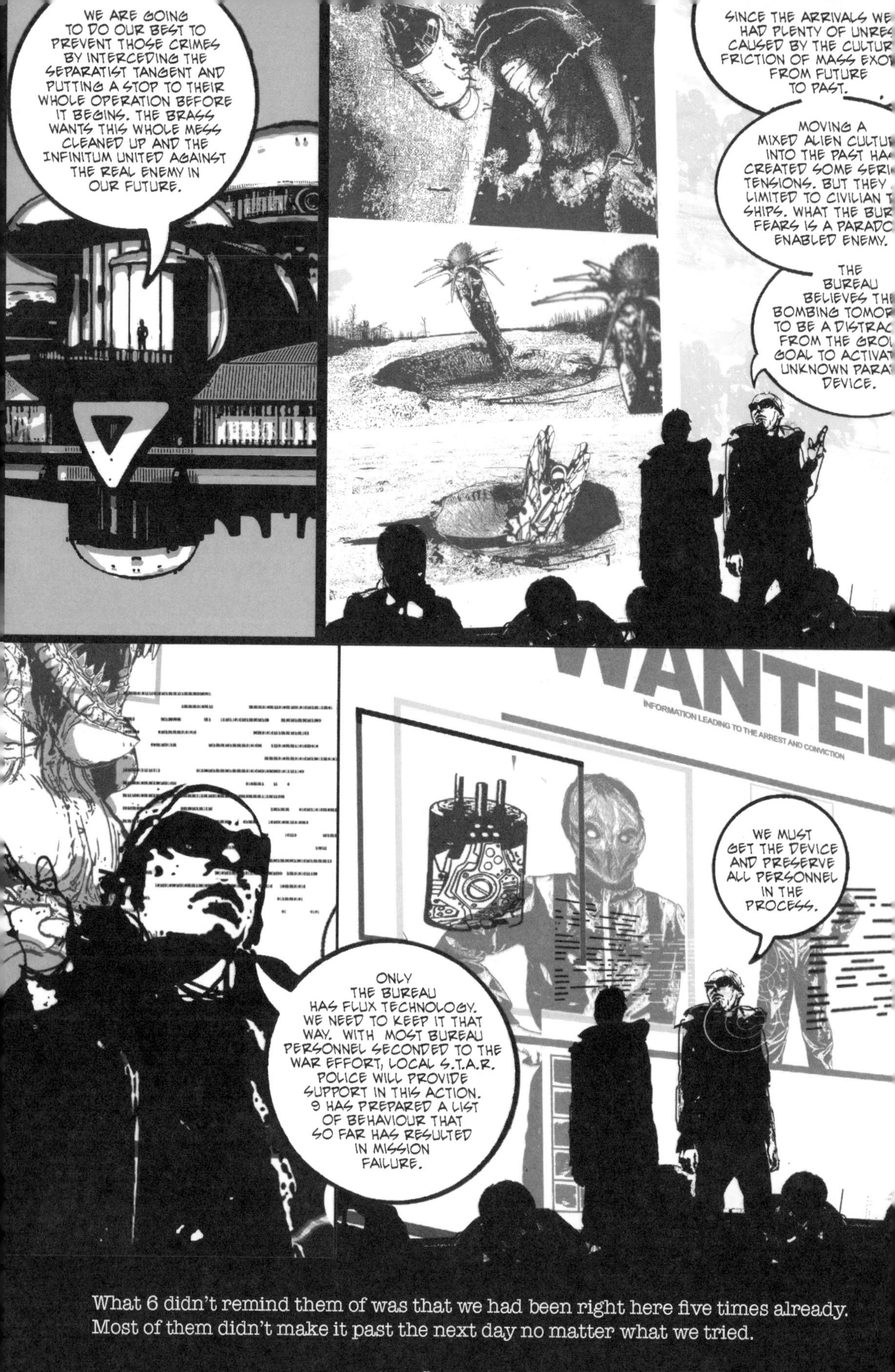
WE ARE GOING TO DO OUR BEST TO PREVENT THOSE CRIMES BY INTERCEDING THE SEPARATIST TANGENT AND PUTTING A STOP TO THEIR WHOLE OPERATION BEFORE IT BEGINS. THE BRASS WANTS THIS WHOLE MESS CLEANED UP AND THE INFINITUM UNITED AGAINST THE REAL ENEMY IN OUR FUTURE.
SINCE THE ARRIVALS WE HAD PLENTY OF UNRE CAUSED BY THE CULTUR FRICTION OF MASS EXO FROM FUTURE TO PAST.
MOVING A MIXED ALIEN CULTU INTO THE PAST HA CREATED SOME SERI TENSIONS. BUT THEY LIMITED TO CIVILIAN SHIPS. WHAT THE BUR FEARS IS A PARADO ENABLED ENEMY.
THE BUREAU BELIEVES TH BOMBING TOMOR TO BE A DISTRAC FROM THE GRO GOAL TO ACTIVAT UNKNOWN PARA DEVICE.
WANTED
INFORMATION LEADING TO THE ARREST AND CONVICTION
WE MUST GET THE DEVICE AND PRESERVE ALL PERSONNEL IN THE PROCESS.
ONLY THE BUREAU HAS FLUX TECHNOLOGY. WE NEED TO KEEP IT THAT WAY. WITH MOST BUREAU PERSONNEL SECONDED TO THE WAR EFFORT, LOCAL S.T.A.R. POLICE WILL PROVIDE SUPPORT IN THIS ACTION. 9 HAS PREPARED A LIST OF BEHAVIOUR THAT SO FAR HAS RESULTED IN MISSION FAILURE.

What 6 didn't remind them of was that we had been right here five times already. Most of them didn't make it past the next day no matter what we tried.

I was sitting in a room with dead people.

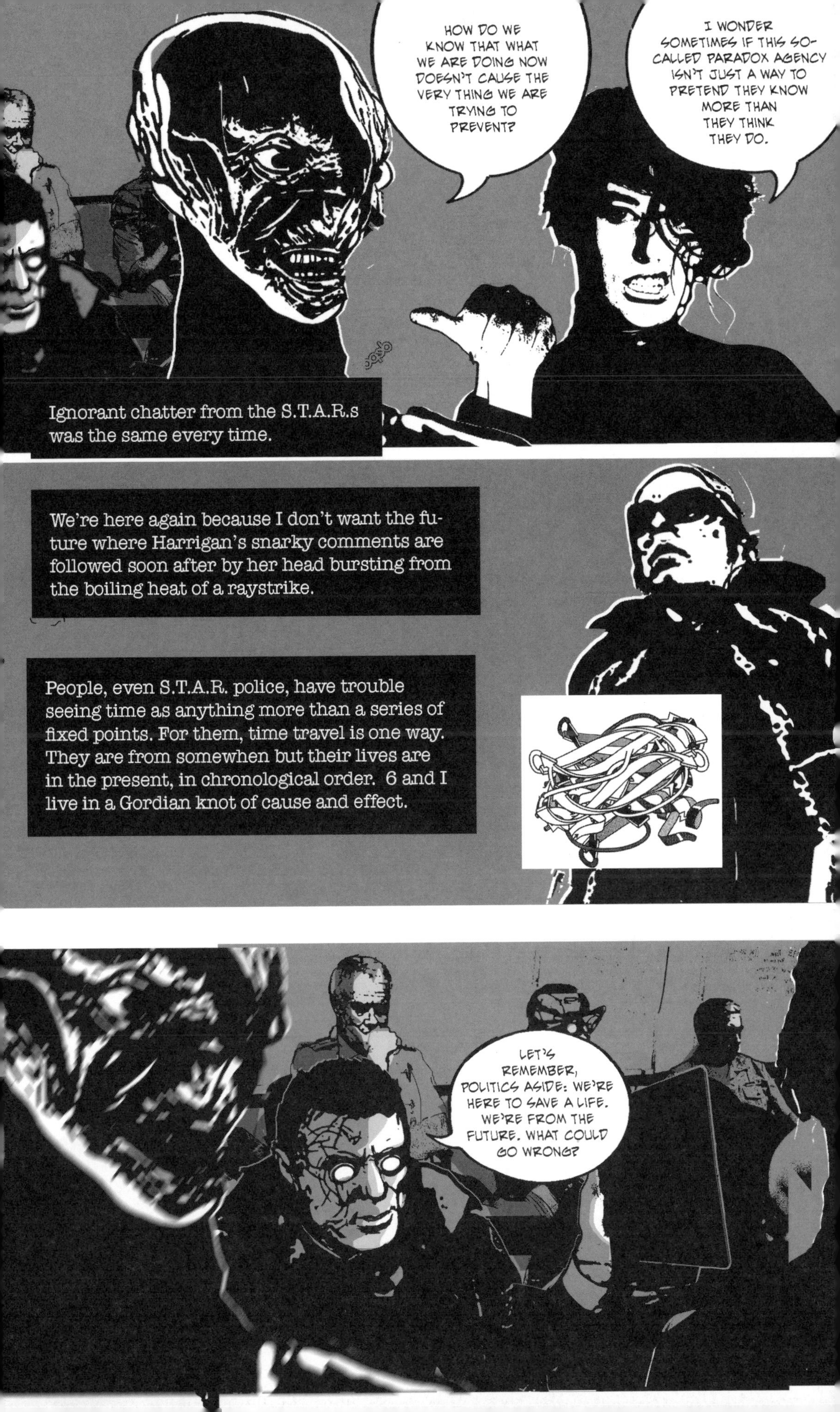
HOW DO WE KNOW THAT WHAT WE ARE DOING NOW DOESN'T CAUSE THE VERY THING WE ARE TRYING TO PREVENT?
I WONDER SOMETIMES IF THIS SO-CALLED PARADOX AGENCY ISN'T JUST A WAY TO PRETEND THEY KNOW MORE THAN THEY THINK THEY DO.
Ignorant chatter from the S.T.A.R.s was the same every time.
We're here again because I don't want the future where Harrigan's snarky comments are followed soon after by her head bursting from the boiling heat of a raystrike.
People, even S.T.A.R. police, have trouble seeing time as anything more than a series of fixed points. For them, time travel is one way. They are from somewhen but their lives are in the present, in chronological order. 6 and I live in a Gordian knot of cause and effect.
LET'S REMEMBER, POLITICS ASIDE: WE'RE HERE TO SAVE A LIFE. WE'RE FROM THE FUTURE. WHAT COULD GO WRONG?

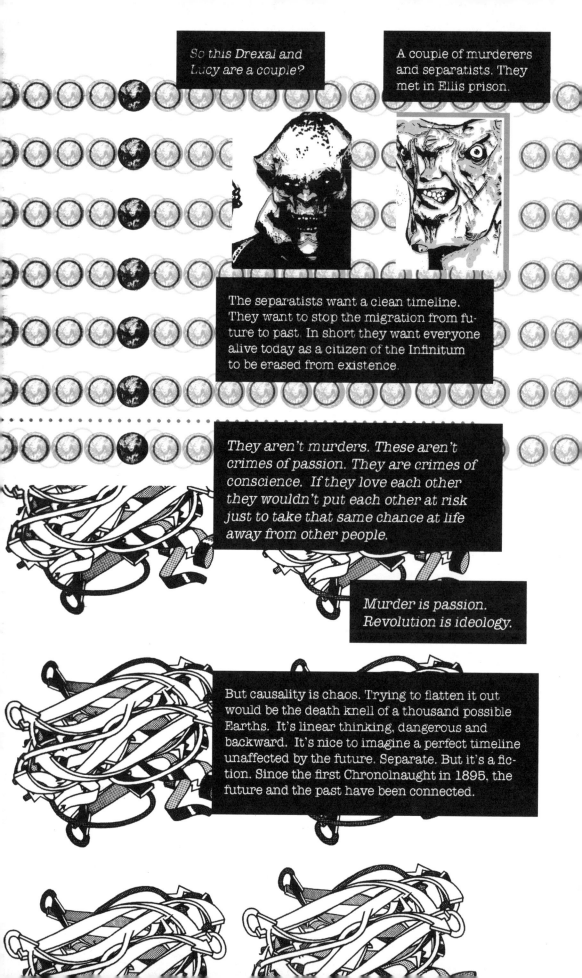

So this Drexal and Lucy are a couple?

A couple of murderers and separatists. They met in Ellis prison.

The separatists want a clean timeline. They want to stop the migration from future to past. In short they want everyone alive today as a citizen of the Infinitum to be erased from existence.

They aren't murders. These aren't crimes of passion. They are crimes of conscience. If they love each other they wouldn't put each other at risk just to take that same chance at life away from other people.

Murder is passion. Revolution is ideology.

But causality is chaos. Trying to flatten it out would be the death knell of a thousand possible Earths. It's linear thinking, dangerous and backward. It's nice to imagine a perfect timeline unaffected by the future. Separate. But it's a fiction. Since the first Chronolnaught in 1895, the future and the past have been connected.

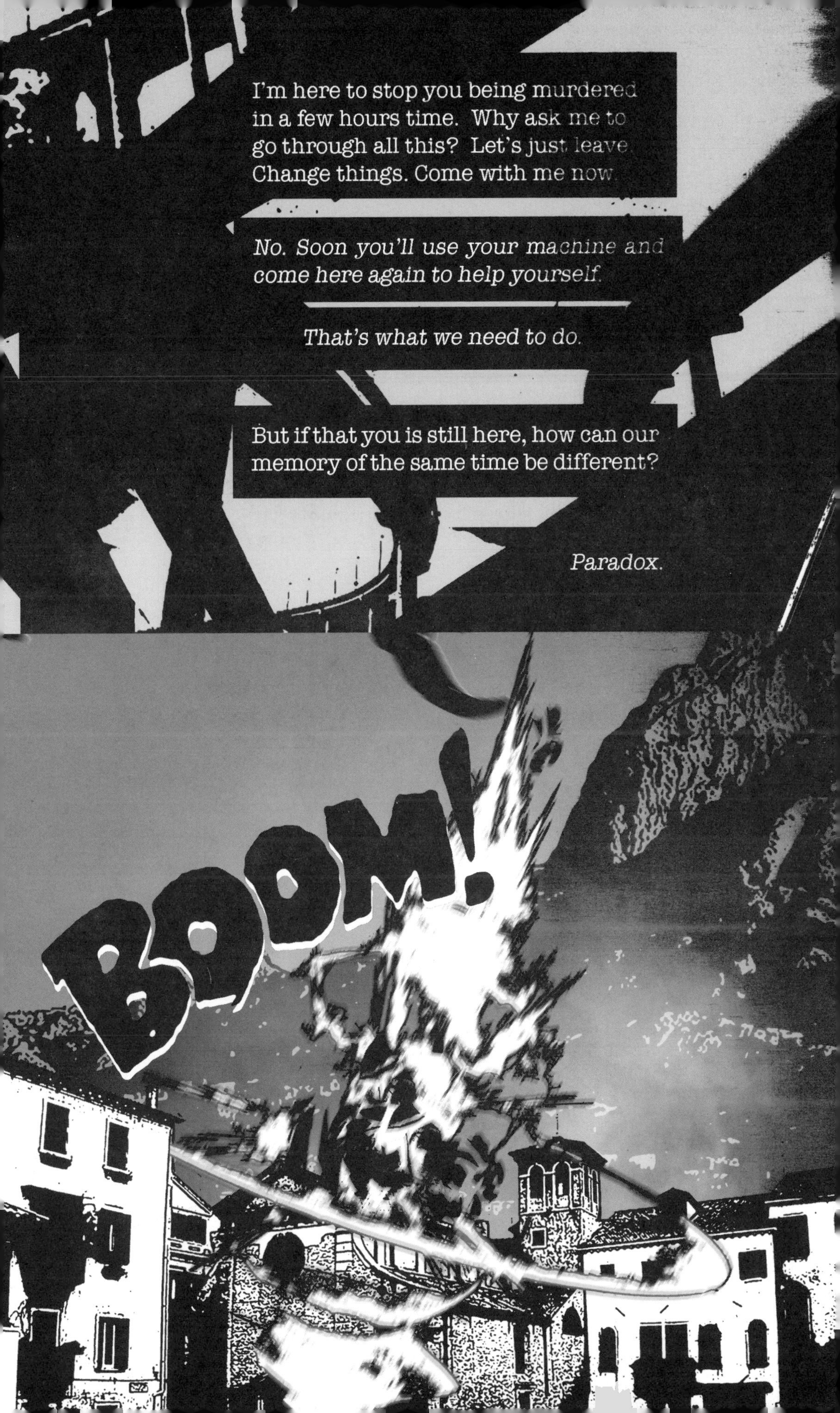
I'm here to stop you being murdered in a few hours time. Why ask me to go through all this? Let's just leave. Change things. Come with me now.
No. Soon you'll use your machine and come here again to help yourself.
That's what we need to do.
But if that you is still here, how can our memory of the same time be different?
Paradox.
BOOM!

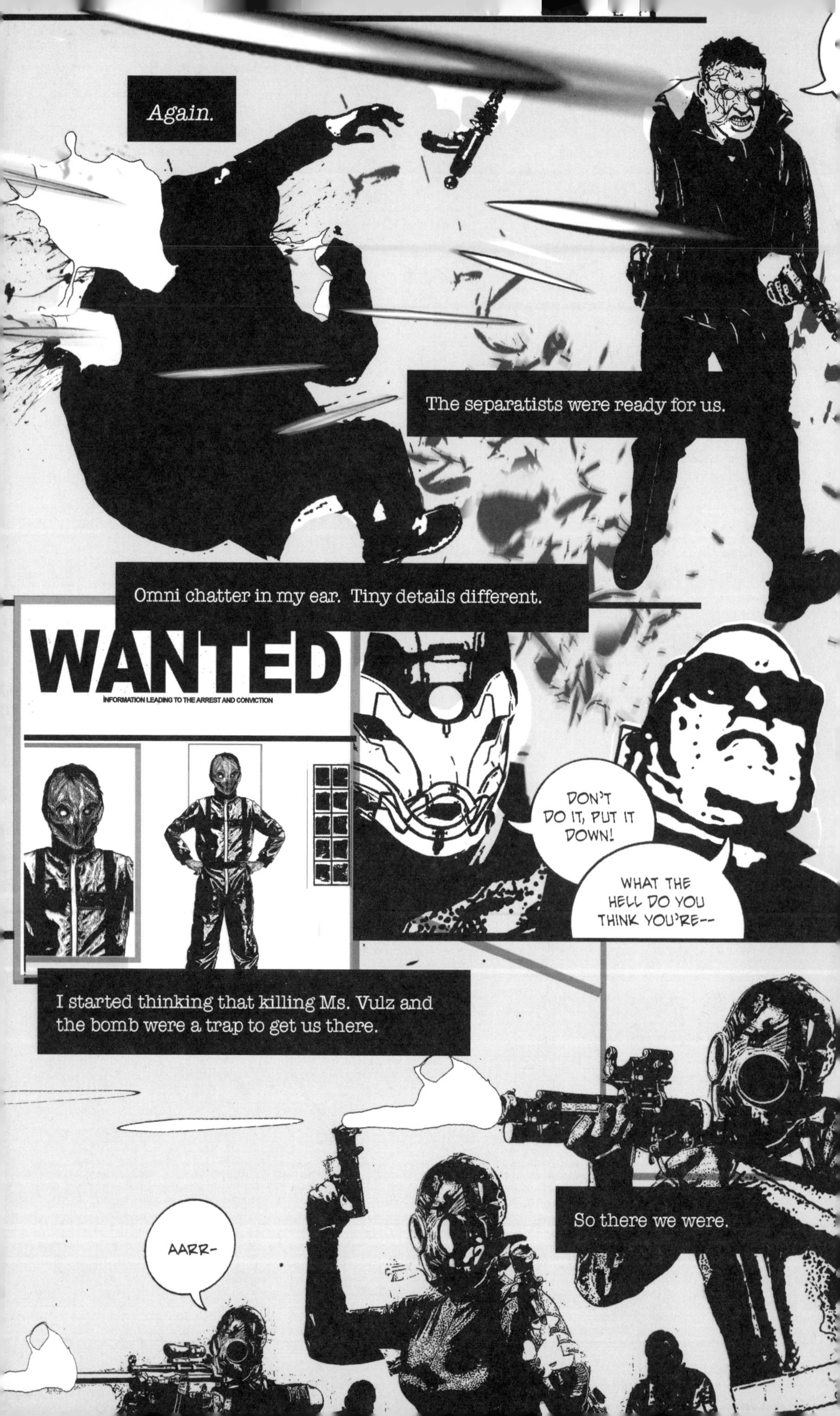
Again.
The separatists were ready for us.
Omni chatter in my ear. Tiny details different.
WANTED
INFORMATION LEADING TO THE ARREST AND CONVICTION
DON'T DO IT, PUT IT DOWN!
WHAT THE HELL DO YOU THINK YOU'RE--
I started thinking that killing Ms. Vulz and the bomb were a trap to get us there.
So there we were.
AARR-

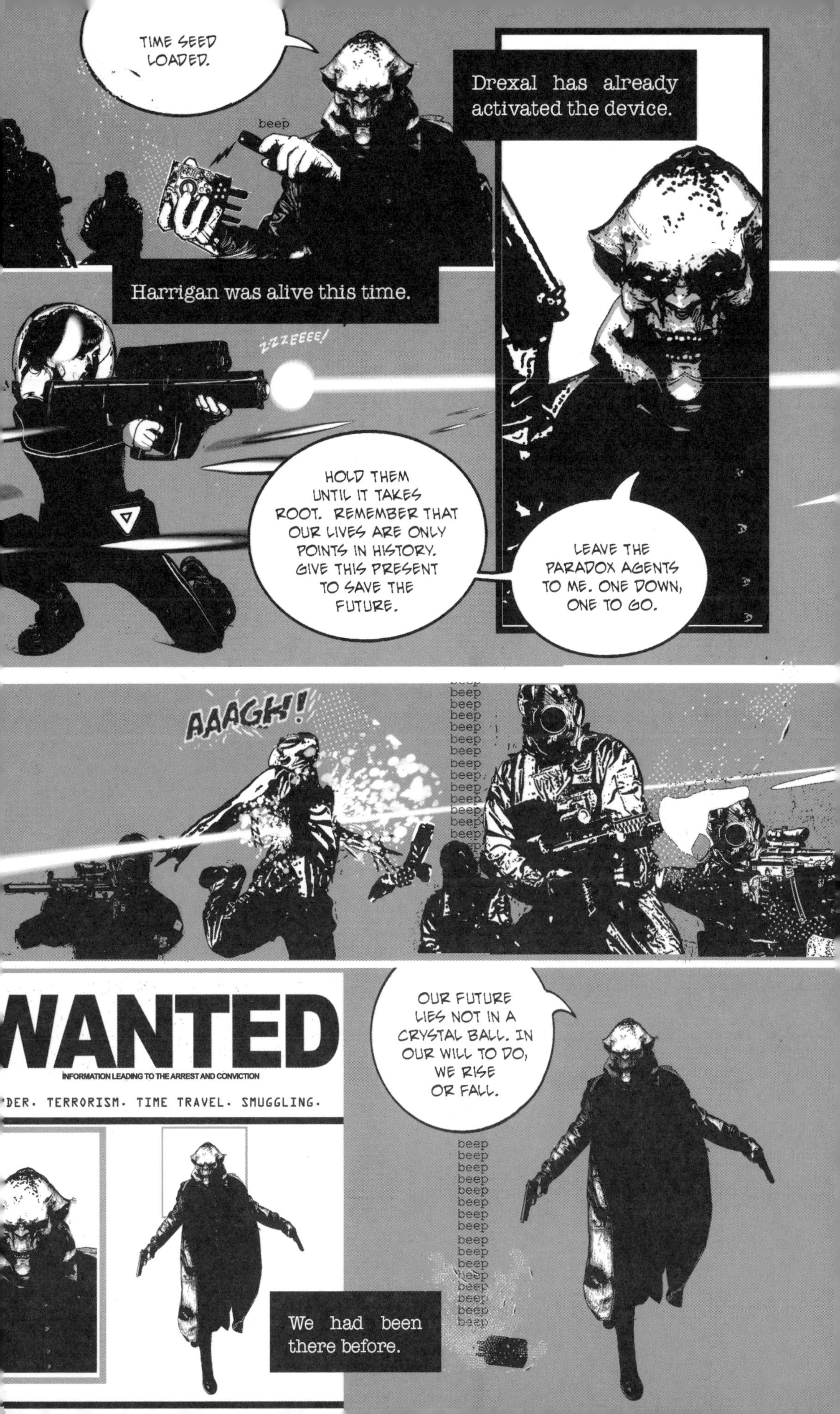

TIME SEED LOADED.
beep
Drexal has already activated the device.
Harrigan was alive this time.
Z-ZZEEEE!
HOLD THEM UNTIL IT TAKES ROOT. REMEMBER THAT OUR LIVES ARE ONLY POINTS IN HISTORY. GIVE THIS PRESENT TO SAVE THE FUTURE.
LEAVE THE PARADOX AGENTS TO ME. ONE DOWN, ONE TO GO.
AAAGH!
beep beep beep beep beep beep beep beep beep beep beep beep beep beep
WANTED
INFORMATION LEADING TO THE ARREST AND CONVICTION
DER. TERRORISM. TIME TRAVEL. SMUGGLING.
OUR FUTURE LIES NOT IN A CRYSTAL BALL. IN OUR WILL TO DO, WE RISE OR FALL.
beep beep beep beep beep beep beep beep beep beep beep beep beep beep beep beep beep
We had been there before.

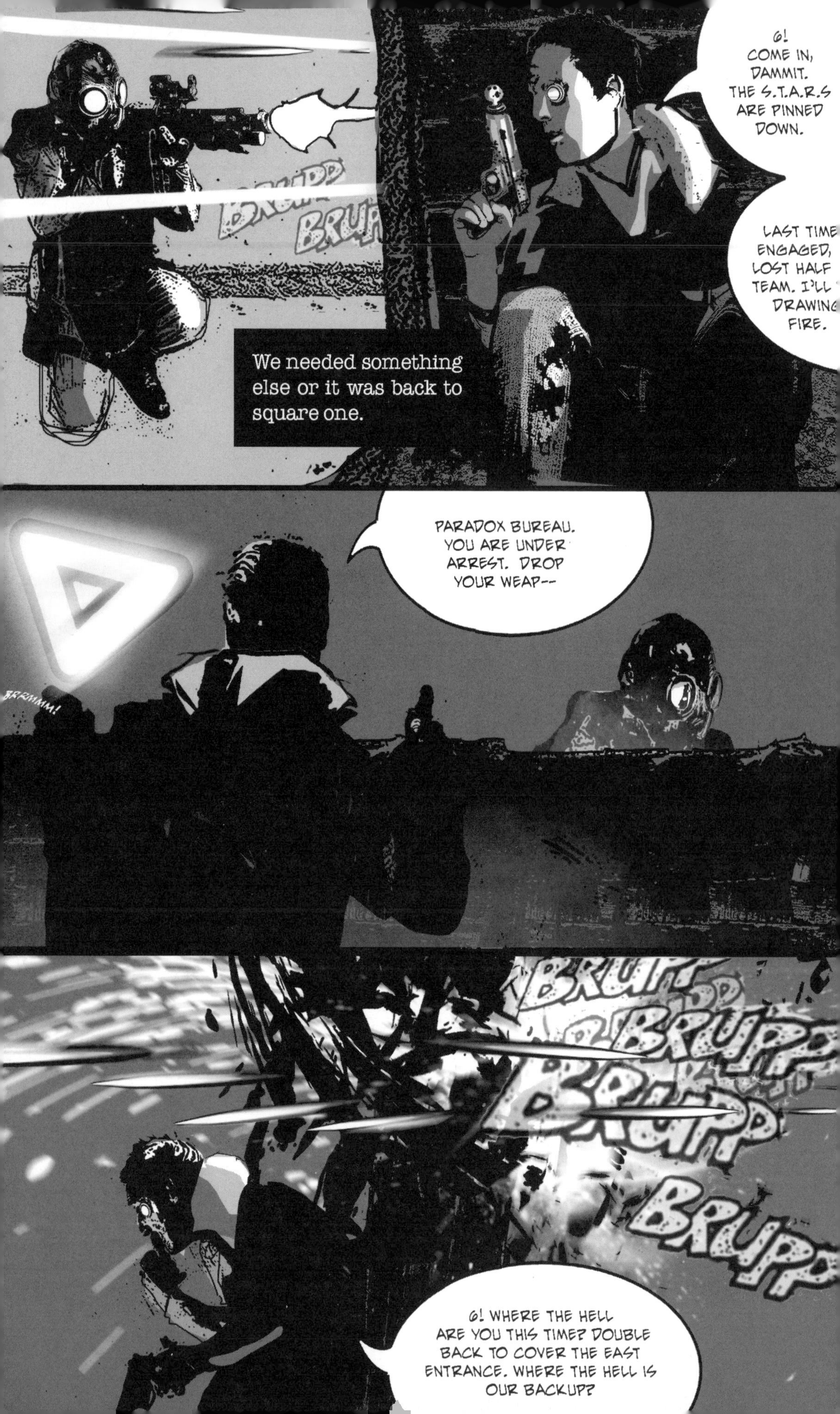

We needed something else or it was back to square one.
G! COME IN, DAMMIT. THE S.T.A.R.S ARE PINNED DOWN.
LAST TIME ENGAGED, LOST HALF TEAM. I'LL DRAWING FIRE.
PARADOX BUREAU. YOU ARE UNDER ARREST. DROP YOUR WEAP--
G! WHERE THE HELL ARE YOU THIS TIME? DOUBLE BACK TO COVER THE EAST ENTRANCE. WHERE THE HELL IS OUR BACKUP?

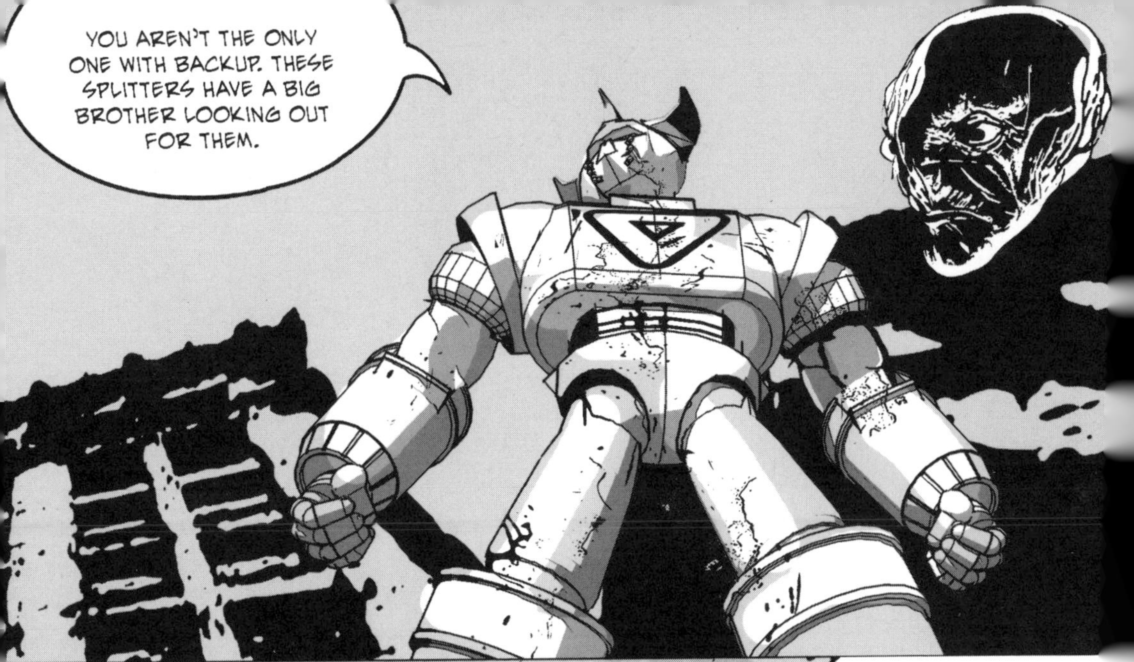
YOU AREN'T THE ONLY ONE WITH BACKUP. THESE SPLITTERS HAVE A BIG BROTHER LOOKING OUT FOR THEM.

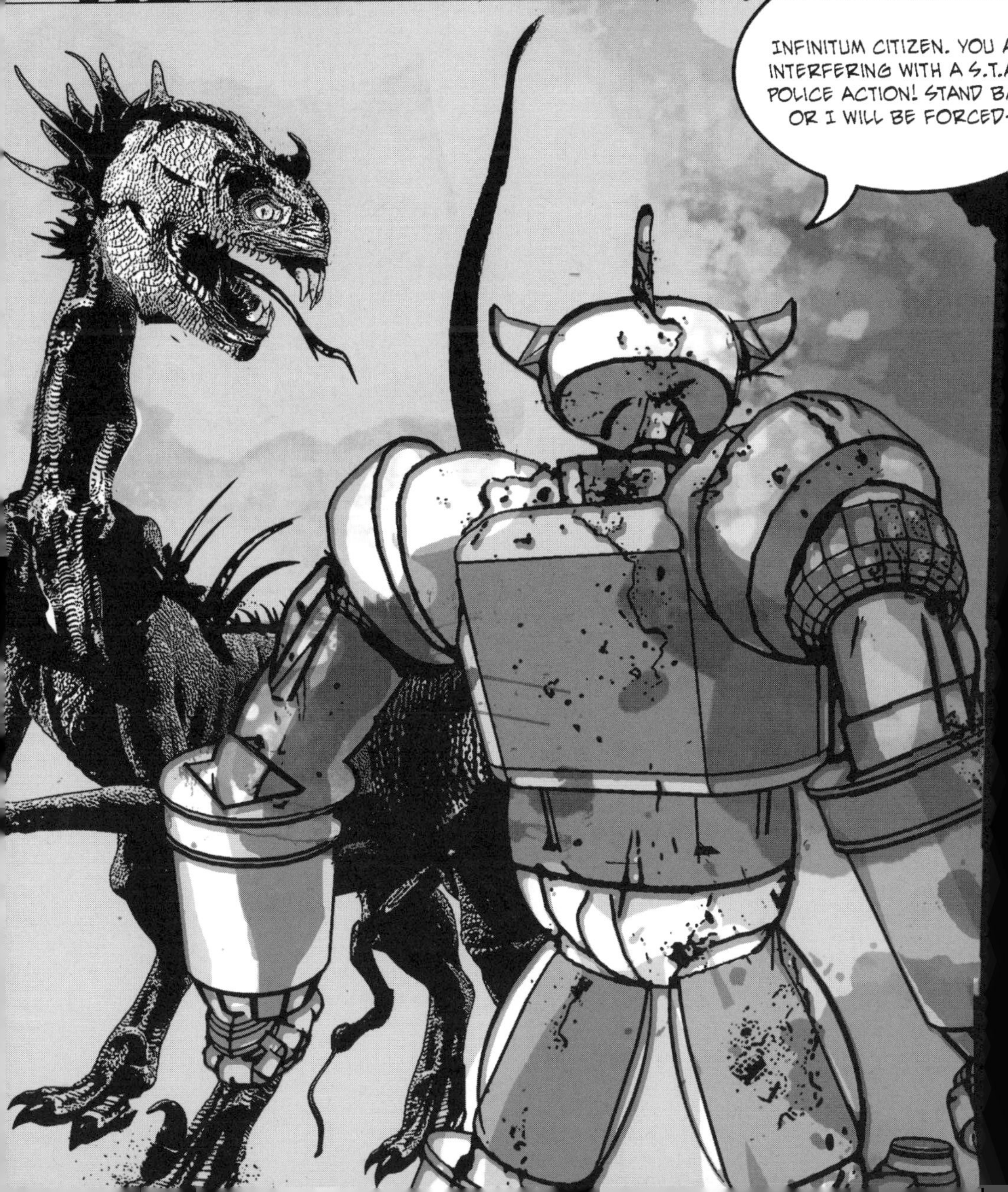
INFINITUM CITIZEN. YOU A INTERFERING WITH A S.T.A POLICE ACTION! STAND BA OR I WILL BE FORCED-

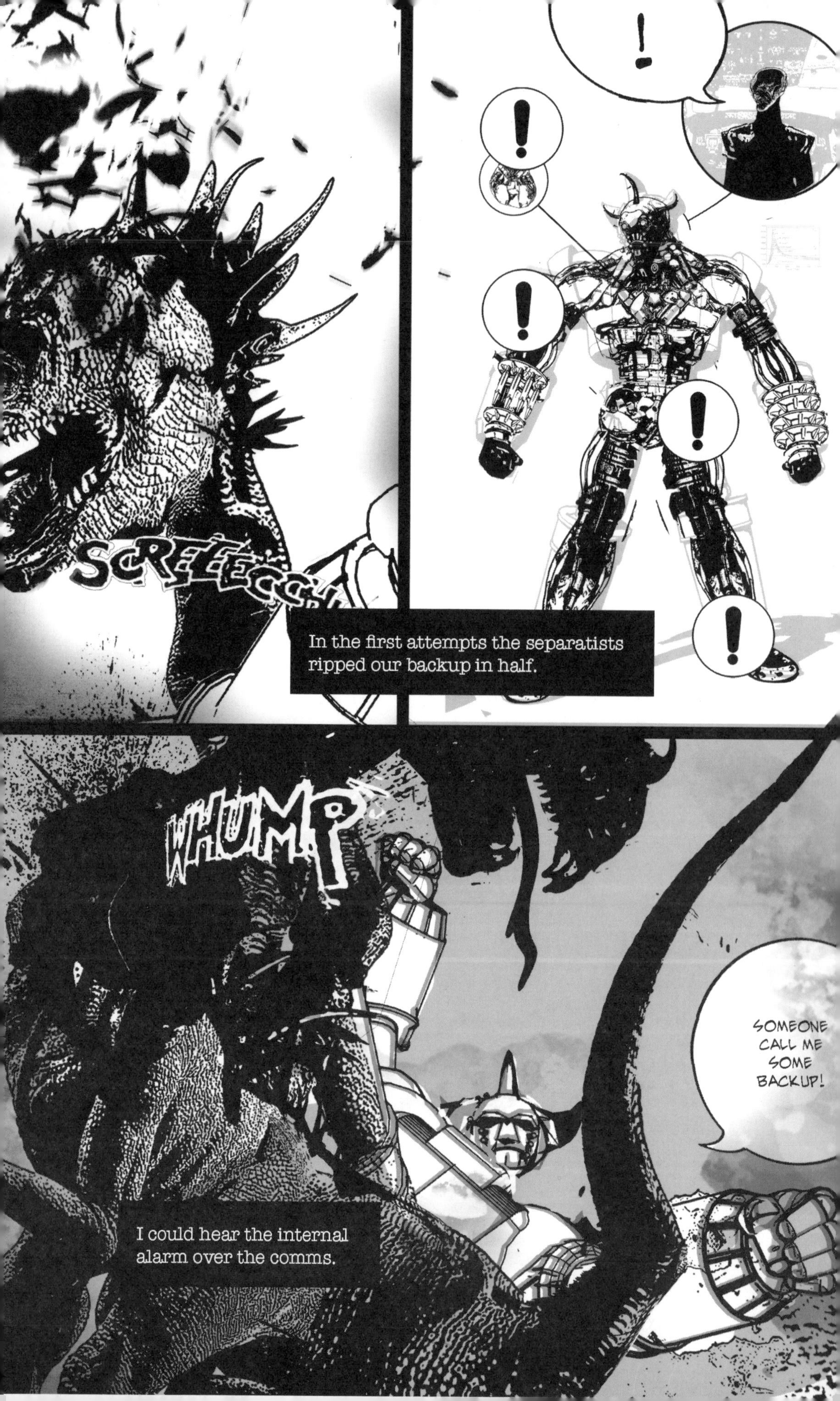
SCREEECCH
!
!
!
!
!
In the first attempts the separatists ripped our backup in half.
WHUMP
SOMEONE CALL ME SOME BACKUP!
I could hear the internal alarm over the comms.

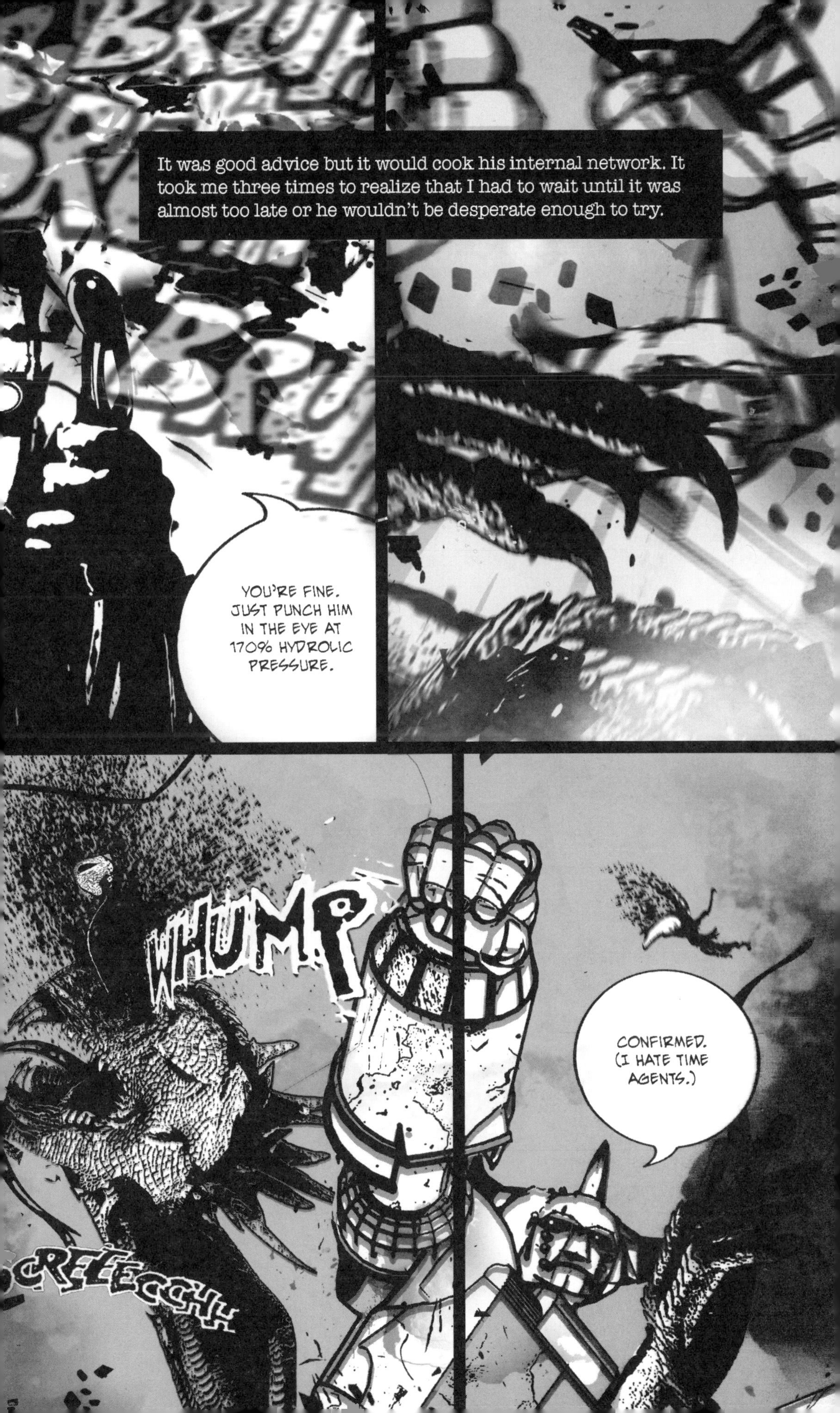
It was good advice but it would cook his internal network. It took me three times to realize that I had to wait until it was almost too late or he wouldn't be desperate enough to try.
YOU'RE FINE. JUST PUNCH HIM IN THE EYE AT 170% HYDROLIC PRESSURE.
WHUMP
CONFIRMED. (I HATE TIME AGENTS.)

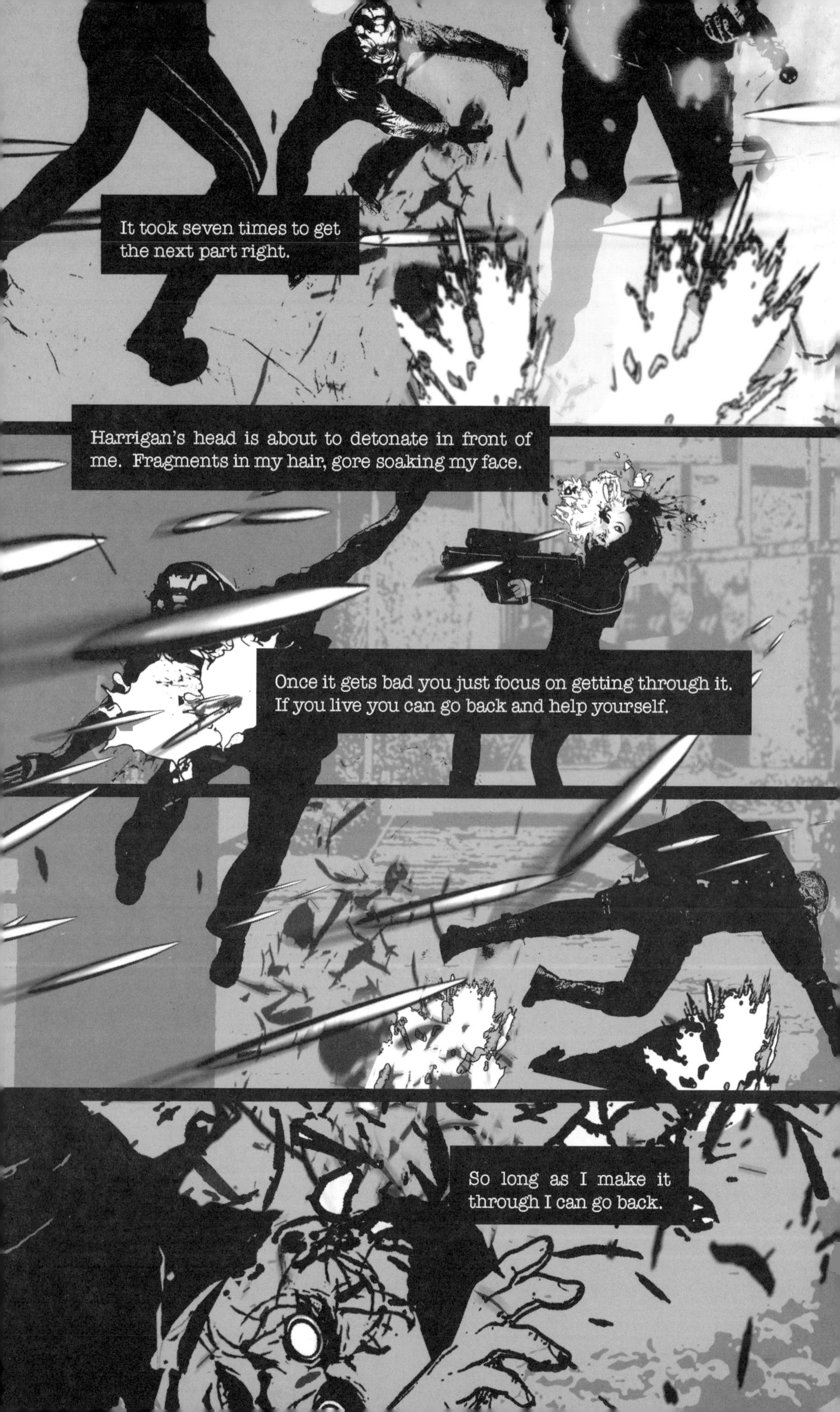
It took seven times to get the next part right.
Harrigan's head is about to detonate in front of me. Fragments in my hair, gore soaking my face.
Once it gets bad you just focus on getting through it. If you live you can go back and help yourself.
So long as I make it through I can go back.

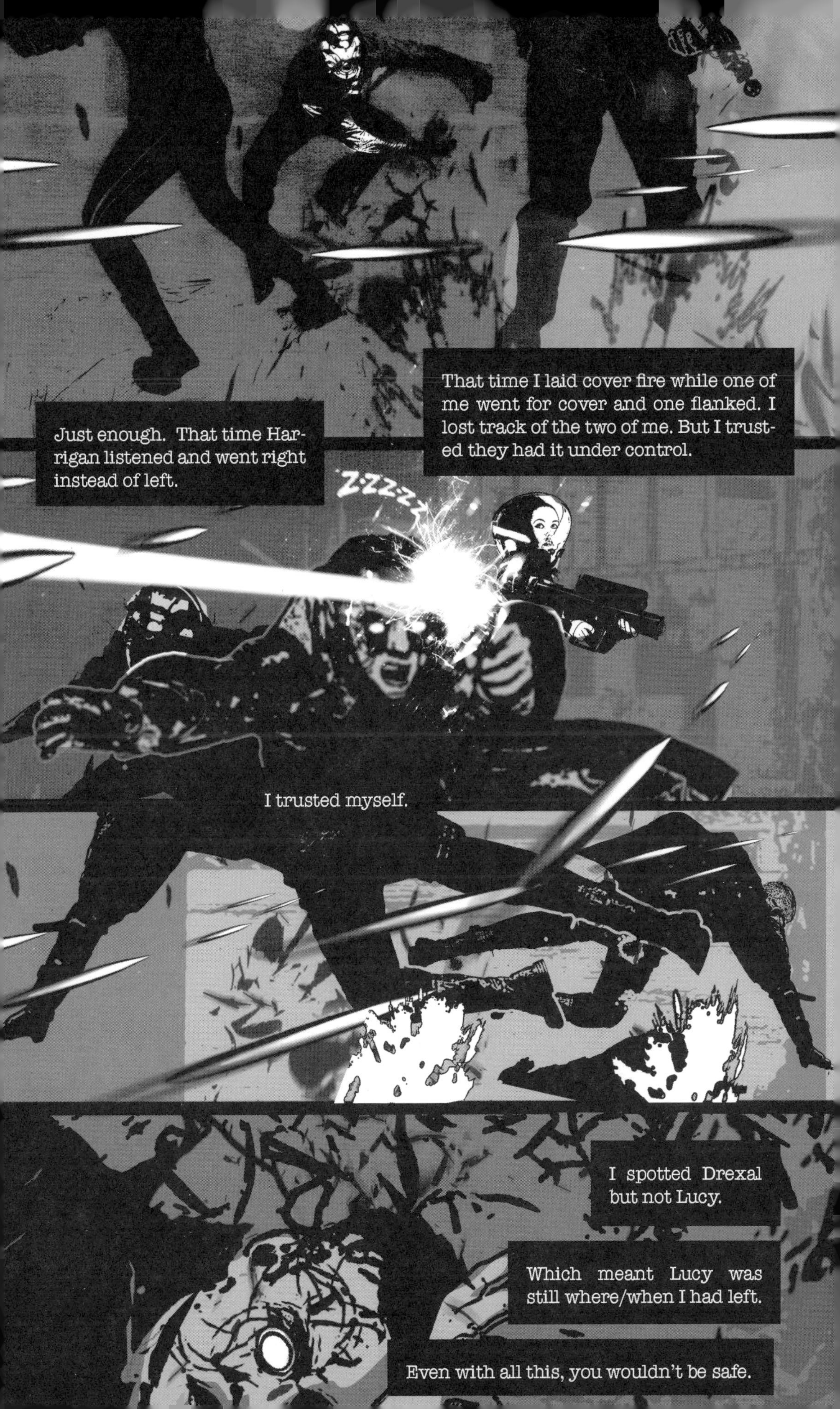

Just enough. That time Harrigan listened and went right instead of left.
That time I laid cover fire while one of me went for cover and one flanked. I lost track of the two of me. But I trusted they had it under control.
Z-Z-Z-Z-Z
I trusted myself.
I spotted Drexal but not Lucy.
Which meant Lucy was still where/when I had left.
Even with all this, you wouldn't be safe.

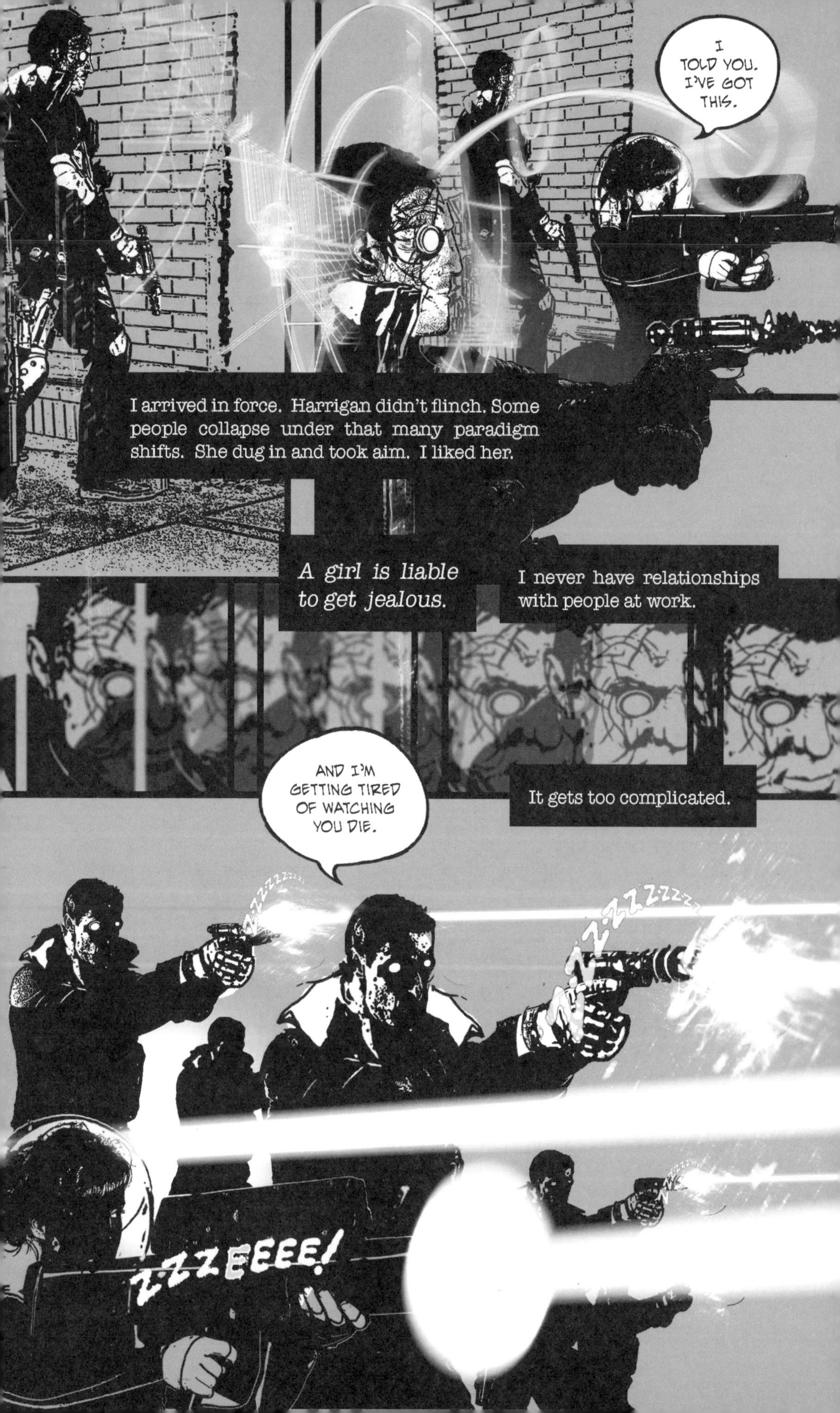

I TOLD YOU. I'VE GOT THIS.
I arrived in force. Harrigan didn't flinch. Some people collapse under that many paradigm shifts. She dug in and took aim. I liked her.
A girl is liable to get jealous.
I never have relationships with people at work.
AND I'M GETTING TIRED OF WATCHING YOU DIE.
It gets too complicated.
ZZZZZZZ
ZZZZZZZZ
ZZZEEEE!

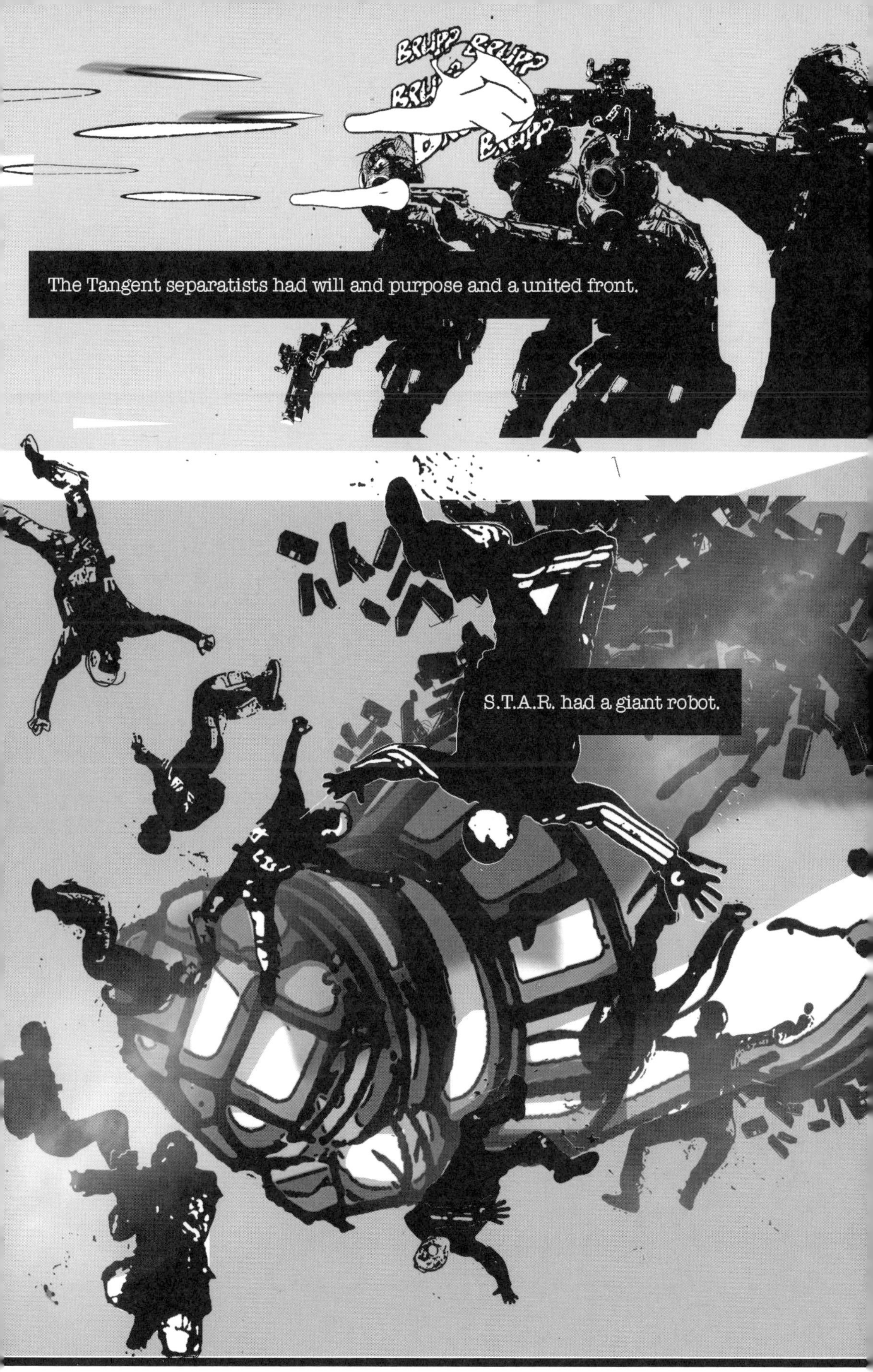
BRUPP
The Tangent separatists had will and purpose and a united front.
S.T.A.R. had a giant robot.

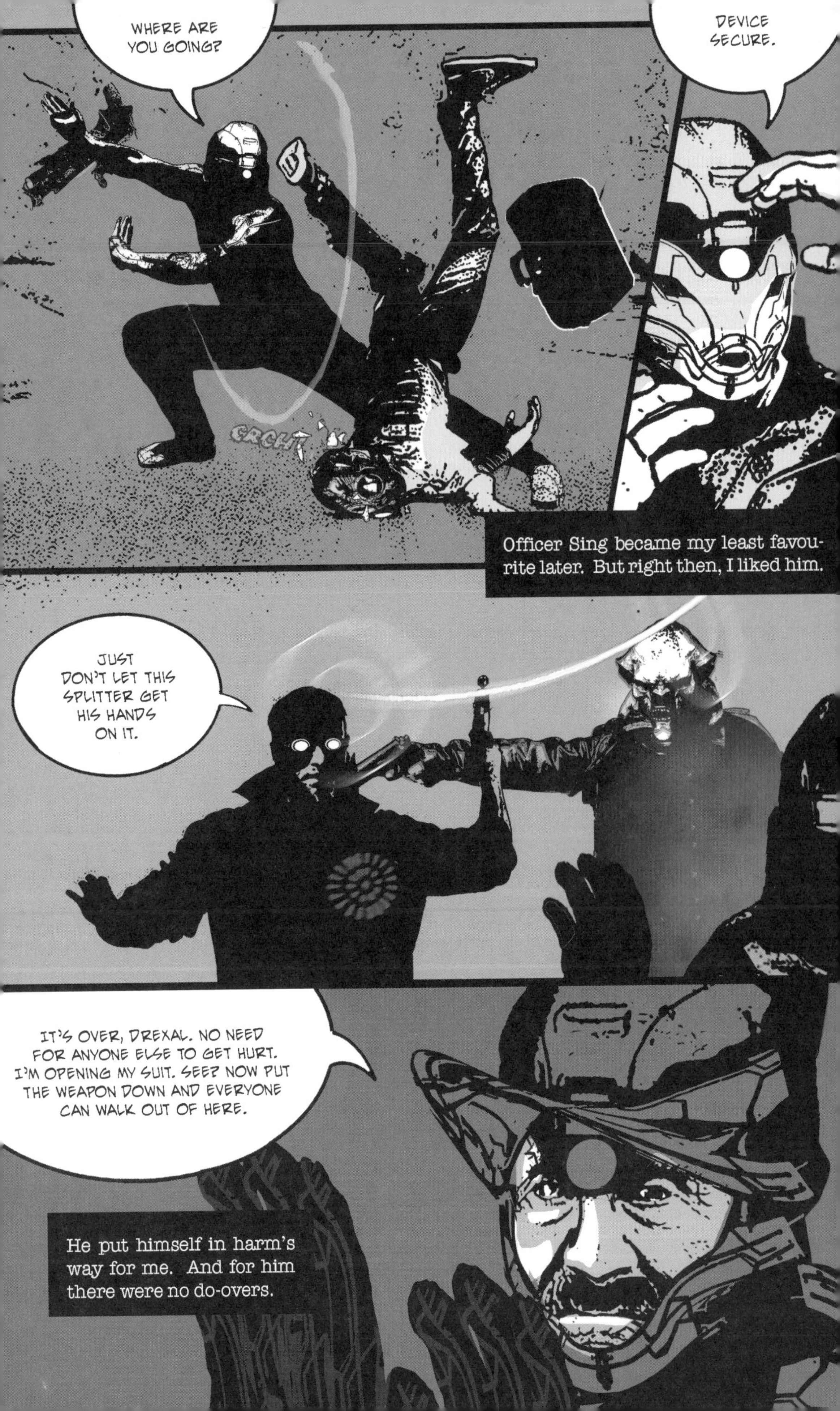
WHERE ARE YOU GOING?
CRCH!
DEVICE SECURE.
Officer Sing became my least favourite later. But right then, I liked him.
JUST DON'T LET THIS SPLITTER GET HIS HANDS ON IT.
IT'S OVER, DREXAL. NO NEED FOR ANYONE ELSE TO GET HURT. I'M OPENING MY SUIT. SEE? NOW PUT THE WEAPON DOWN AND EVERYONE CAN WALK OUT OF HERE.
He put himself in harm's way for me. And for him there were no do-overs.

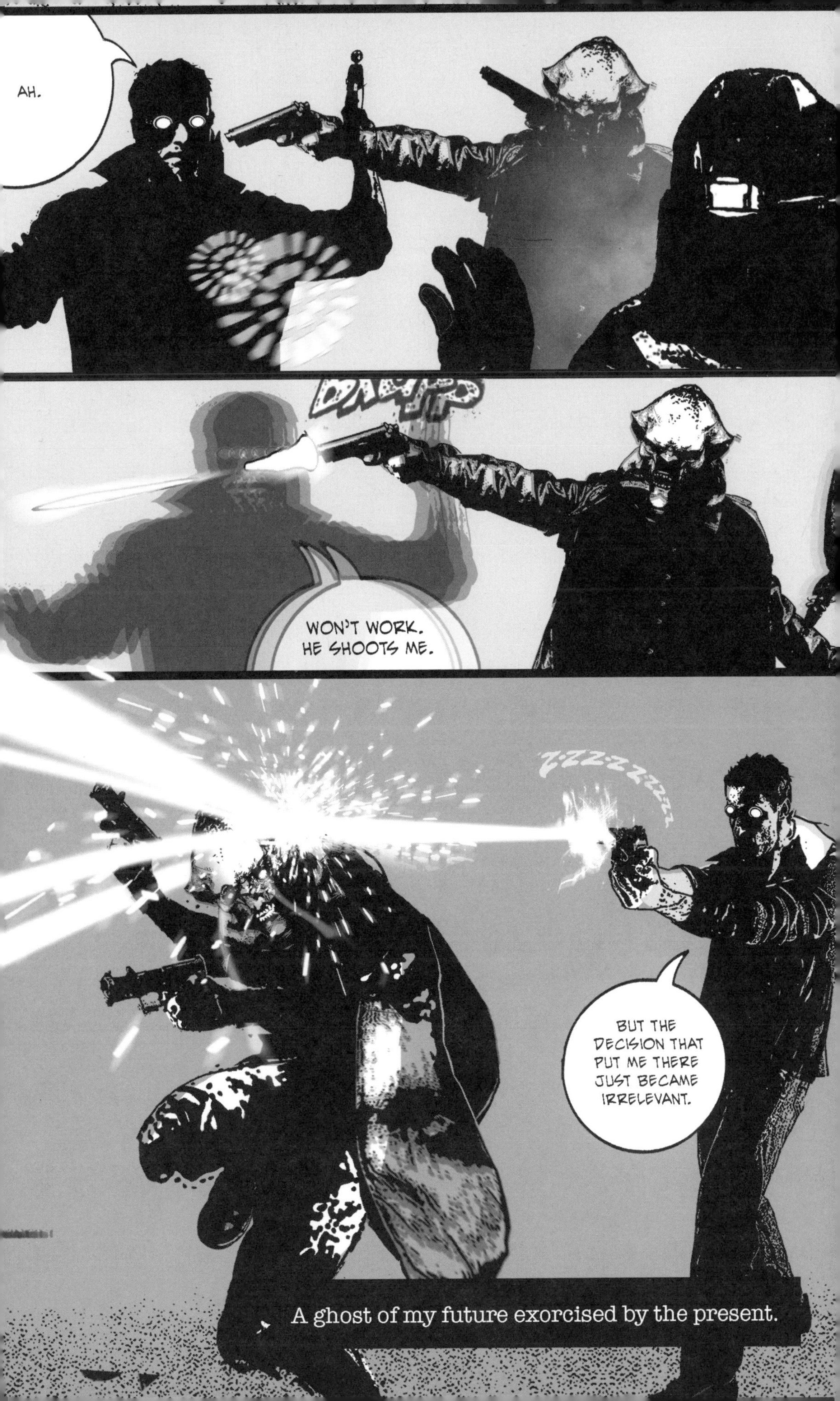
AH.
WON'T WORK. HE SHOOTS ME.
BUT THE DECISION THAT PUT ME THERE JUST BECAME IRRELEVANT.
A ghost of my future exorcised by the present.

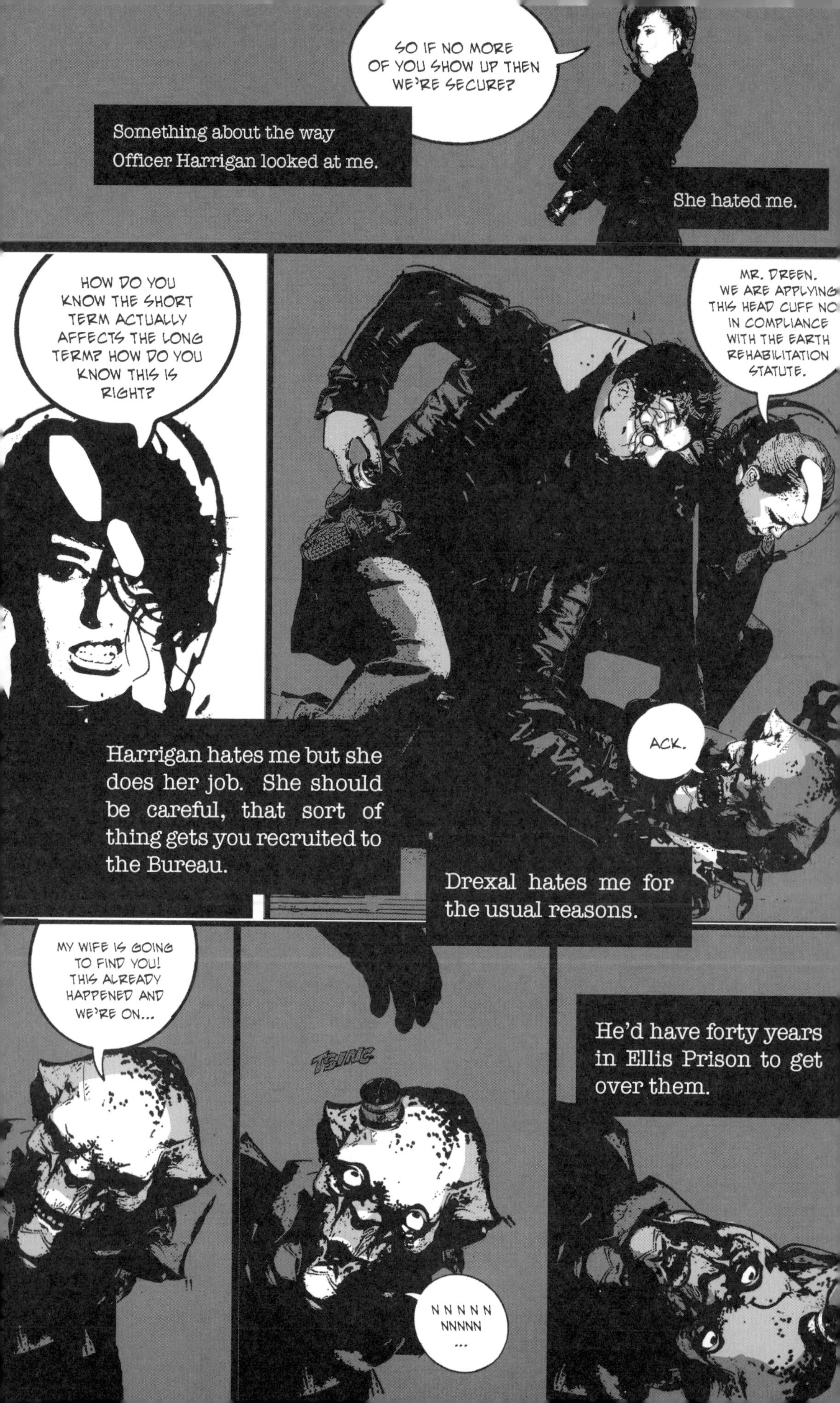
SO IF NO MORE OF YOU SHOW UP THEN WE'RE SECURE?
Something about the way Officer Harrigan looked at me.
She hated me.
HOW DO YOU KNOW THE SHORT TERM ACTUALLY AFFECTS THE LONG TERM? HOW DO YOU KNOW THIS IS RIGHT?
MR. DREEN. WE ARE APPLYING THIS HEAD CUFF NO IN COMPLIANCE WITH THE EARTH REHABILITATION STATUTE.
ACK.
Harrigan hates me but she does her job. She should be careful, that sort of thing gets you recruited to the Bureau.
Drexal hates me for the usual reasons.
MY WIFE IS GOING TO FIND YOU! THIS ALREADY HAPPENED AND WE'RE ON...
TSING
N N N N N NNNNN ...
He'd have forty years in Ellis Prison to get over them.

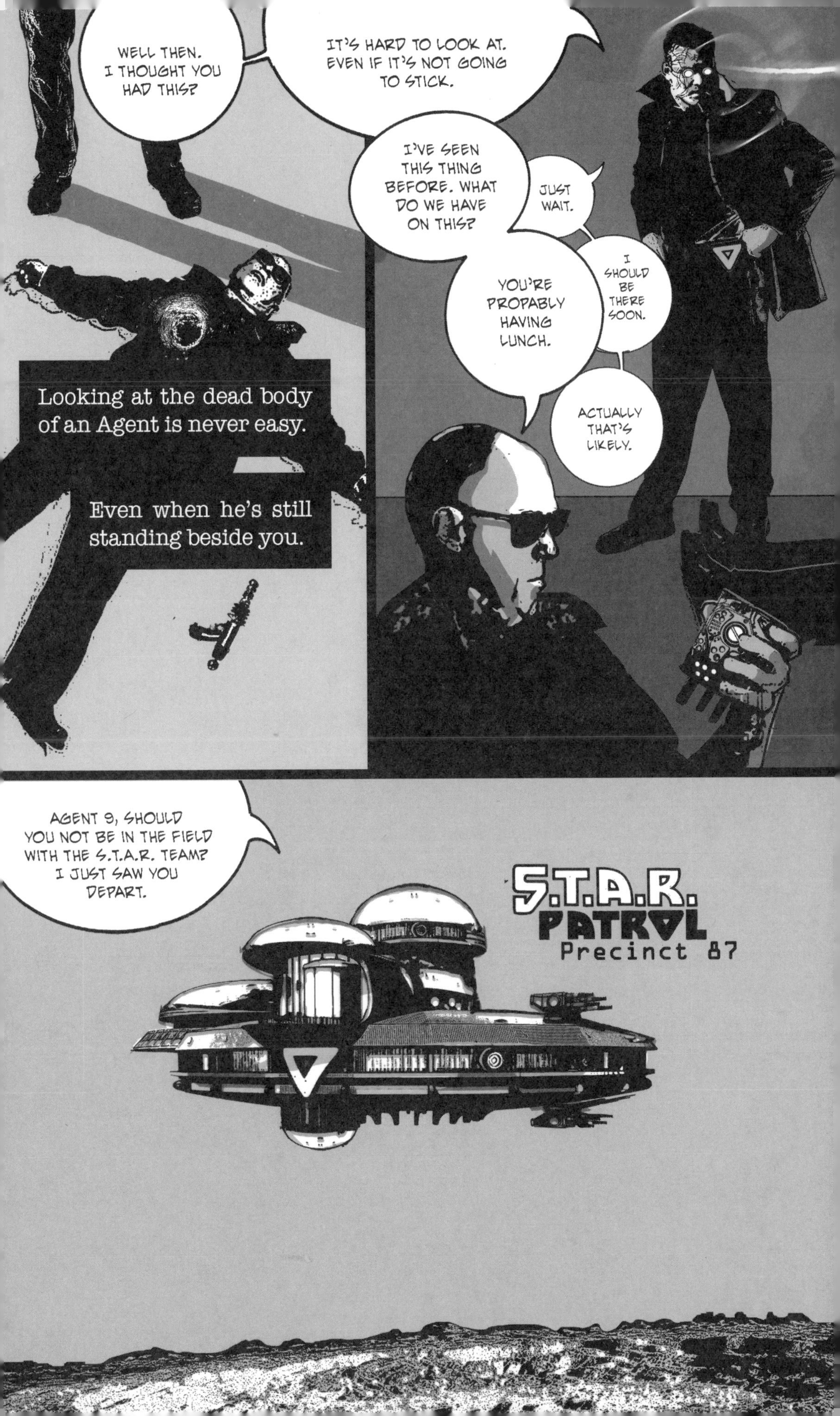
WELL THEN. I THOUGHT YOU HAD THIS?
IT'S HARD TO LOOK AT. EVEN IF IT'S NOT GOING TO STICK.
Looking at the dead body of an Agent is never easy.
Even when he's still standing beside you.
I'VE SEEN THIS THING BEFORE. WHAT DO WE HAVE ON THIS?
JUST WAIT.
YOU'RE PROPABLY HAVING LUNCH.
I SHOULD BE THERE SOON.
ACTUALLY THAT'S LIKELY.
AGENT 9, SHOULD YOU NOT BE IN THE FIELD WITH THE S.T.A.R. TEAM? I JUST SAW YOU DEPART.
S.T.A.R. PATROL
Precinct 87

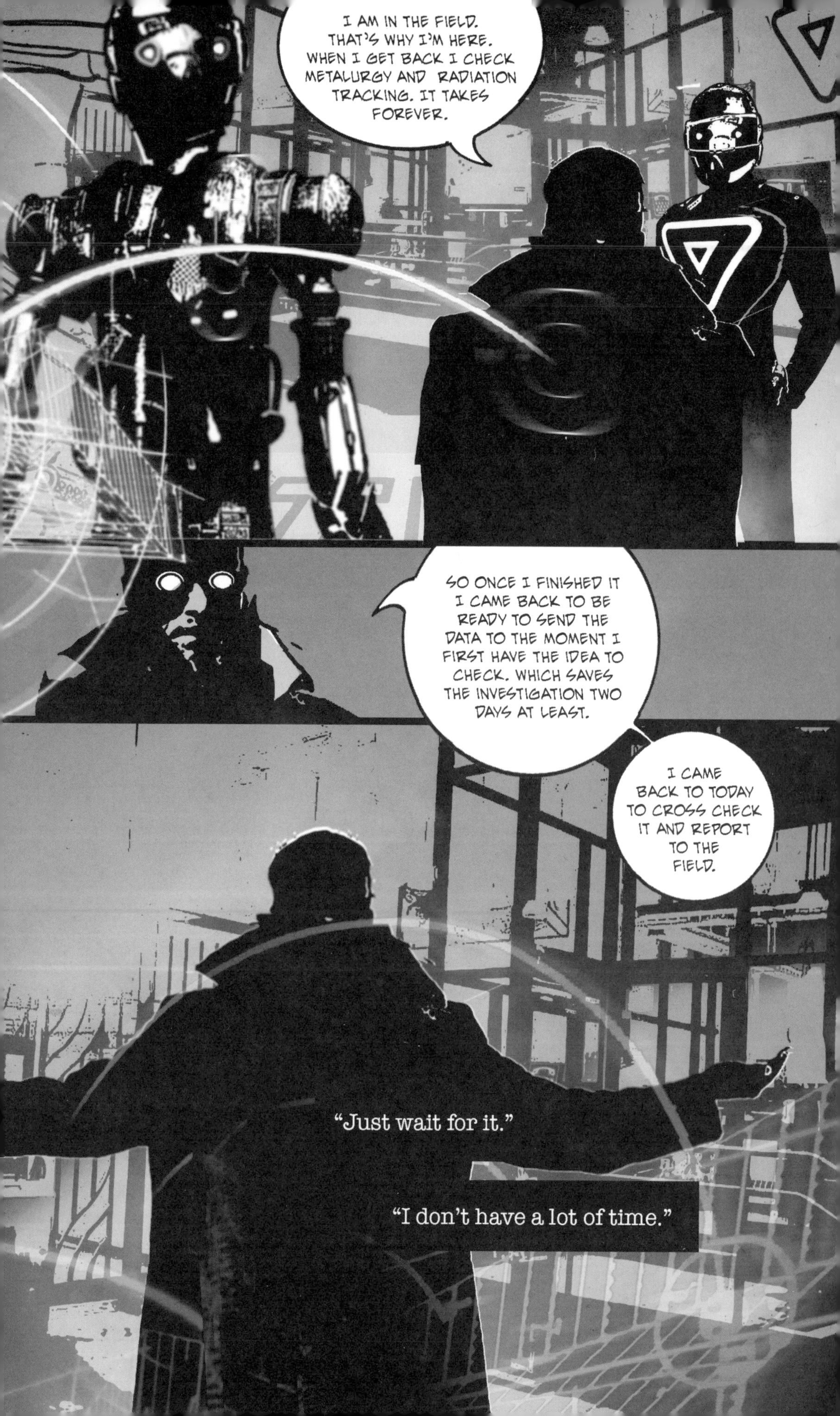
I AM IN THE FIELD. THAT'S WHY I'M HERE. WHEN I GET BACK I CHECK METALURGY AND RADIATION TRACKING. IT TAKES FOREVER.
SO ONCE I FINISHED IT I CAME BACK TO BE READY TO SEND THE DATA TO THE MOMENT I FIRST HAVE THE IDEA TO CHECK. WHICH SAVES THE INVESTIGATION TWO DAYS AT LEAST.
I CAME BACK TO TODAY TO CROSS CHECK IT AND REPORT TO THE FIELD.
"Just wait for it."
"I don't have a lot of time."

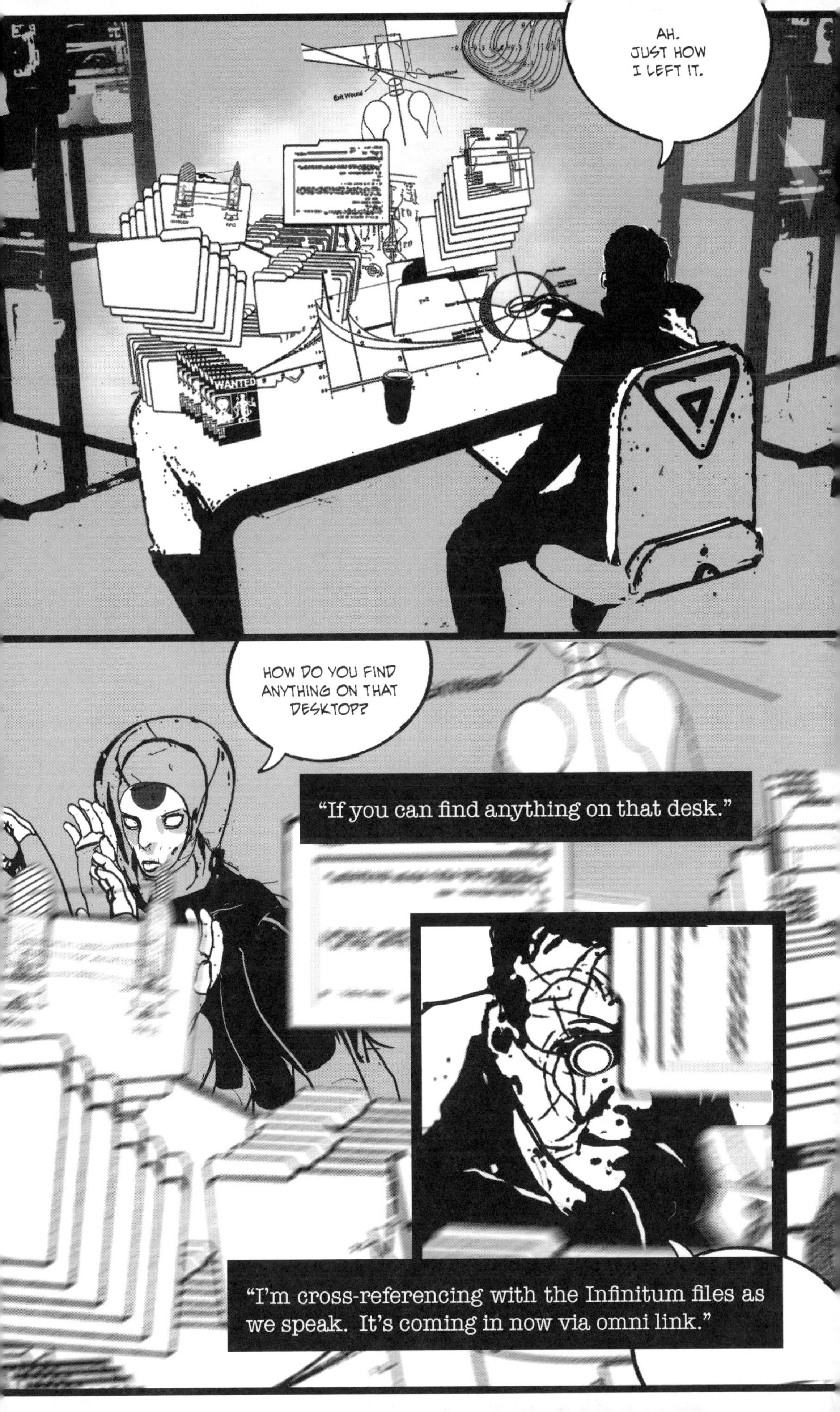
AH. JUST HOW I LEFT IT.
HOW DO YOU FIND ANYTHING ON THAT DESKTOP?
"If you can find anything on that desk."
"I'm cross-referencing with the Infinitum files as we speak. It's coming in now via omni link."

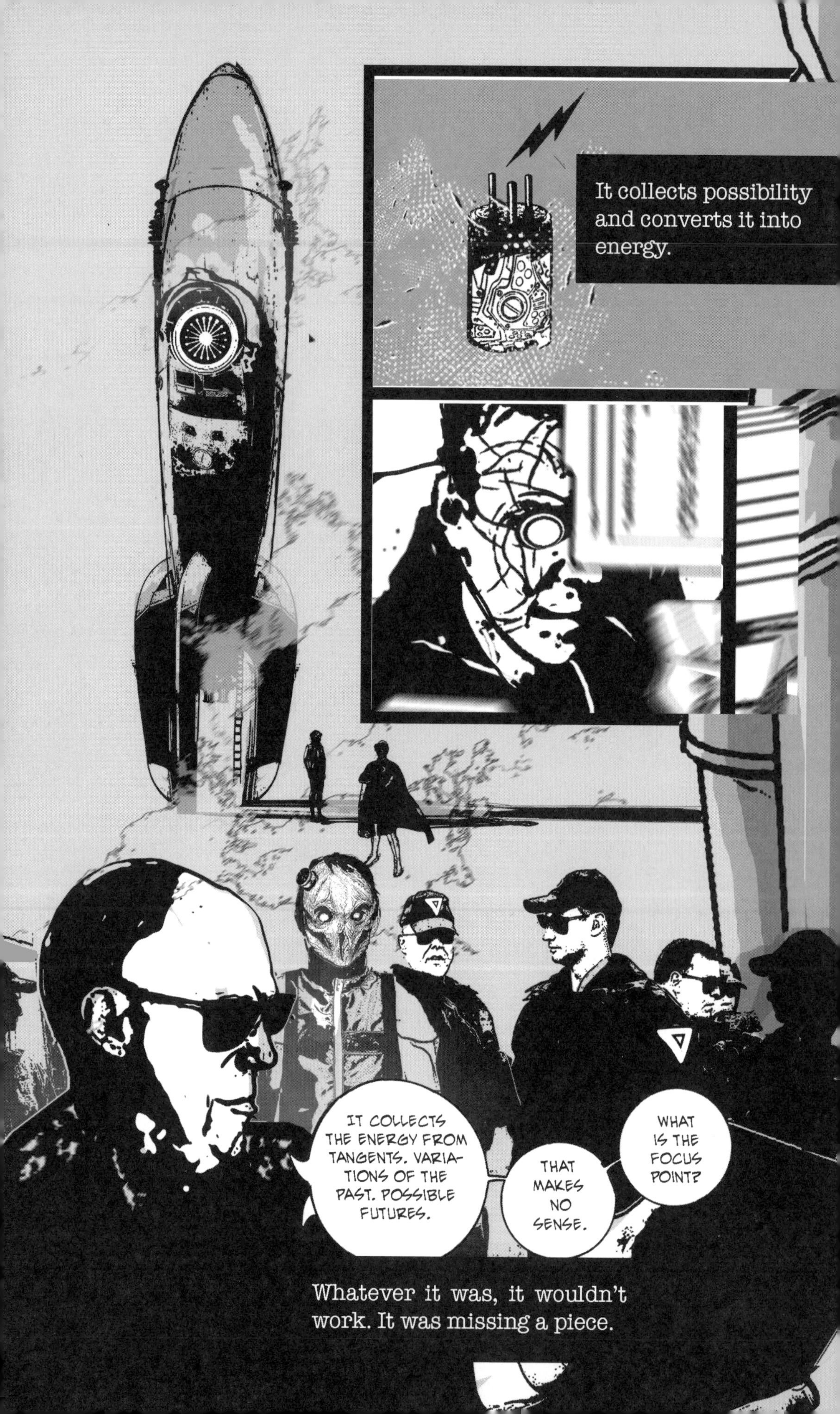
It collects possibility and converts it into energy.
IT COLLECTS THE ENERGY FROM TANGENTS. VARIATIONS OF THE PAST. POSSIBLE FUTURES.
THAT MAKES NO SENSE.
WHAT IS THE FOCUS POINT?
Whatever it was, it wouldn't work. It was missing a piece.

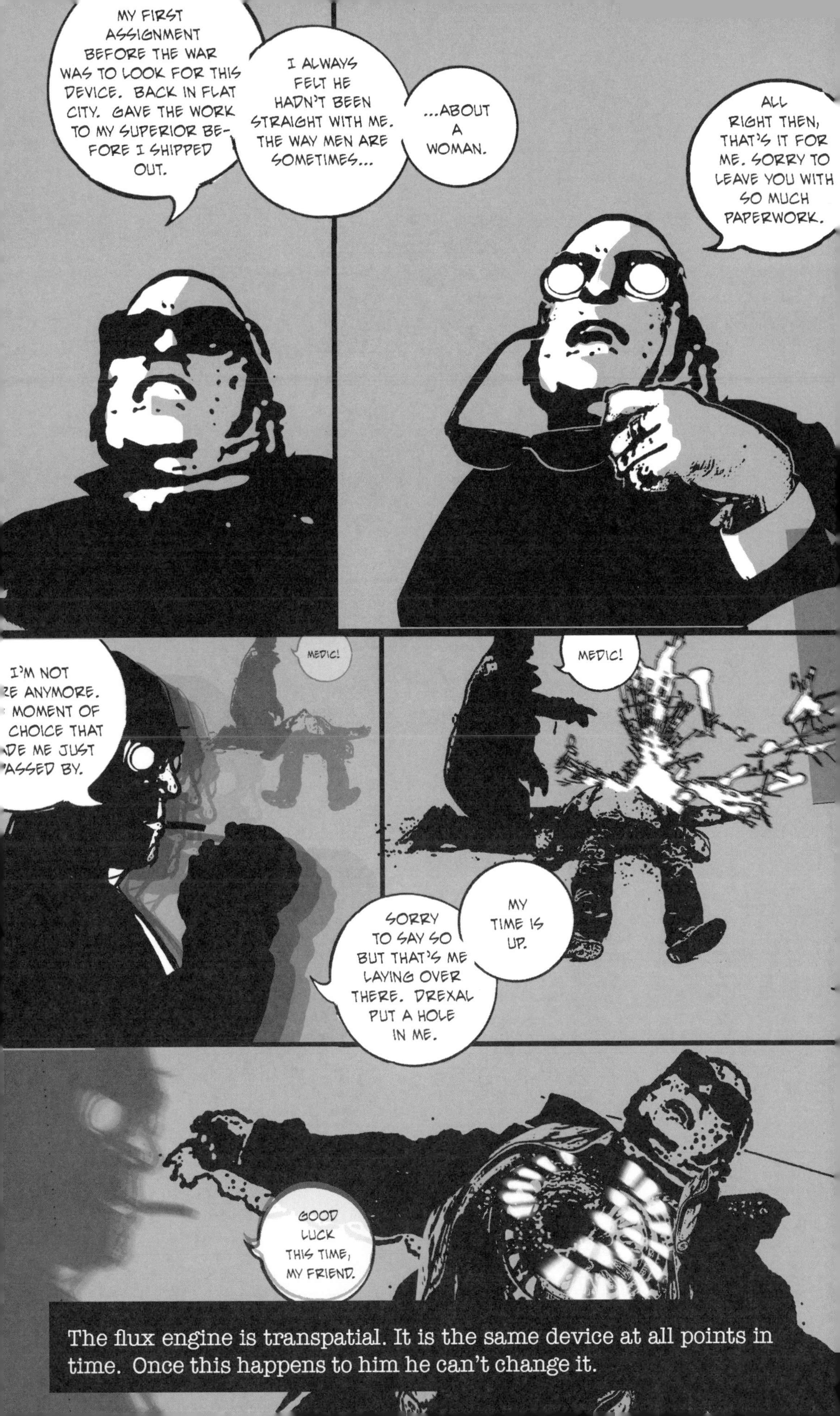
MY FIRST ASSIGNMENT BEFORE THE WAR WAS TO LOOK FOR THIS DEVICE. BACK IN FLAT CITY. GAVE THE WORK TO MY SUPERIOR BEFORE I SHIPPED OUT.
I ALWAYS FELT HE HADN'T BEEN STRAIGHT WITH ME. THE WAY MEN ARE SOMETIMES...
...ABOUT A WOMAN.
ALL RIGHT THEN, THAT'S IT FOR ME. SORRY TO LEAVE YOU WITH SO MUCH PAPERWORK.
I'M NOT ANYMORE. MOMENT OF CHOICE THAT ME JUST ASSED BY.
MEDIC!
MEDIC!
SORRY TO SAY SO BUT THAT'S ME LAYING OVER THERE. DREXAL PUT A HOLE IN ME.
MY TIME IS UP.
GOOD LUCK THIS TIME, MY FRIEND.
The flux engine is transpatial. It is the same device at all points in time. Once this happens to him he can't change it.

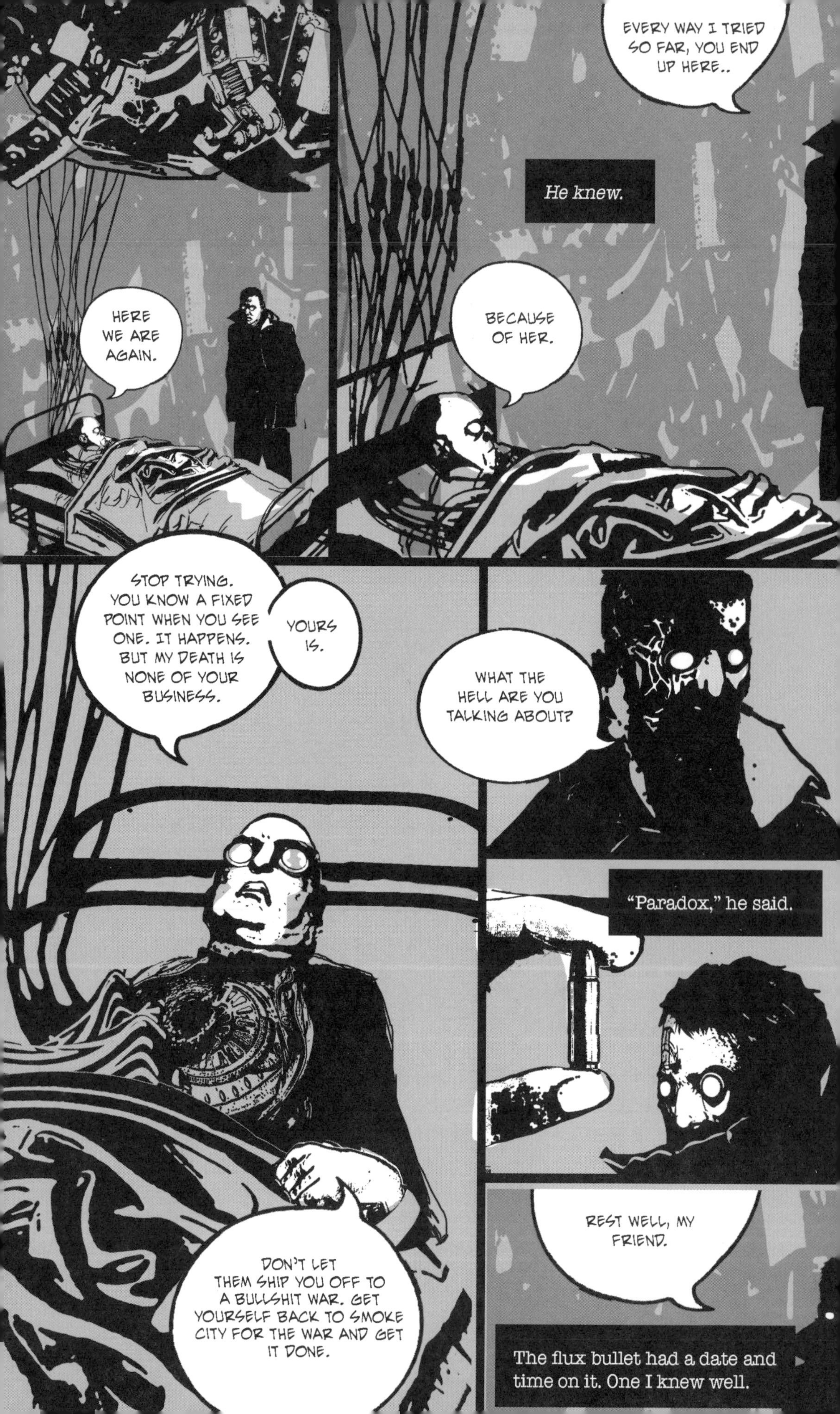
HERE WE ARE AGAIN.
EVERY WAY I TRIED SO FAR, YOU END UP HERE..
He knew.
BECAUSE OF HER.
STOP TRYING. YOU KNOW A FIXED POINT WHEN YOU SEE ONE. IT HAPPENS. BUT MY DEATH IS NONE OF YOUR BUSINESS.
YOURS IS.
WHAT THE HELL ARE YOU TALKING ABOUT?
"Paradox," he said.
DON'T LET THEM SHIP YOU OFF TO A BULLSHIT WAR. GET YOURSELF BACK TO SMOKE CITY FOR THE WAR AND GET IT DONE.
REST WELL, MY FRIEND.
The flux bullet had a date and time on it. One I knew well.

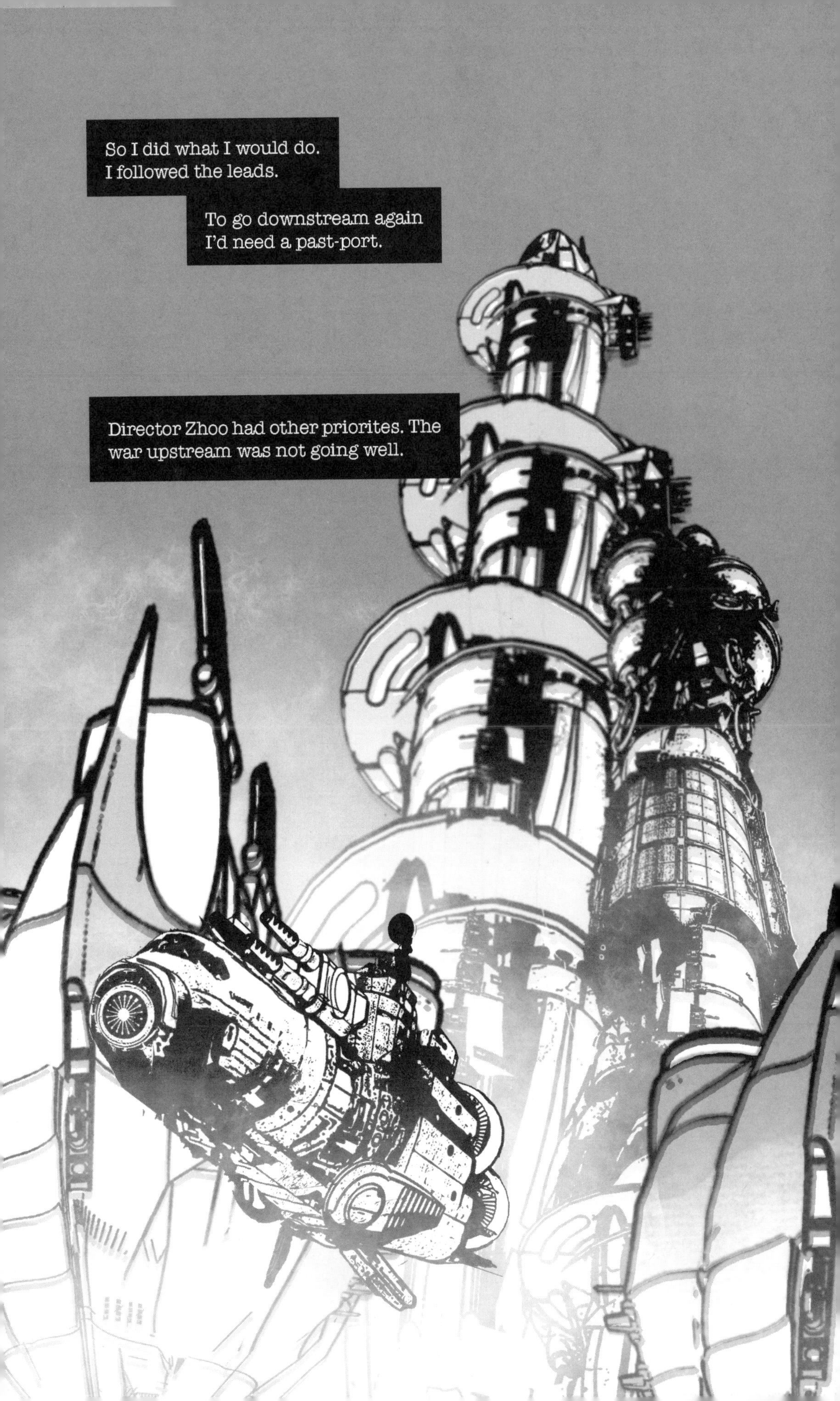
So I did what I would do.
I followed the leads.
To go downstream again
I'd need a past-port.
Director Zhoo had other priorites. The
war upstream was not going well.

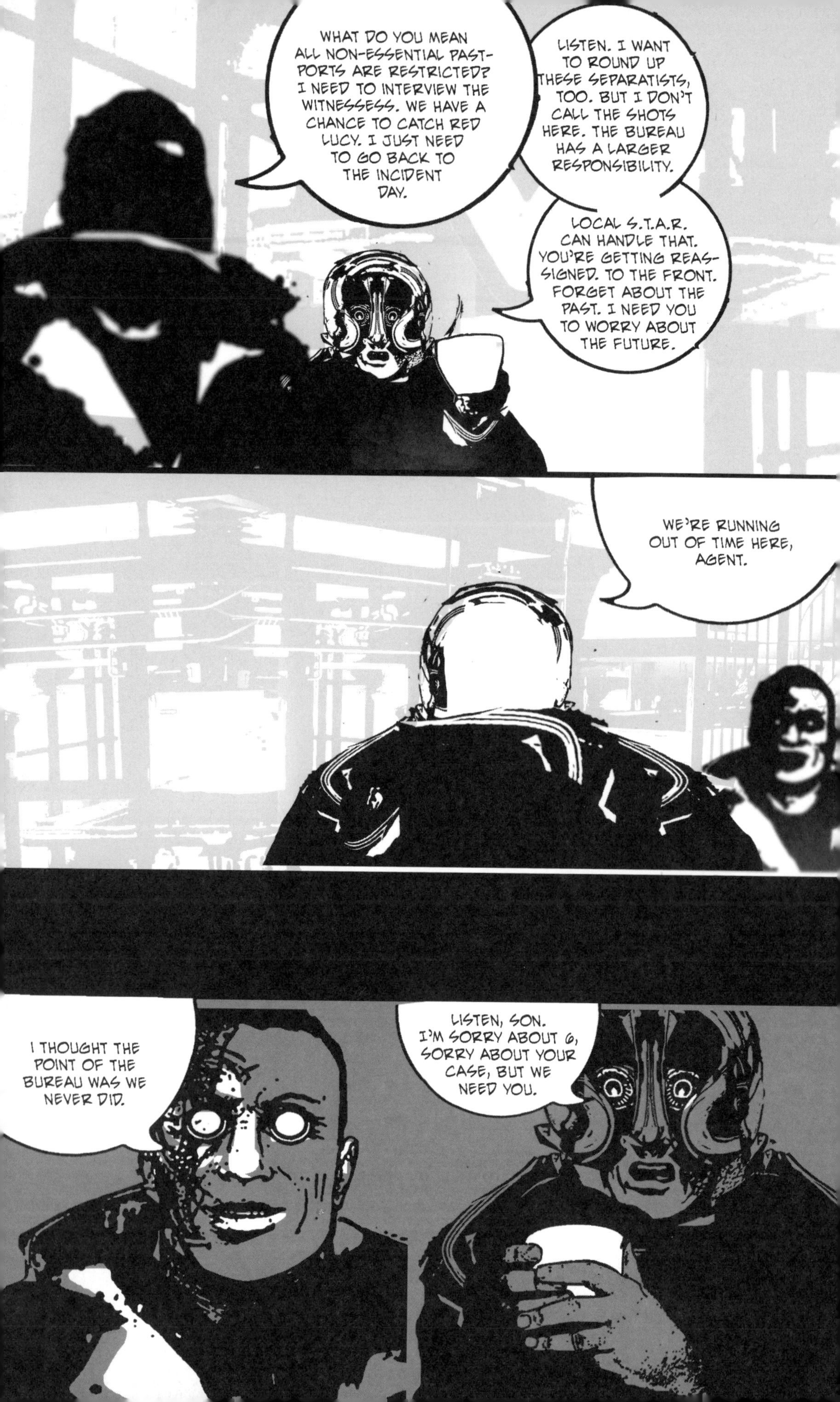
WHAT DO YOU MEAN ALL NON-ESSENTIAL PASSPORTS ARE RESTRICTED? I NEED TO INTERVIEW THE WITNESSESS. WE HAVE A CHANCE TO CATCH RED LUCY. I JUST NEED TO GO BACK TO THE INCIDENT DAY.
LISTEN. I WANT TO ROUND UP THESE SEPARATISTS, TOO. BUT I DON'T CALL THE SHOTS HERE. THE BUREAU HAS A LARGER RESPONSIBILITY.
LOCAL S.T.A.R. CAN HANDLE THAT. YOU'RE GETTING REASSIGNED. TO THE FRONT. FORGET ABOUT THE PAST. I NEED YOU TO WORRY ABOUT THE FUTURE.
WE'RE RUNNING OUT OF TIME HERE, AGENT.
I THOUGHT THE POINT OF THE BUREAU WAS WE NEVER DID.
LISTEN, SON. I'M SORRY ABOUT 6, SORRY ABOUT YOUR CASE, BUT WE NEED YOU.

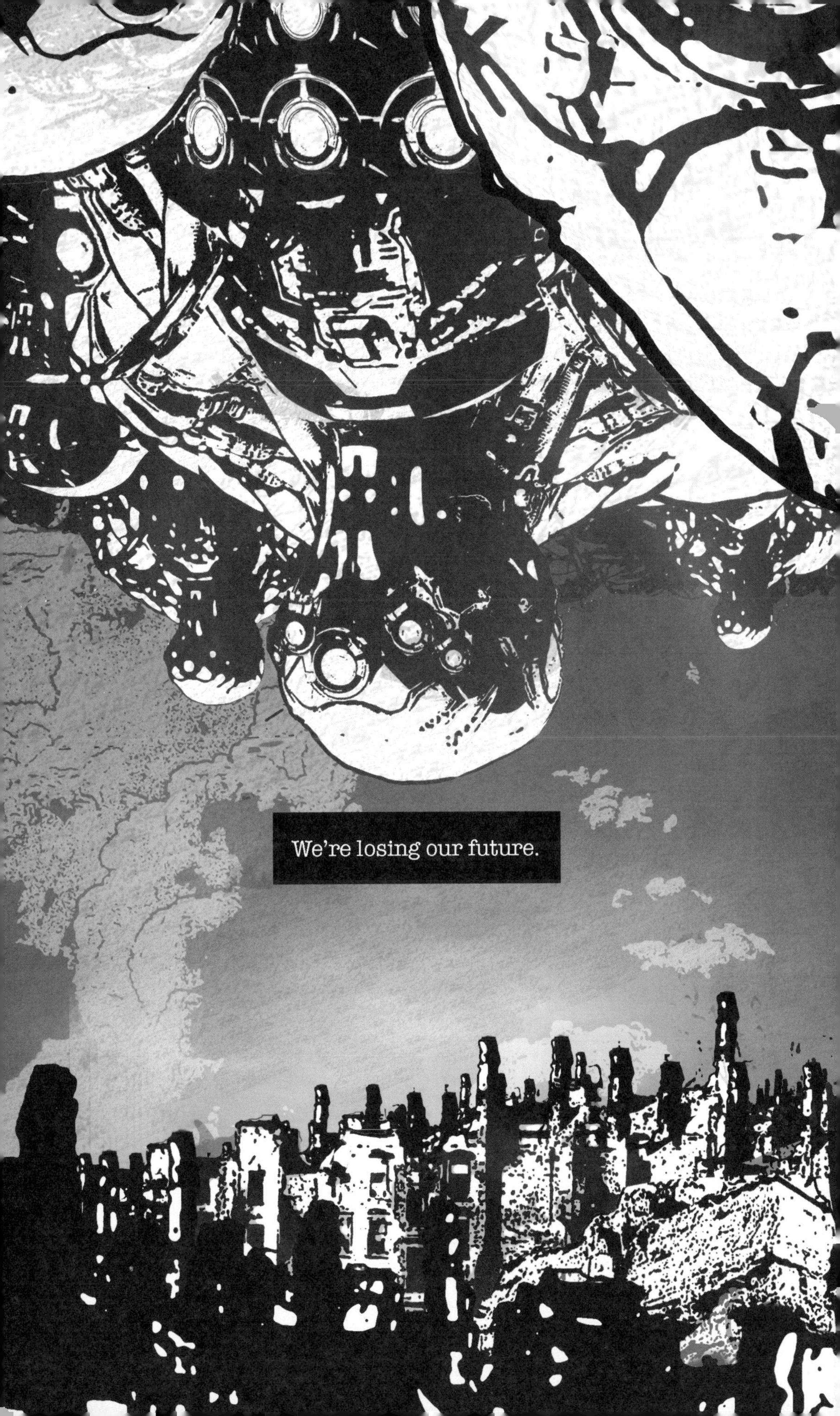
We're losing our future.

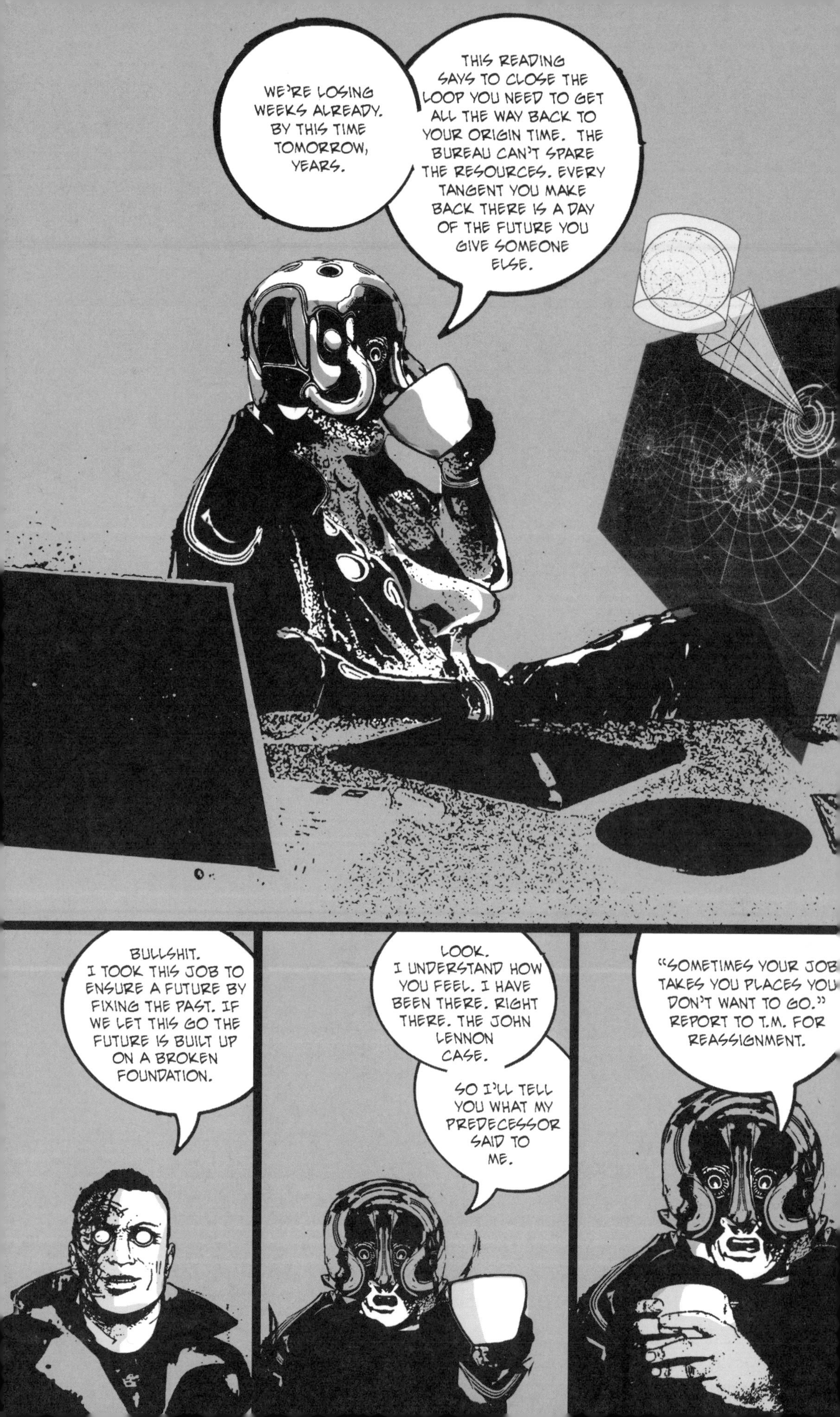
WE'RE LOSING WEEKS ALREADY. BY THIS TIME TOMORROW, YEARS.
THIS READING SAYS TO CLOSE THE LOOP YOU NEED TO GET ALL THE WAY BACK TO YOUR ORIGIN TIME. THE BUREAU CAN'T SPARE THE RESOURCES. EVERY TANGENT YOU MAKE BACK THERE IS A DAY OF THE FUTURE YOU GIVE SOMEONE ELSE.
BULLSHIT. I TOOK THIS JOB TO ENSURE A FUTURE BY FIXING THE PAST. IF WE LET THIS GO THE FUTURE IS BUILT UP ON A BROKEN FOUNDATION.
LOOK. I UNDERSTAND HOW YOU FEEL. I HAVE BEEN THERE. RIGHT THERE. THE JOHN LENNON CASE.
SO I'LL TELL YOU WHAT MY PREDECESSOR SAID TO ME.
"SOMETIMES YOUR JOB TAKES YOU PLACES YOU DON'T WANT TO GO." REPORT TO T.M. FOR REASSIGNMENT.

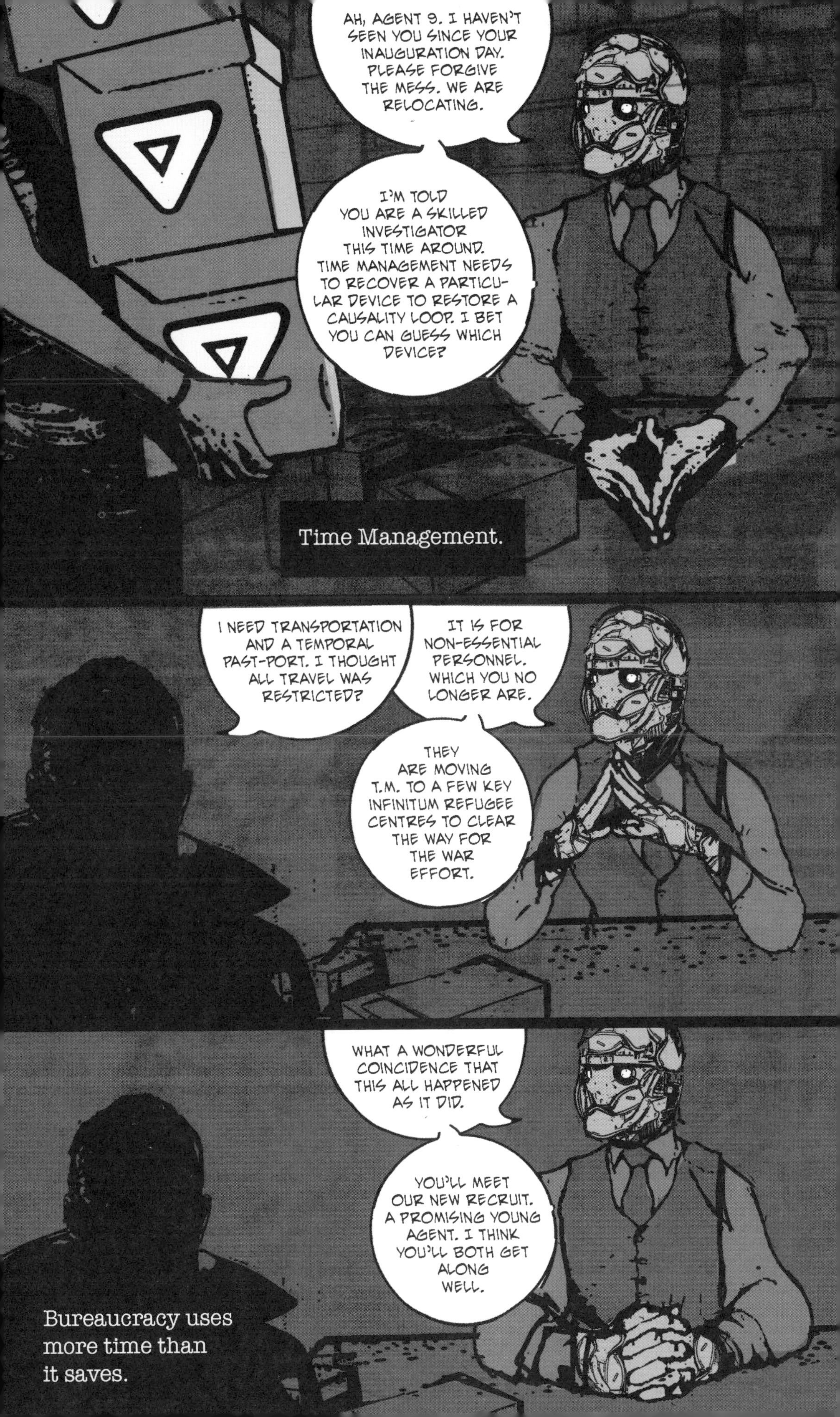
AH, AGENT 9. I HAVEN'T SEEN YOU SINCE YOUR INAUGURATION DAY. PLEASE FORGIVE THE MESS. WE ARE RELOCATING.
I'M TOLD YOU ARE A SKILLED INVESTIGATOR THIS TIME AROUND. TIME MANAGEMENT NEEDS TO RECOVER A PARTICU-LAR DEVICE TO RESTORE A CAUSALITY LOOP. I BET YOU CAN GUESS WHICH DEVICE?
Time Management.
I NEED TRANSPORTATION AND A TEMPORAL PAST-PORT. I THOUGHT ALL TRAVEL WAS RESTRICTED?
IT IS FOR NON-ESSENTIAL PERSONNEL. WHICH YOU NO LONGER ARE.
THEY ARE MOVING T.M. TO A FEW KEY INFINITUM REFUGEE CENTRES TO CLEAR THE WAY FOR THE WAR EFFORT.
WHAT A WONDERFUL COINCIDENCE THAT THIS ALL HAPPENED AS IT DID.
YOU'LL MEET OUR NEW RECRUIT. A PROMISING YOUNG AGENT. I THINK YOU'LL BOTH GET ALONG WELL.
Bureaucracy uses more time than it saves.

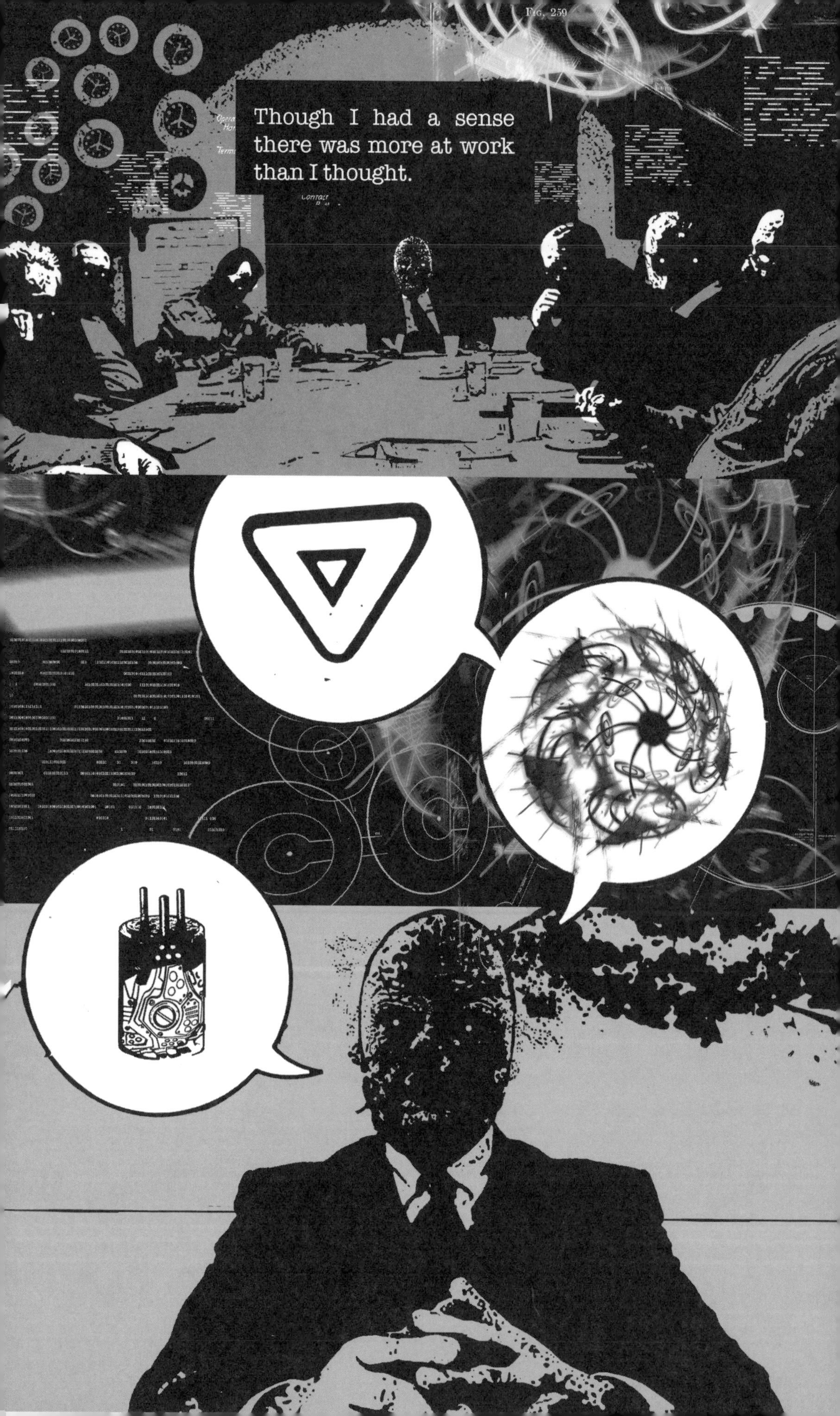
Fig. 259
Though I had a sense there was more at work than I thought.

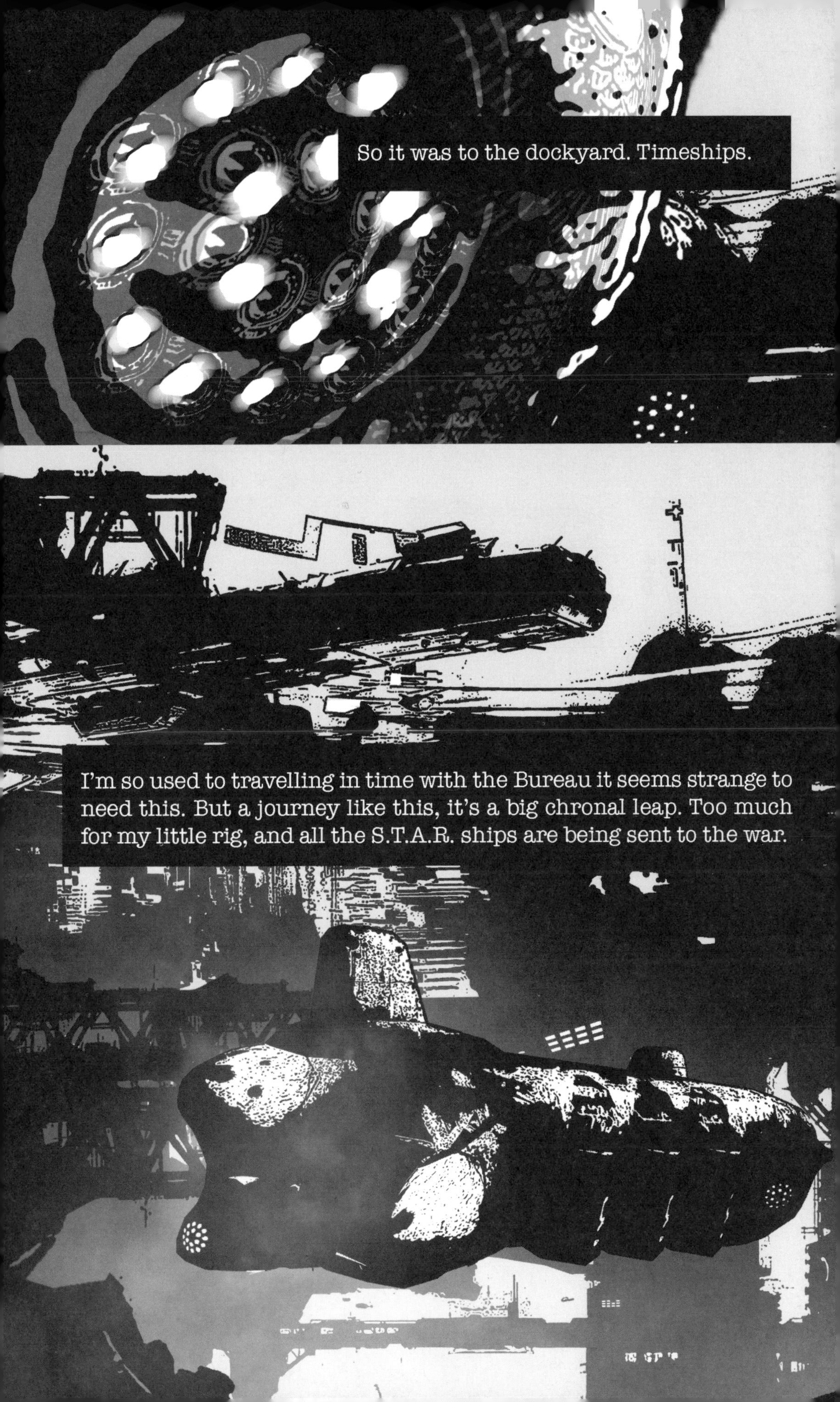
So it was to the dockyard. Timeships.
I'm so used to travelling in time with the Bureau it seems strange to need this. But a journey like this, it's a big chronal leap. Too much for my little rig, and all the S.T.A.R. ships are being sent to the war.

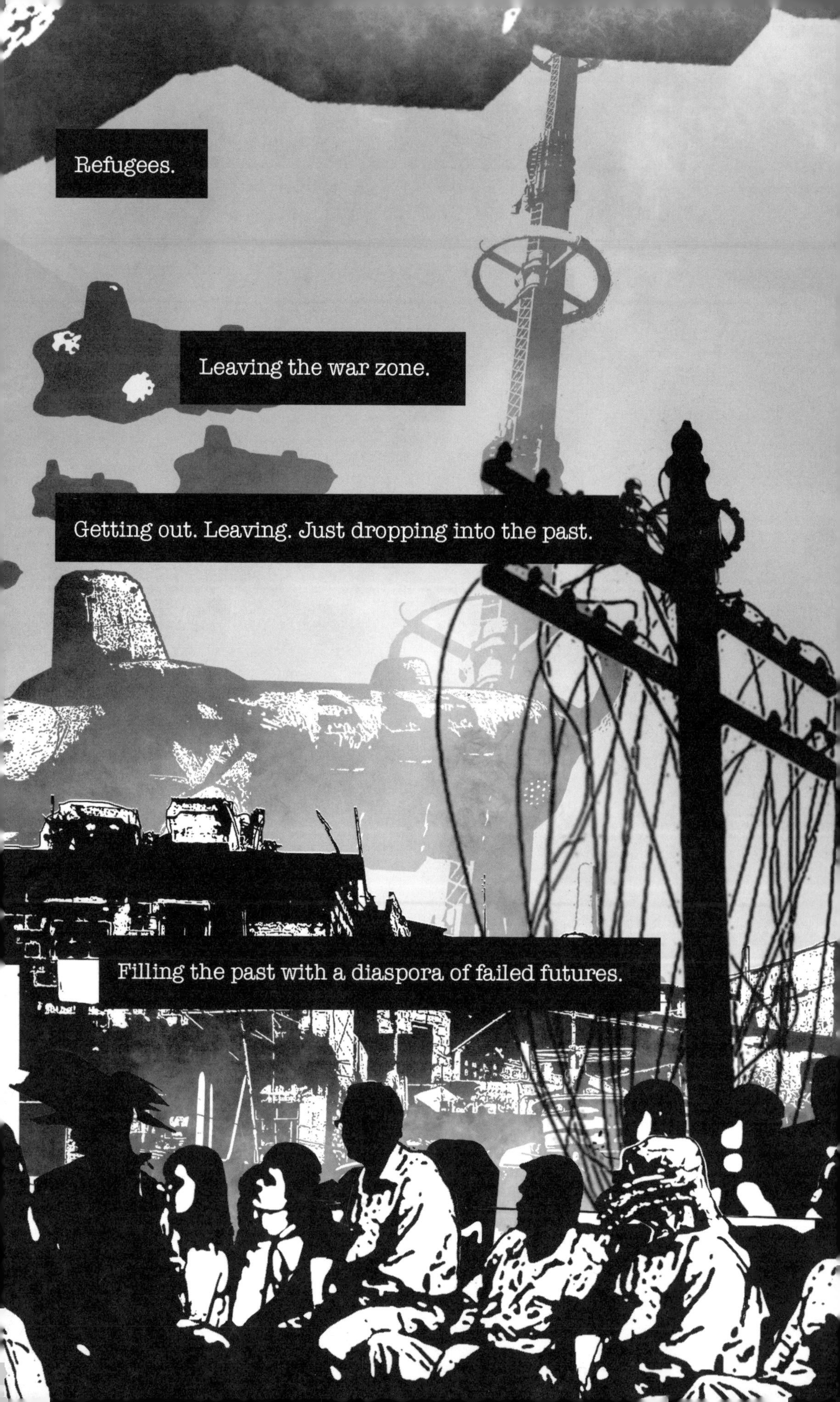

Refugees.
Leaving the war zone.
Getting out. Leaving. Just dropping into the past.
Filling the past with a diaspora of failed futures.

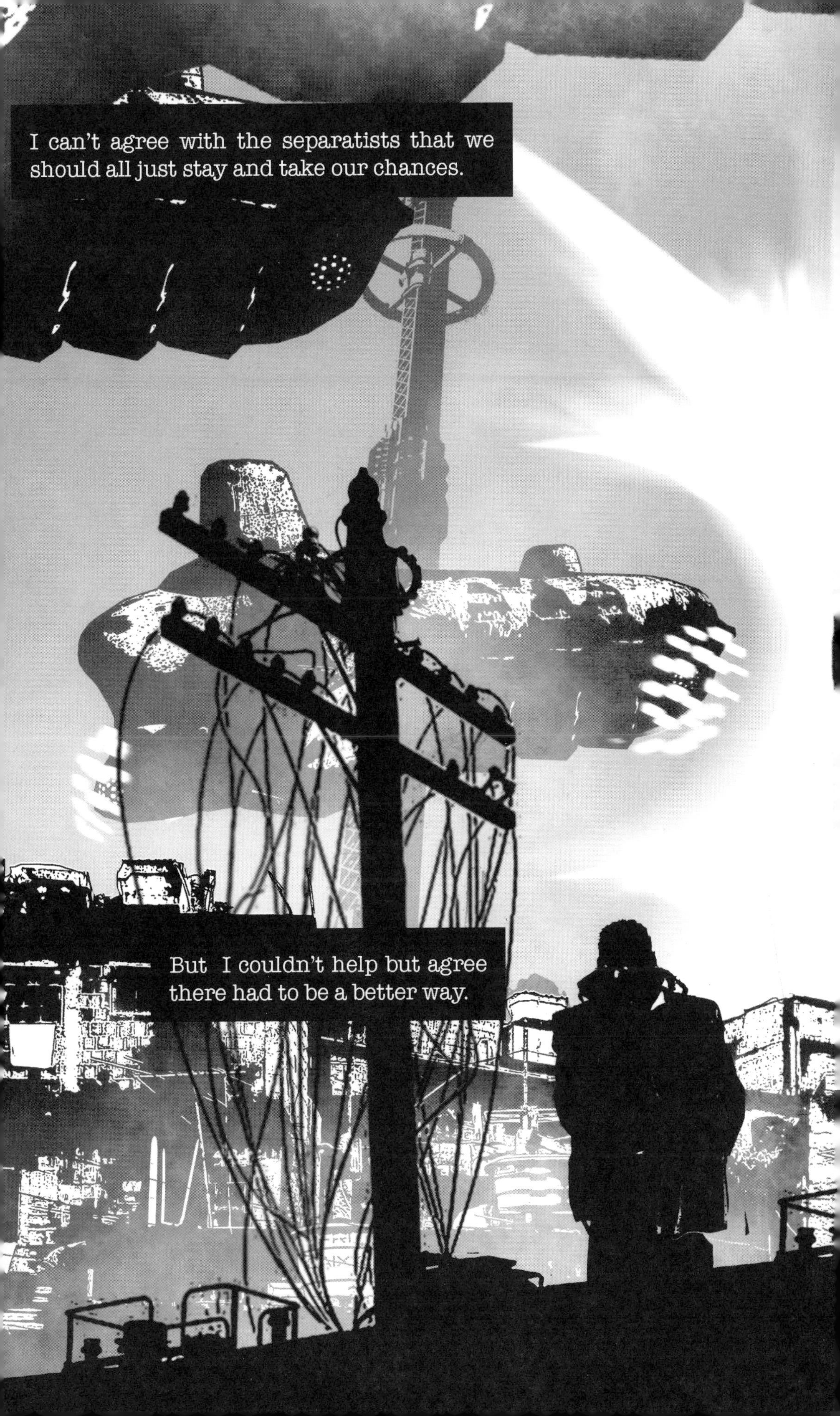
I can't agree with the separatists that we should all just stay and take our chances.
But I couldn't help but agree there had to be a better way.

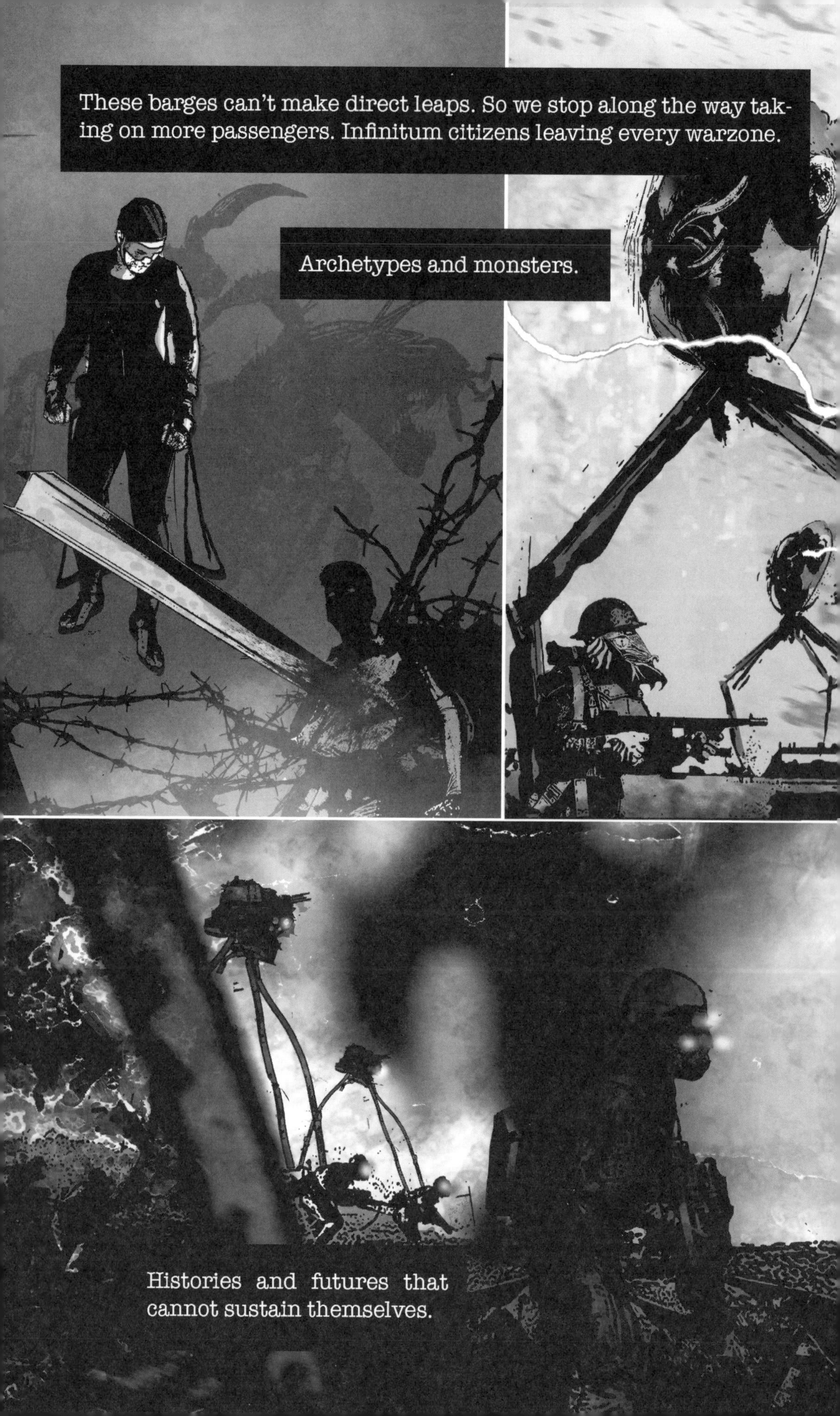
These barges can't make direct leaps. So we stop along the way tak-ing on more passengers. Infinitum citizens leaving every warzone.
Archetypes and monsters.
Histories and futures that cannot sustain themselves.

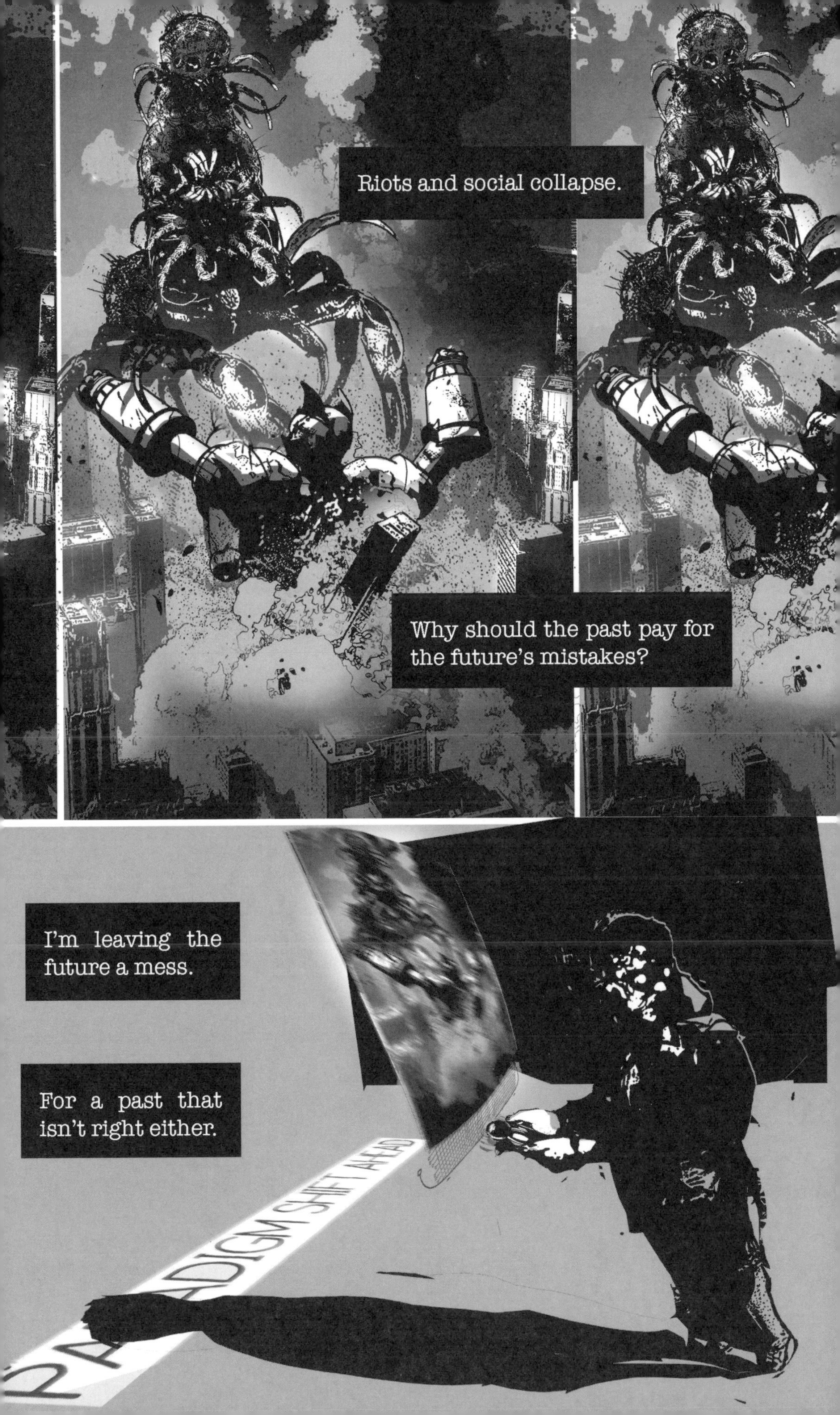
Riots and social collapse.
Why should the past pay for the future's mistakes?
I'm leaving the future a mess.
For a past that isn't right either.
DIGM SHIFT AHEAD

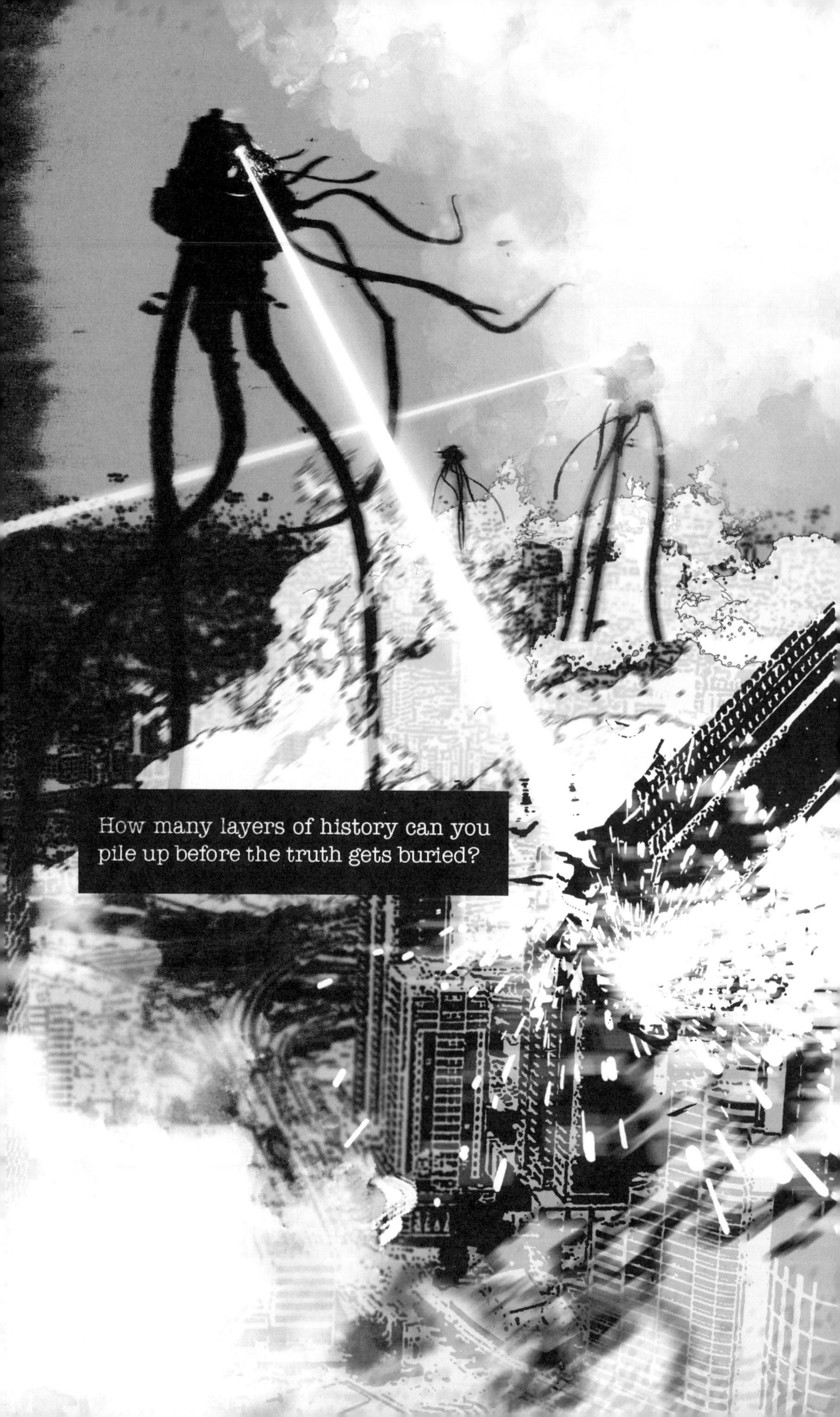
How many layers of history can you pile up before the truth gets buried?

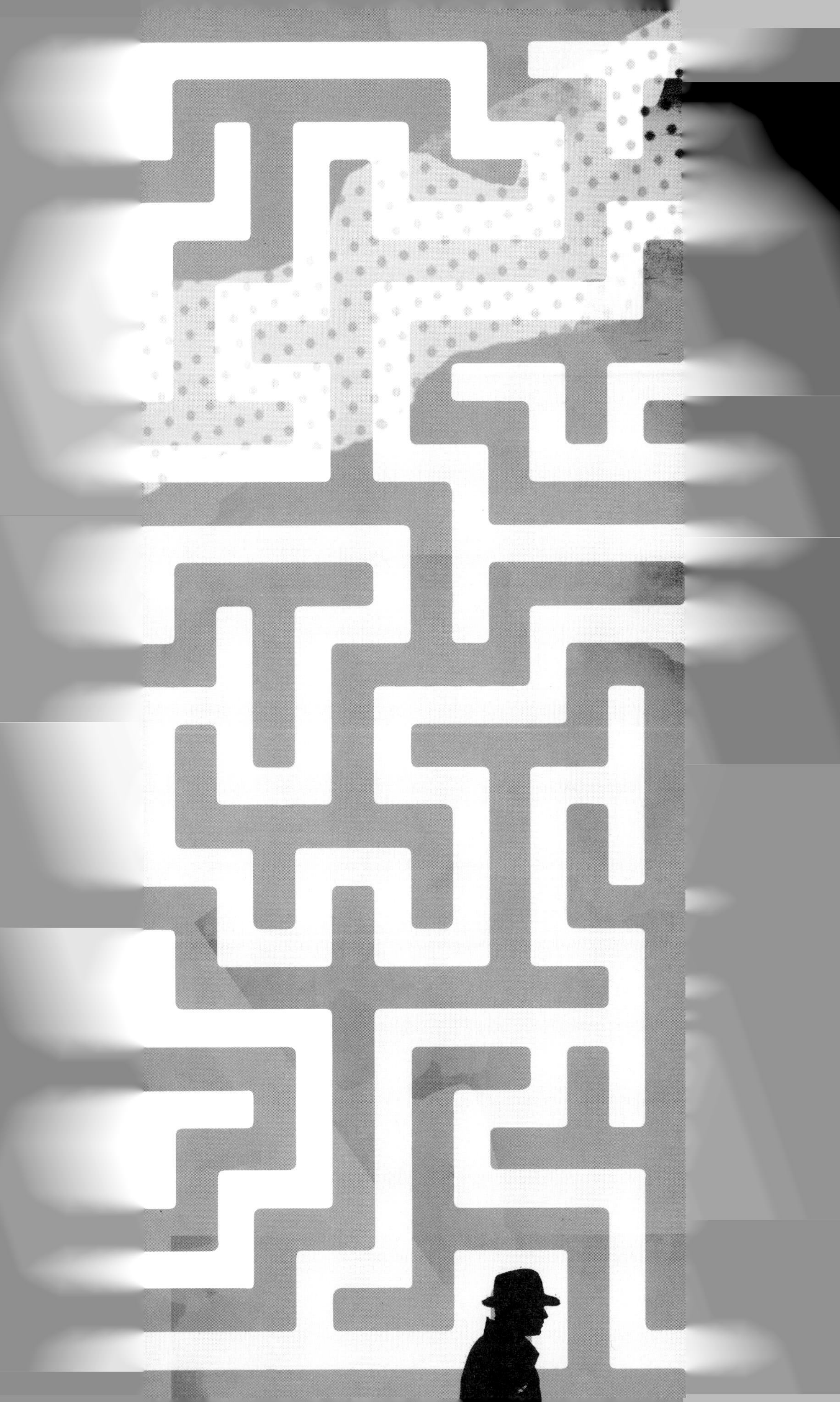

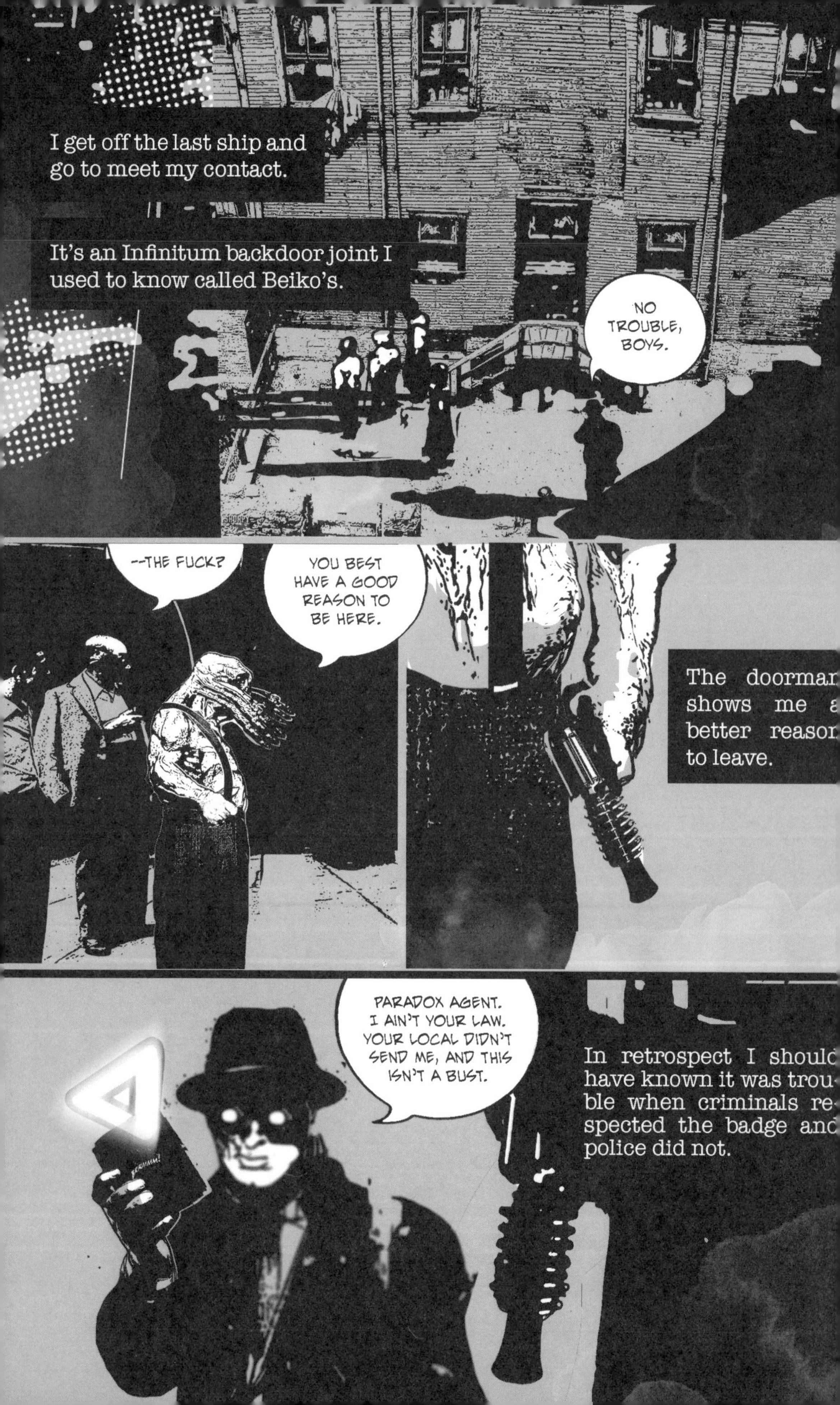

I get off the last ship and go to meet my contact.
It's an Infinitum backdoor joint I used to know called Beiko's.
NO TROUBLE, BOYS.
--THE FUCK?
YOU BEST HAVE A GOOD REASON TO BE HERE.
The doorman shows me a better reason to leave.
PARADOX AGENT. I AIN'T YOUR LAW. YOUR LOCAL DIDN'T SEND ME, AND THIS ISN'T A BUST.
In retrospect I should have known it was trouble when criminals respected the badge and police did not.

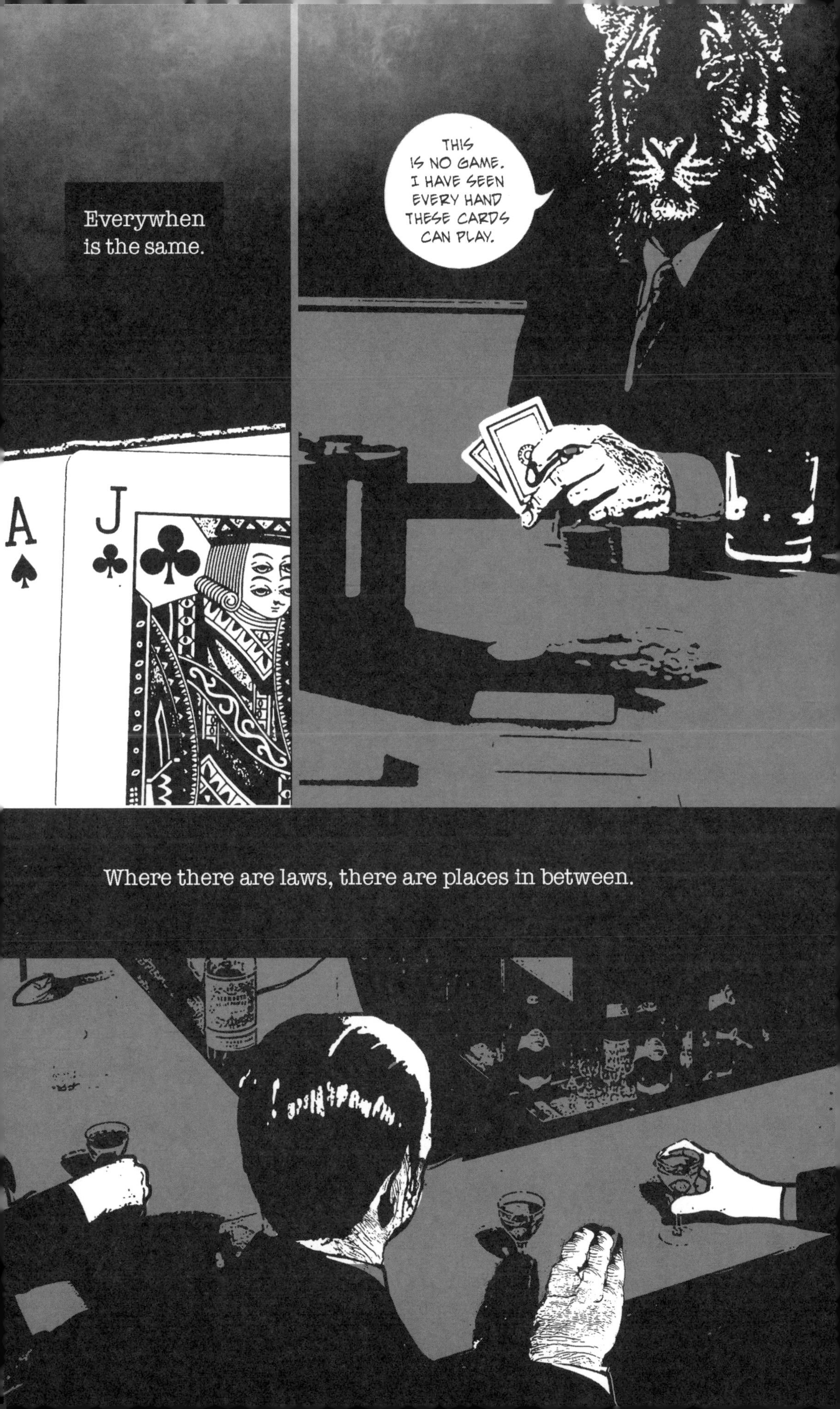
Everywhen
is the same.
THIS IS NO GAME. I HAVE SEEN EVERY HAND THESE CARDS CAN PLAY.
A
J
Where there are laws, there are places in between.

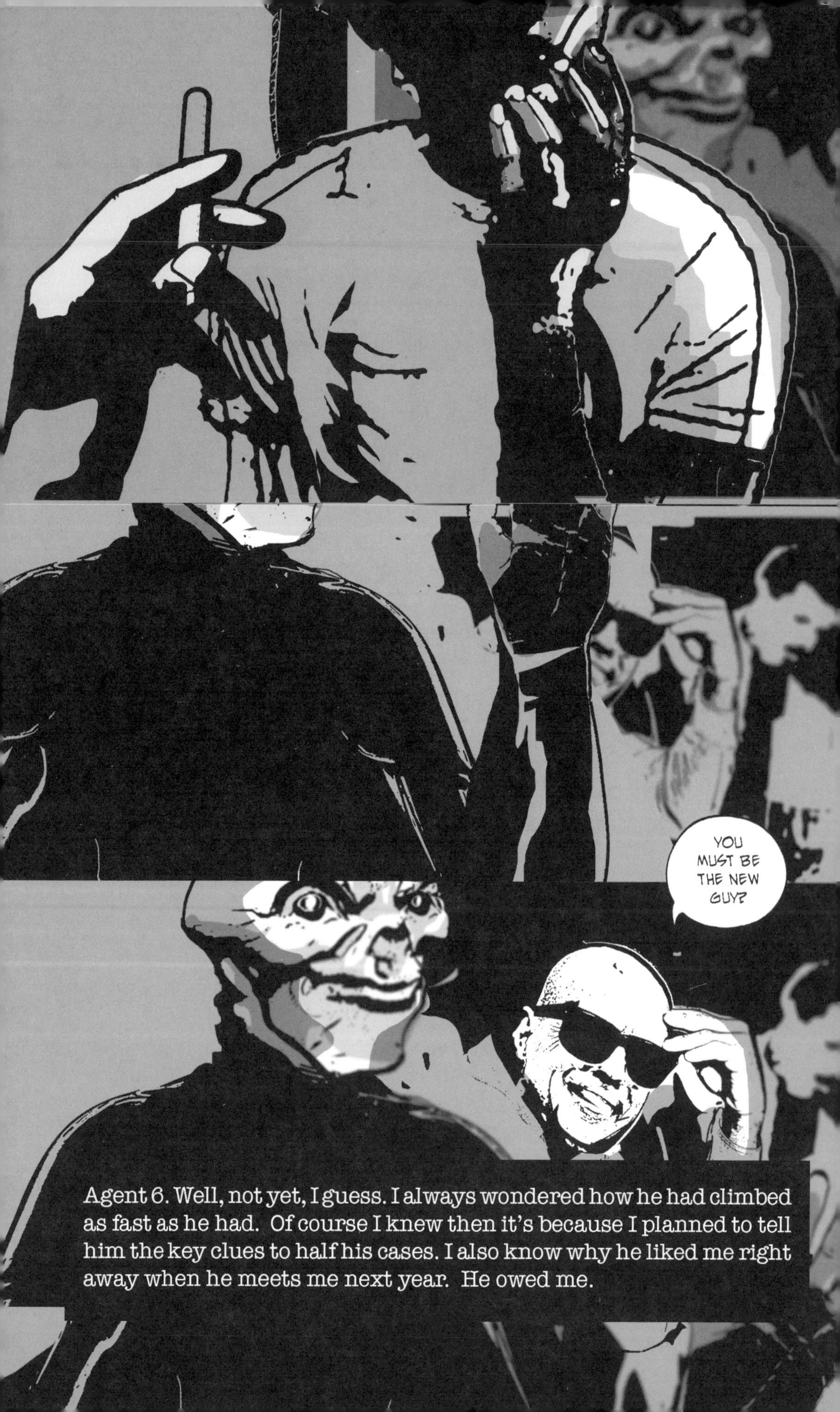
YOU MUST BE THE NEW GUY?
Agent 6. Well, not yet, I guess. I always wondered how he had climbed as fast as he had. Of course I knew then it's because I planned to tell him the key clues to half his cases. I also know why he liked me right away when he meets me next year. He owed me.

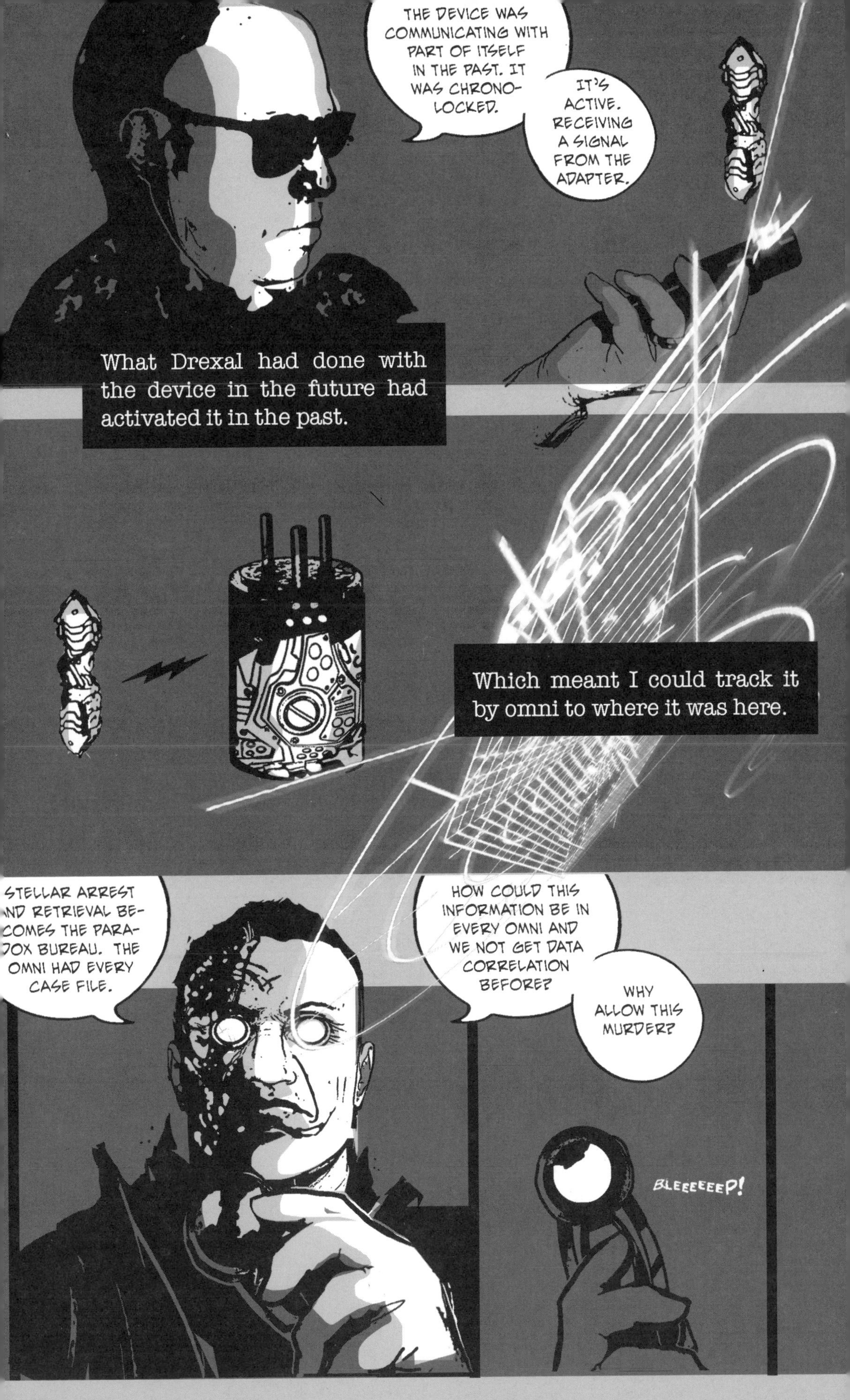
THE DEVICE WAS COMMUNICATING WITH PART OF ITSELF IN THE PAST. IT WAS CHRONO-LOCKED.
IT'S ACTIVE. RECEIVING A SIGNAL FROM THE ADAPTER.
What Drexal had done with the device in the future had activated it in the past.
Which meant I could track it by omni to where it was here.
STELLAR ARREST ND RETRIEVAL BE-COMES THE PARA-OX BUREAU. THE OMNI HAD EVERY CASE FILE.
HOW COULD THIS INFORMATION BE IN EVERY OMNI AND WE NOT GET DATA CORRELATION BEFORE?
WHY ALLOW THIS MURDER?
BLEEEEEEP!

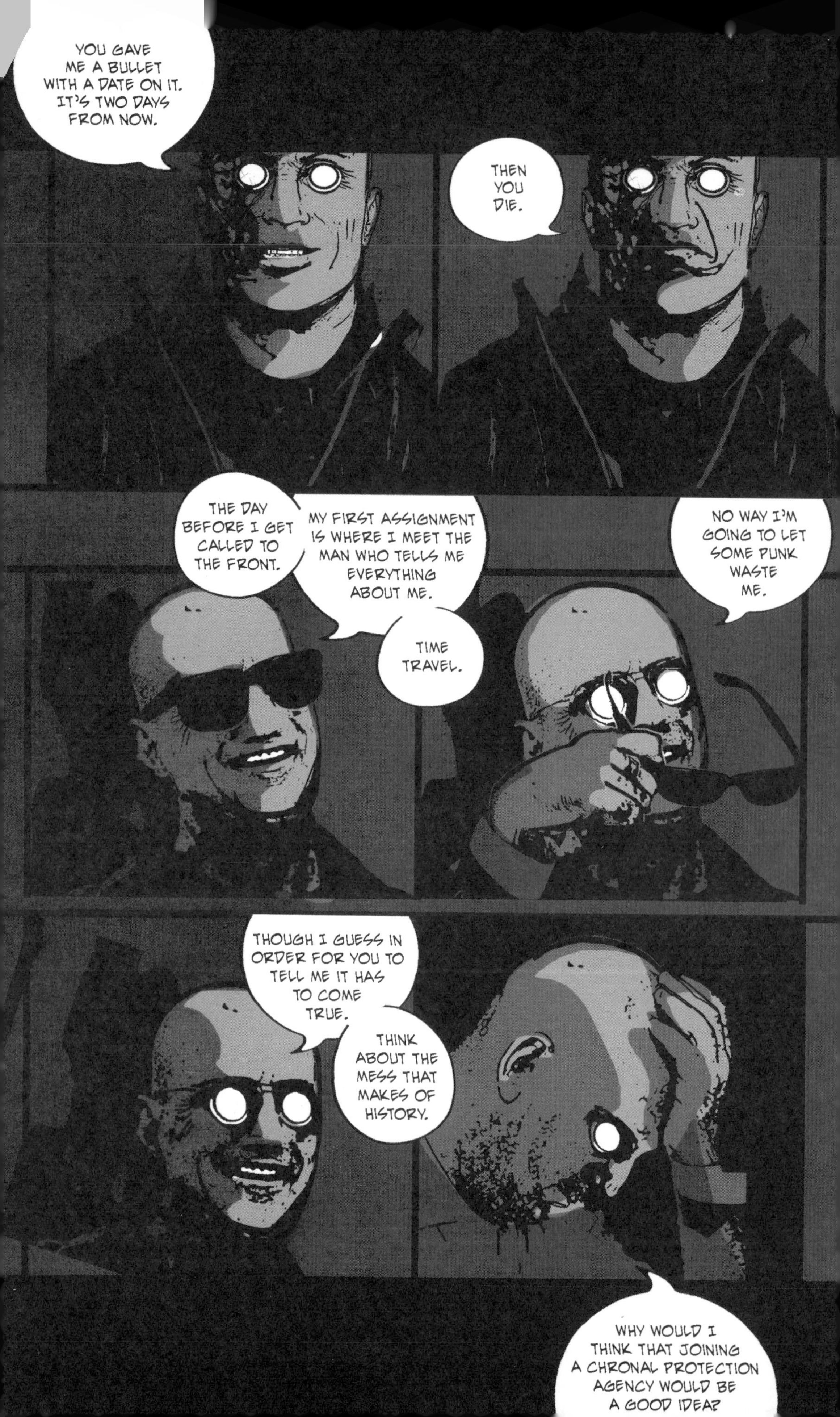
YOU GAVE ME A BULLET WITH A DATE ON IT. IT'S TWO DAYS FROM NOW.
THEN YOU DIE.
THE DAY BEFORE I GET CALLED TO THE FRONT.
MY FIRST ASSIGNMENT IS WHERE I MEET THE MAN WHO TELLS ME EVERYTHING ABOUT ME.
TIME TRAVEL.
NO WAY I'M GOING TO LET SOME PUNK WASTE ME.
THOUGH I GUESS IN ORDER FOR YOU TO TELL ME IT HAS TO COME TRUE.
THINK ABOUT THE MESS THAT MAKES OF HISTORY.
WHY WOULD I THINK THAT JOINING A CHRONAL PROTECTION AGENCY WOULD BE A GOOD IDEA?

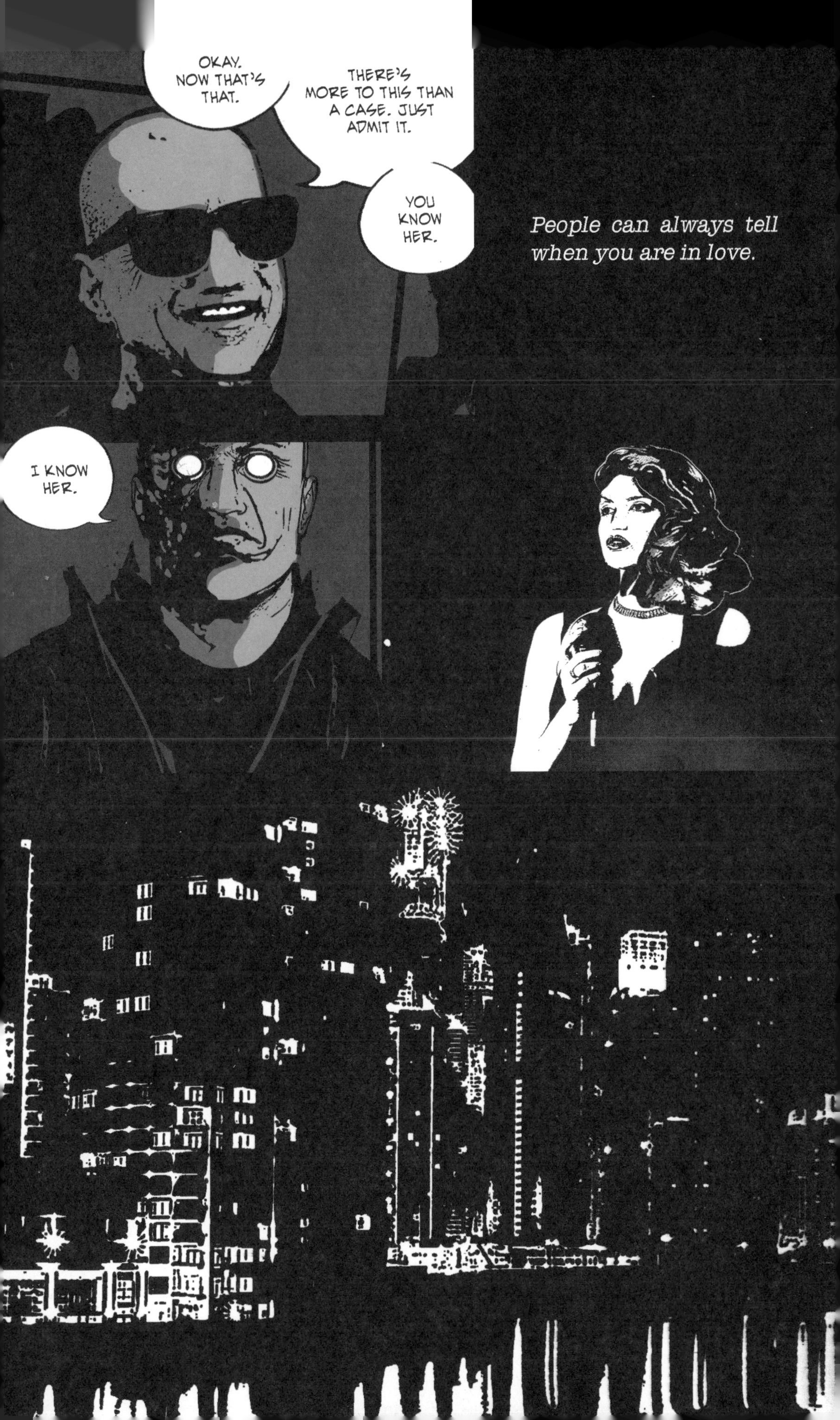
OKAY. NOW THAT'S THAT.
THERE'S MORE TO THIS THAN A CASE. JUST ADMIT IT.
YOU KNOW HER.
People can always tell when you are in love.
I KNOW HER.

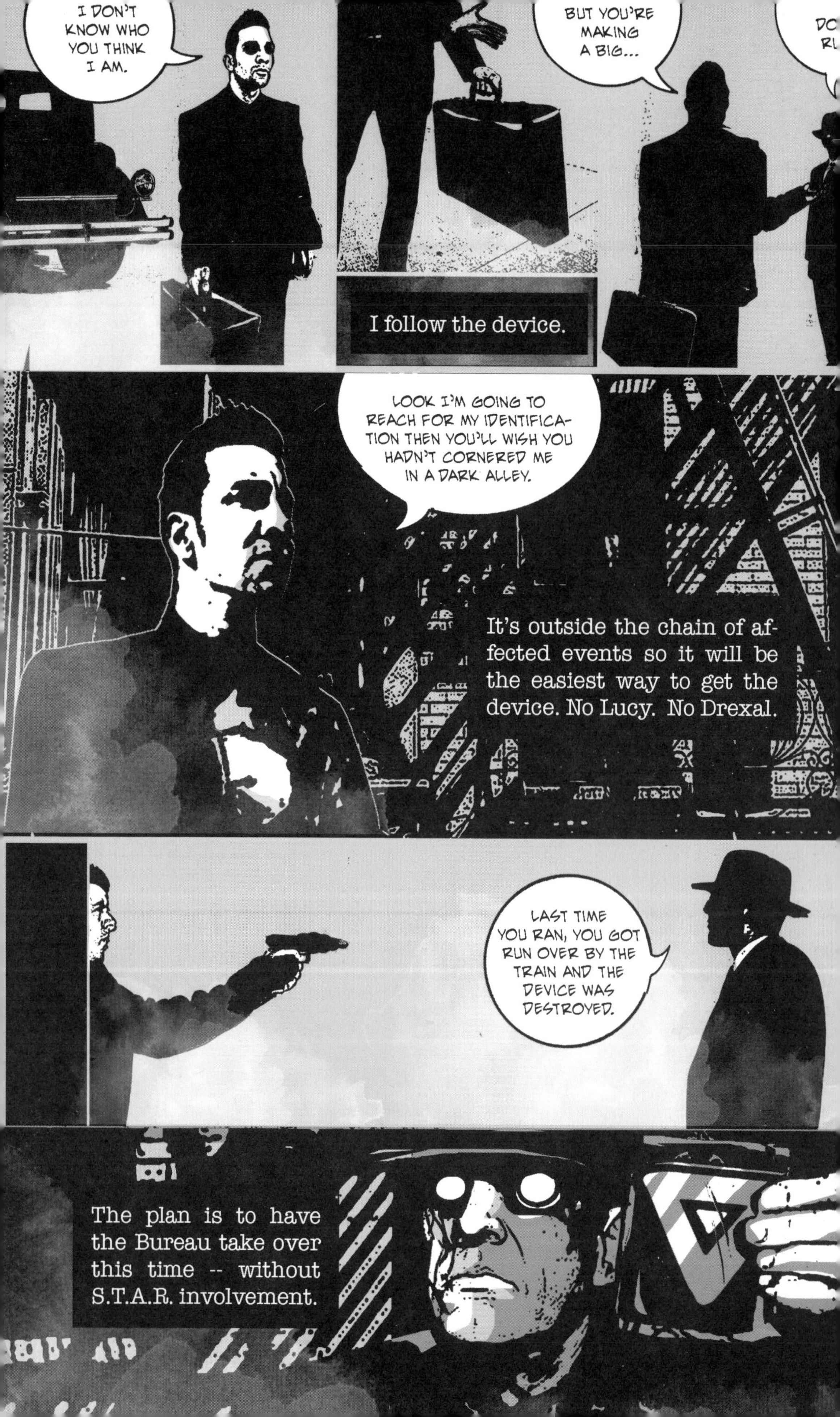
I DON'T KNOW WHO YOU THINK I AM.
BUT YOU'RE MAKING A BIG...
I follow the device.
LOOK I'M GOING TO REACH FOR MY IDENTIFICATION THEN YOU'LL WISH YOU HADN'T CORNERED ME IN A DARK ALLEY.
It's outside the chain of affected events so it will be the easiest way to get the device. No Lucy. No Drexal.
LAST TIME YOU RAN, YOU GOT RUN OVER BY THE TRAIN AND THE DEVICE WAS DESTROYED.
The plan is to have the Bureau take over this time -- without S.T.A.R. involvement.

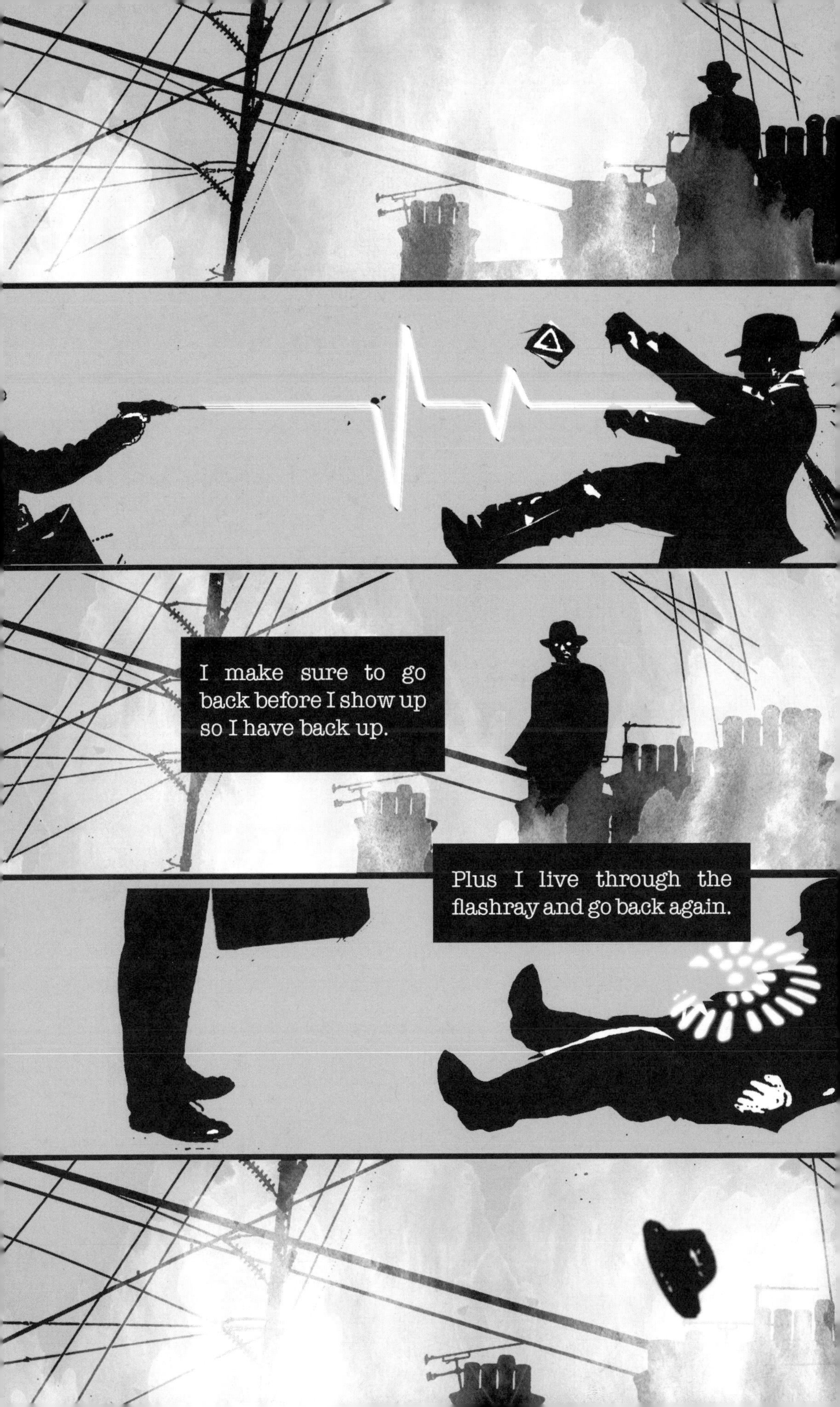
I make sure to go back before I show up so I have back up.
Plus I live through the flashray and go back again.

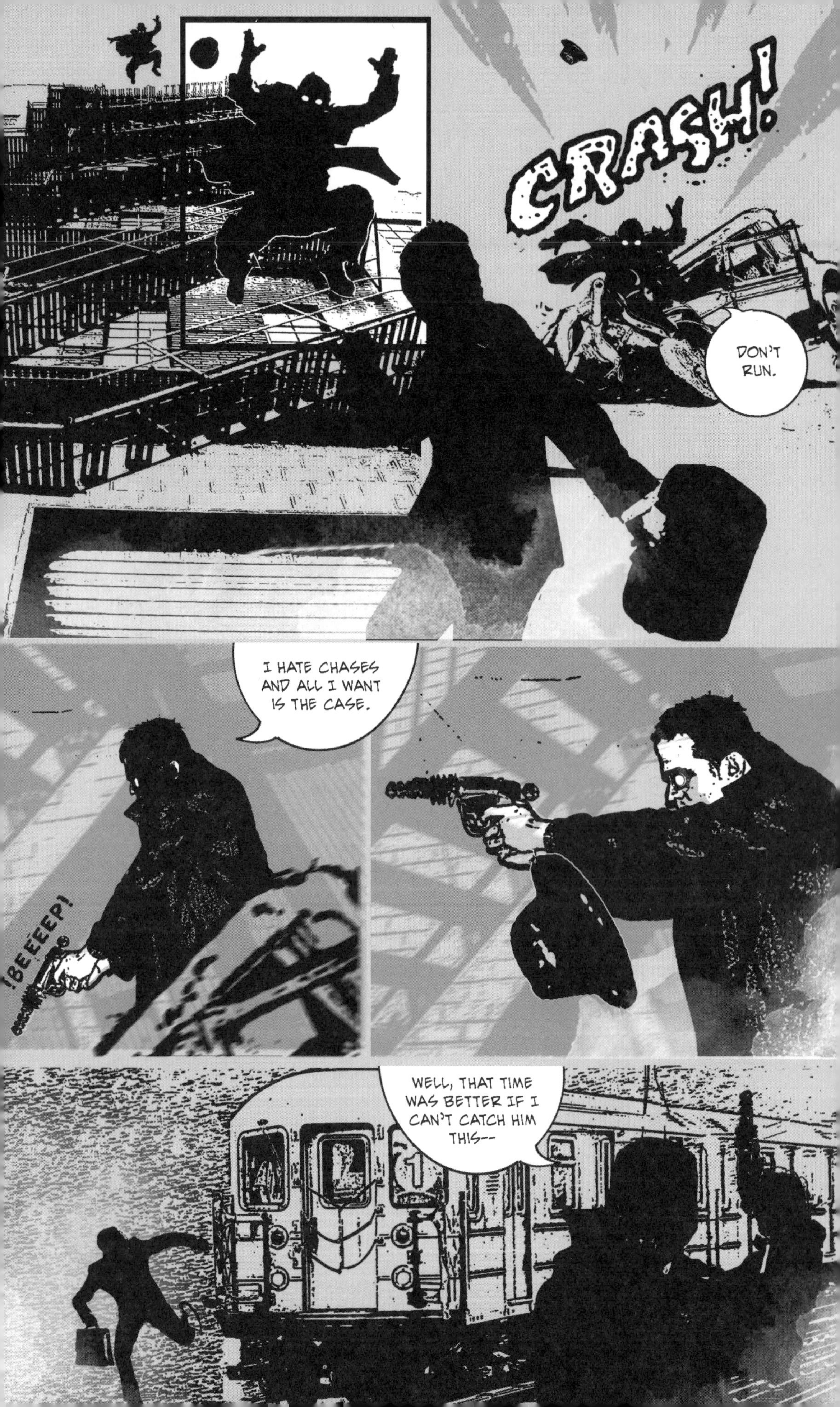
CRASH!
DON'T RUN.
I HATE CHASES AND ALL I WANT IS THE CASE.
!BEEEEEP!
WELL, THAT TIME WAS BETTER IF I CAN'T CATCH HIM THIS--

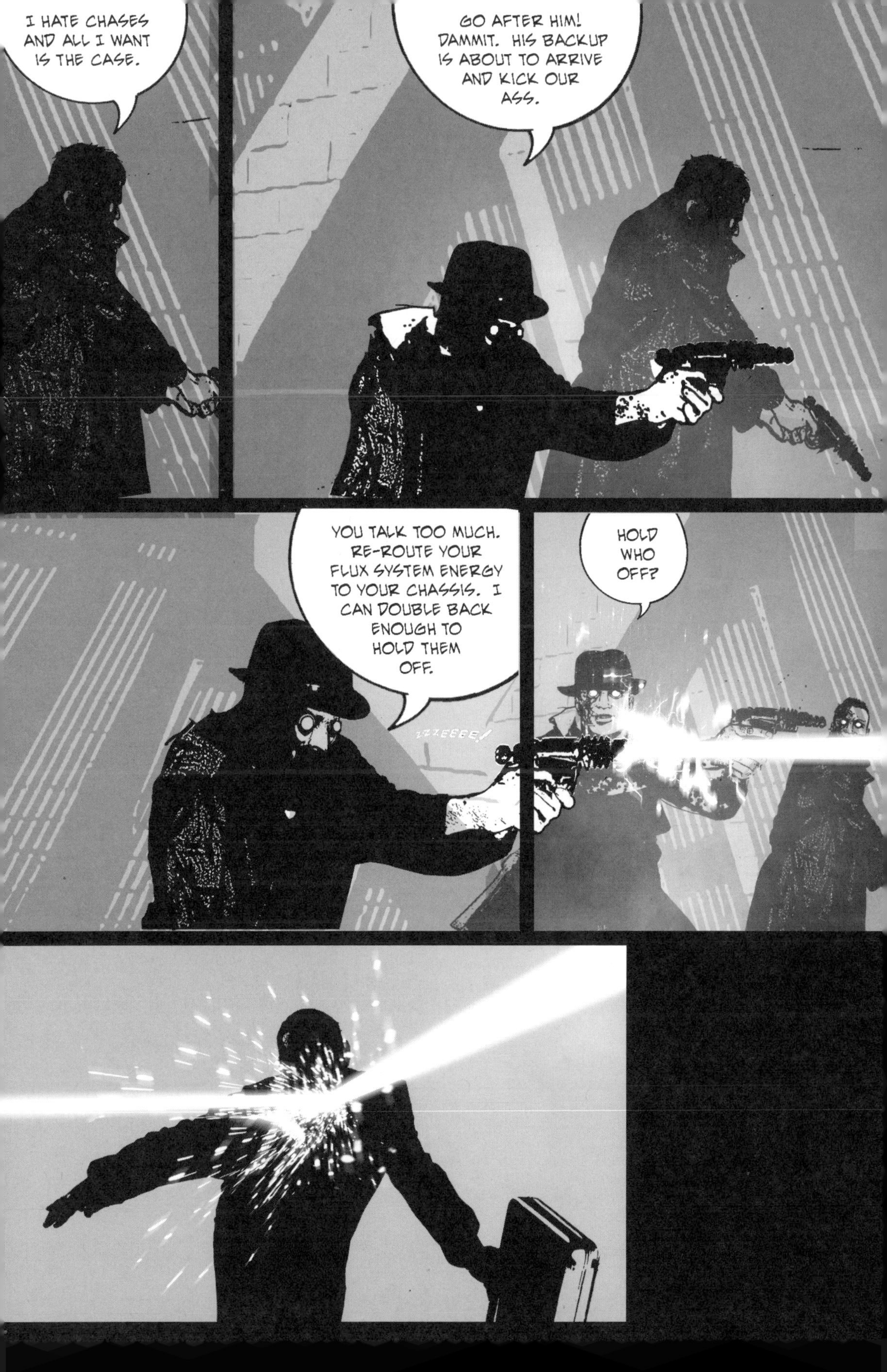
I HATE CHASES AND ALL I WANT IS THE CASE.
GO AFTER HIM! DAMMIT. HIS BACKUP IS ABOUT TO ARRIVE AND KICK OUR ASS.
YOU TALK TOO MUCH. RE-ROUTE YOUR FLUX SYSTEM ENERGY TO YOUR CHASSIS. I CAN DOUBLE BACK ENOUGH TO HOLD THEM OFF.
HOLD WHO OFF?

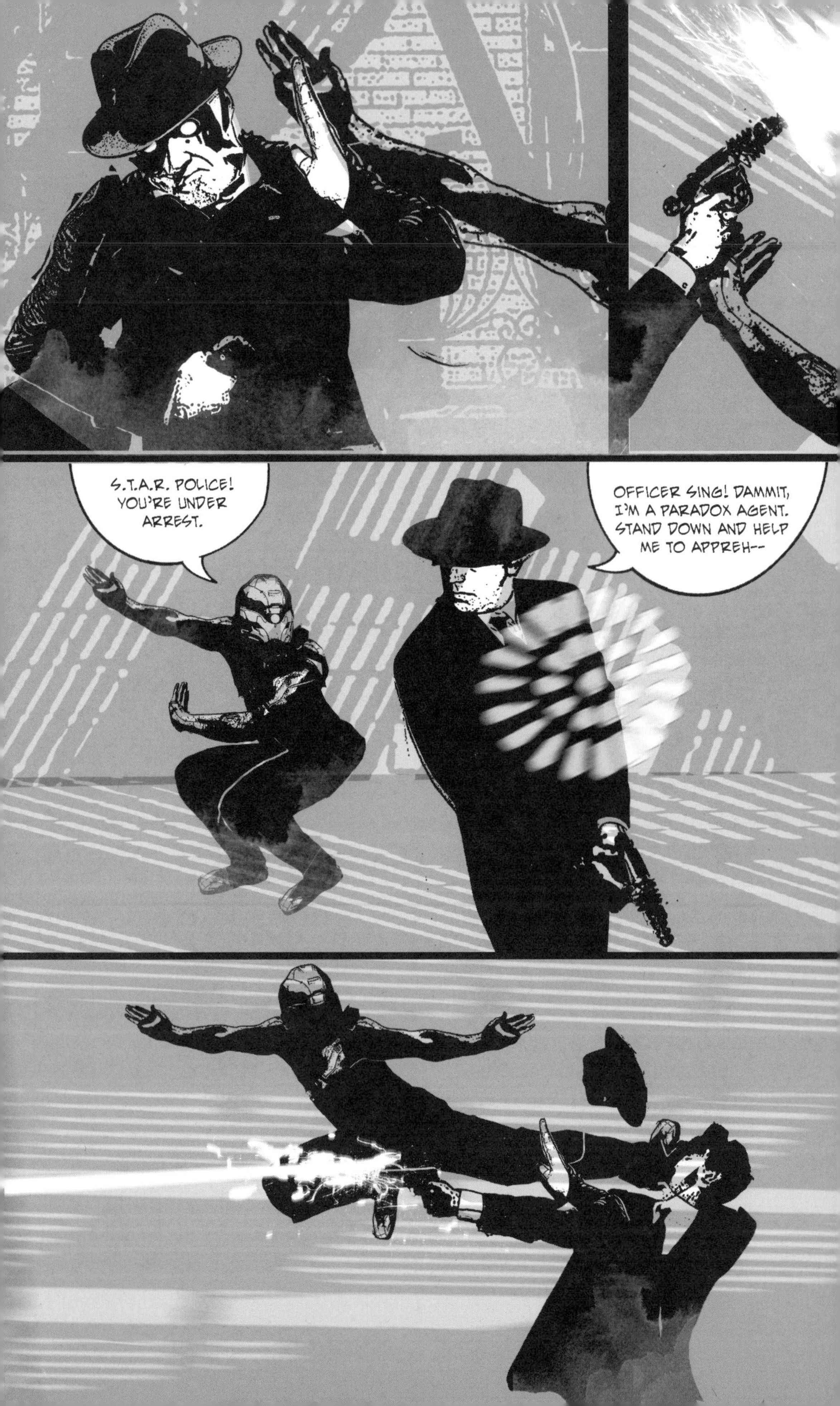
S.T.A.R. POLICE! YOU'RE UNDER ARREST.
OFFICER SING! DAMMIT, I'M A PARADOX AGENT. STAND DOWN AND HELP ME TO APPREH--

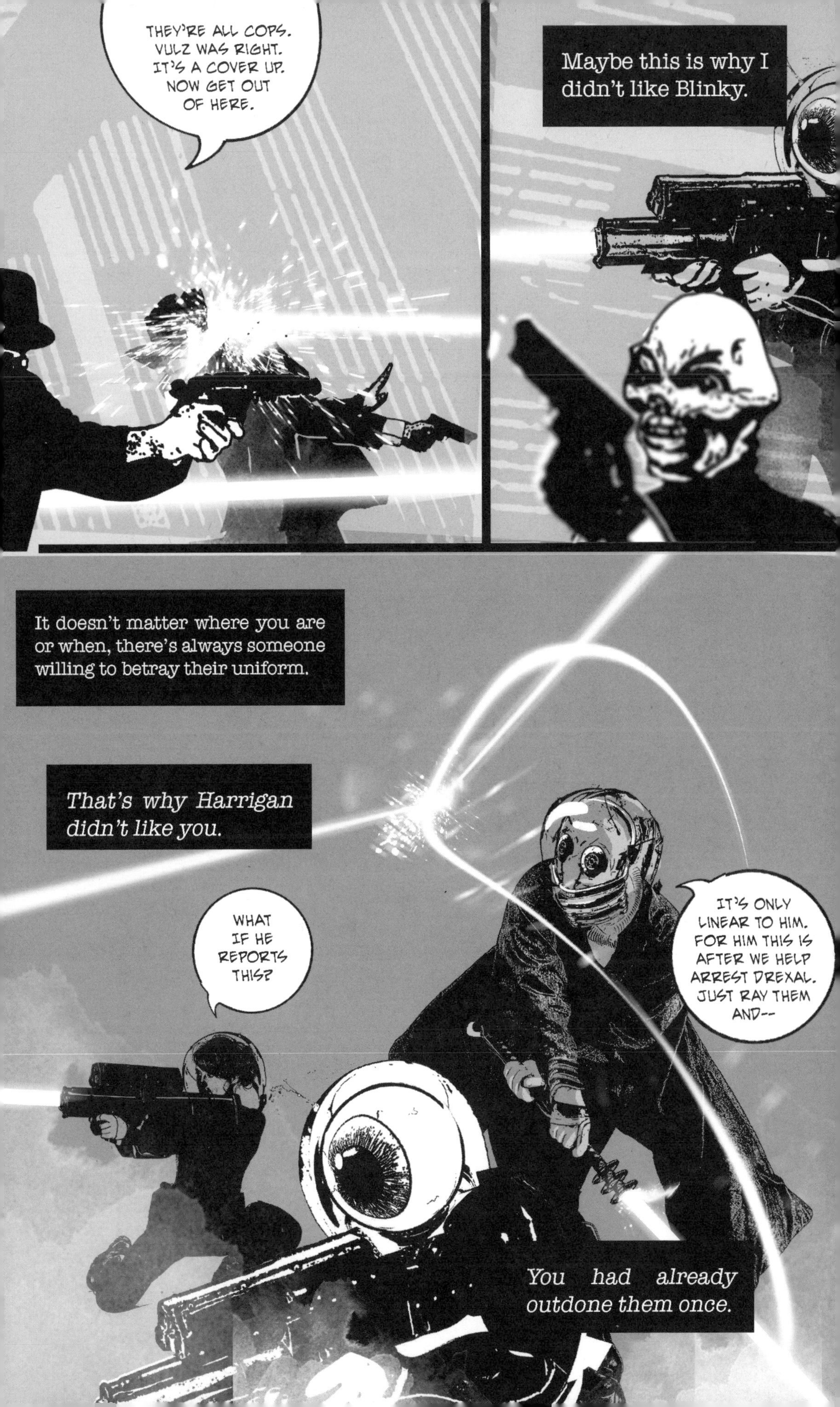

THEY'RE ALL COPS. VULZ WAS RIGHT. IT'S A COVER UP. NOW GET OUT OF HERE.
Maybe this is why I didn't like Blinky.
It doesn't matter where you are or when, there's always someone willing to betray their uniform.
That's why Harrigan didn't like you.
WHAT IF HE REPORTS THIS?
IT'S ONLY LINEAR TO HIM. FOR HIM THIS IS AFTER WE HELP ARREST DREXAL. JUST RAY THEM AND--
You had already outdone them once.

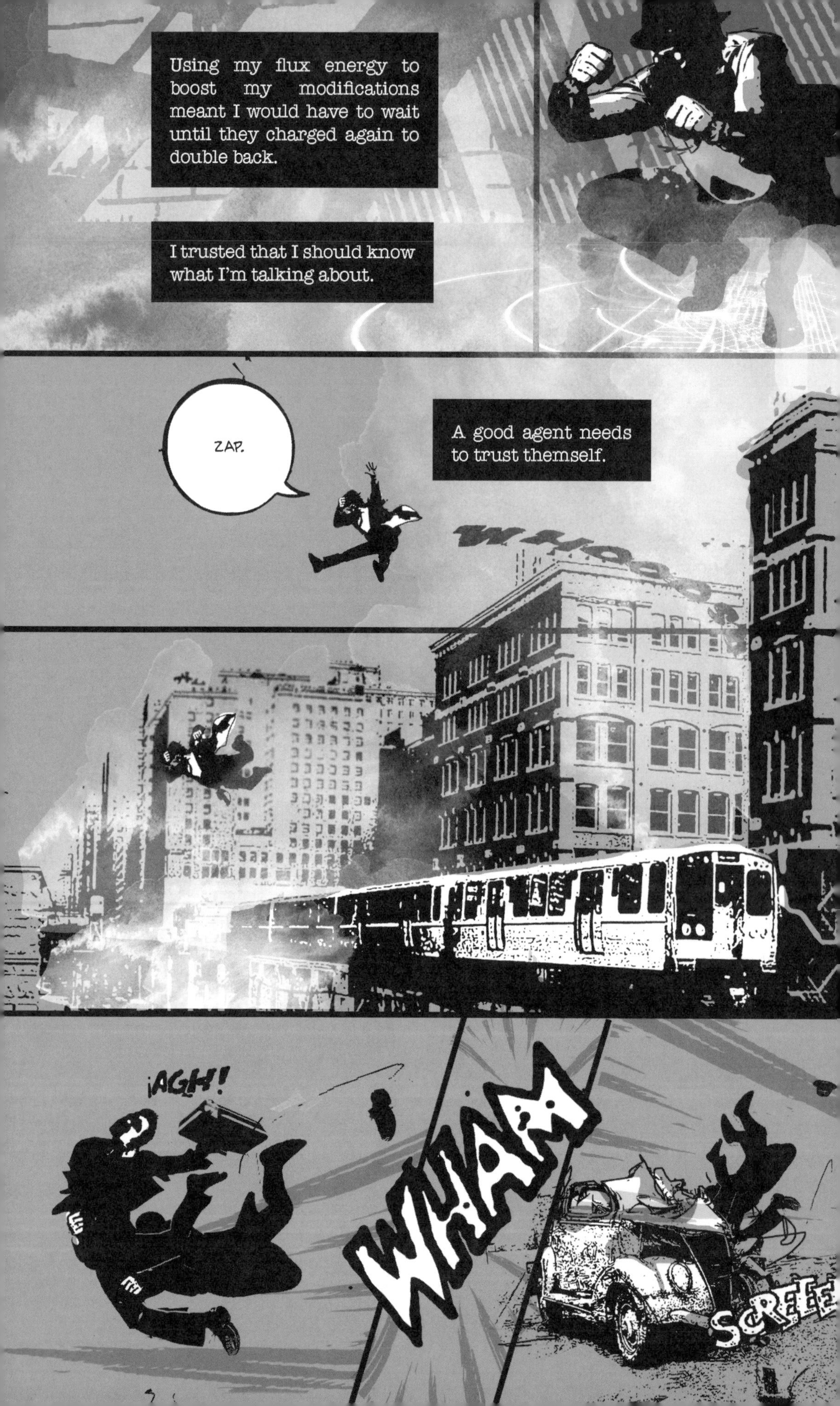

Using my flux energy to boost my modifications meant I would have to wait until they charged again to double back.
I trusted that I should know what I'm talking about.
ZAP.
A good agent needs to trust themself.
¡AGH!
WHAM
SCREEE

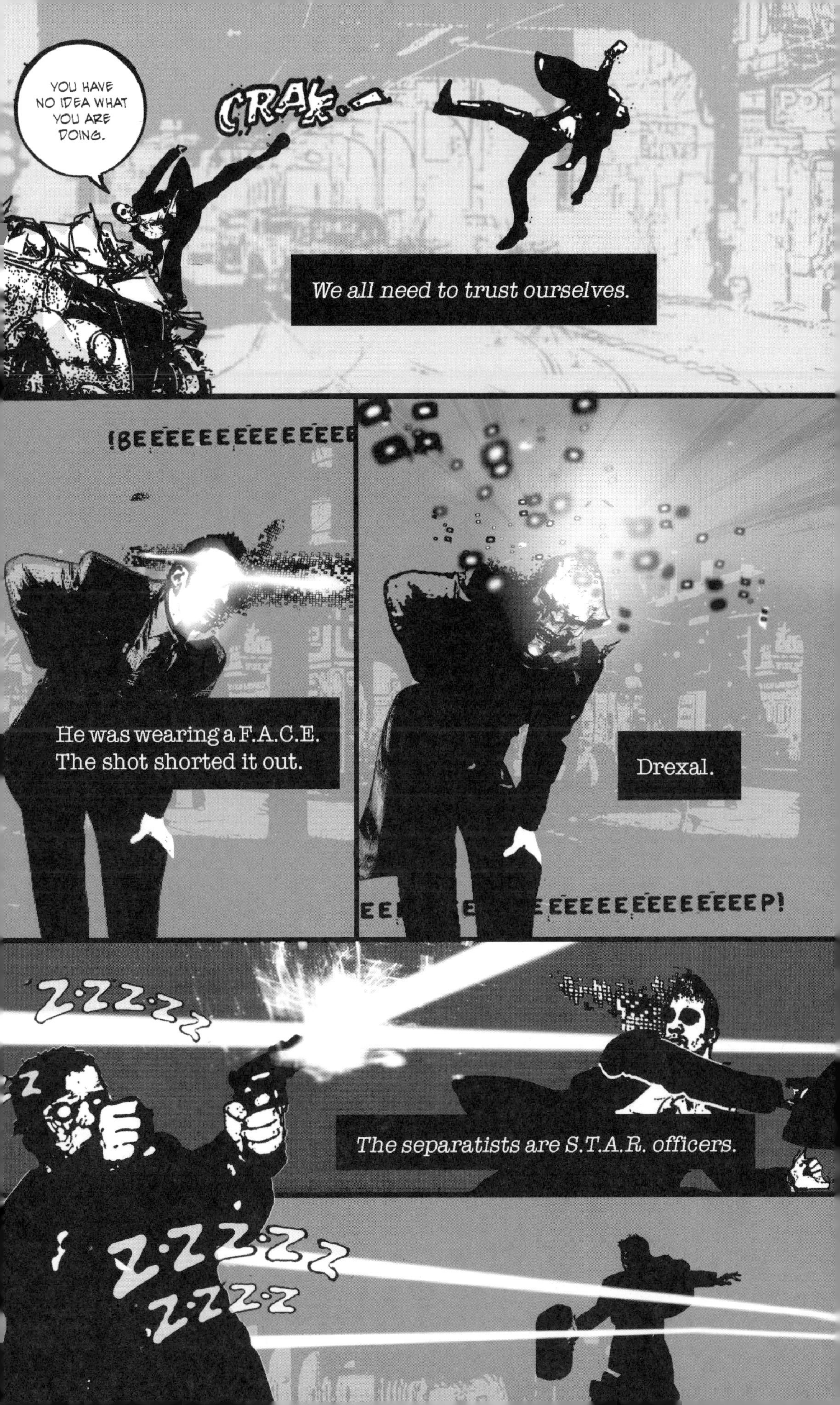
YOU HAVE NO IDEA WHAT YOU ARE DOING.
CRAK...
We all need to trust ourselves.
!BEEEEEEEEEEEEEE
He was wearing a F.A.C.E. The shot shorted it out.
Drexal.
EEEEEEEEEEEEEEEEEEEEP!
Z-ZZ-ZZ
The separatists are S.T.A.R. officers.
Z-ZZ-ZZ
Z-ZZ-Z

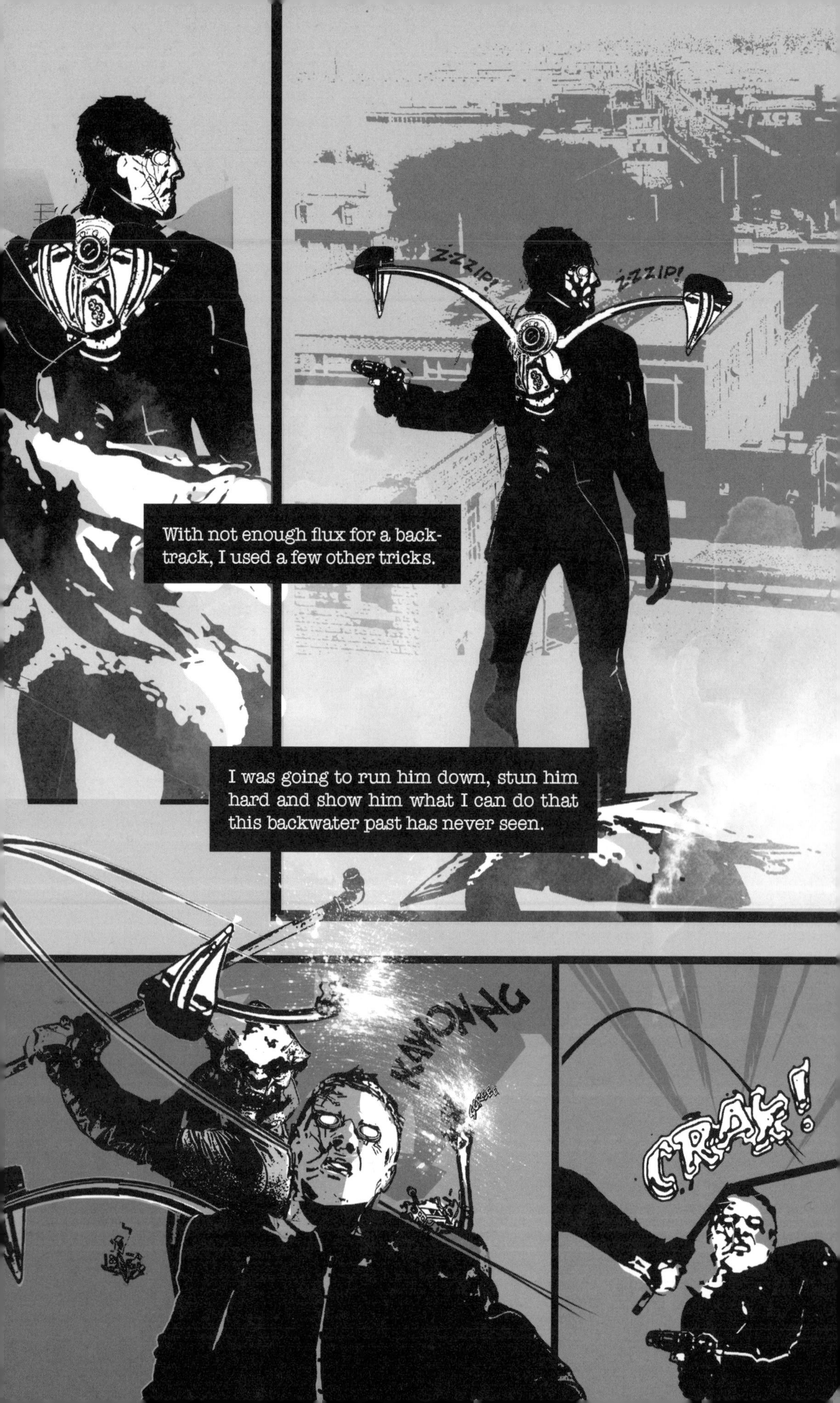
ZZZIP!
ZZZIP!
With not enough flux for a back-track, I used a few other tricks.
I was going to run him down, stun him hard and show him what I can do that this backwater past has never seen.
KAWONG
SCREEE
CRAK!

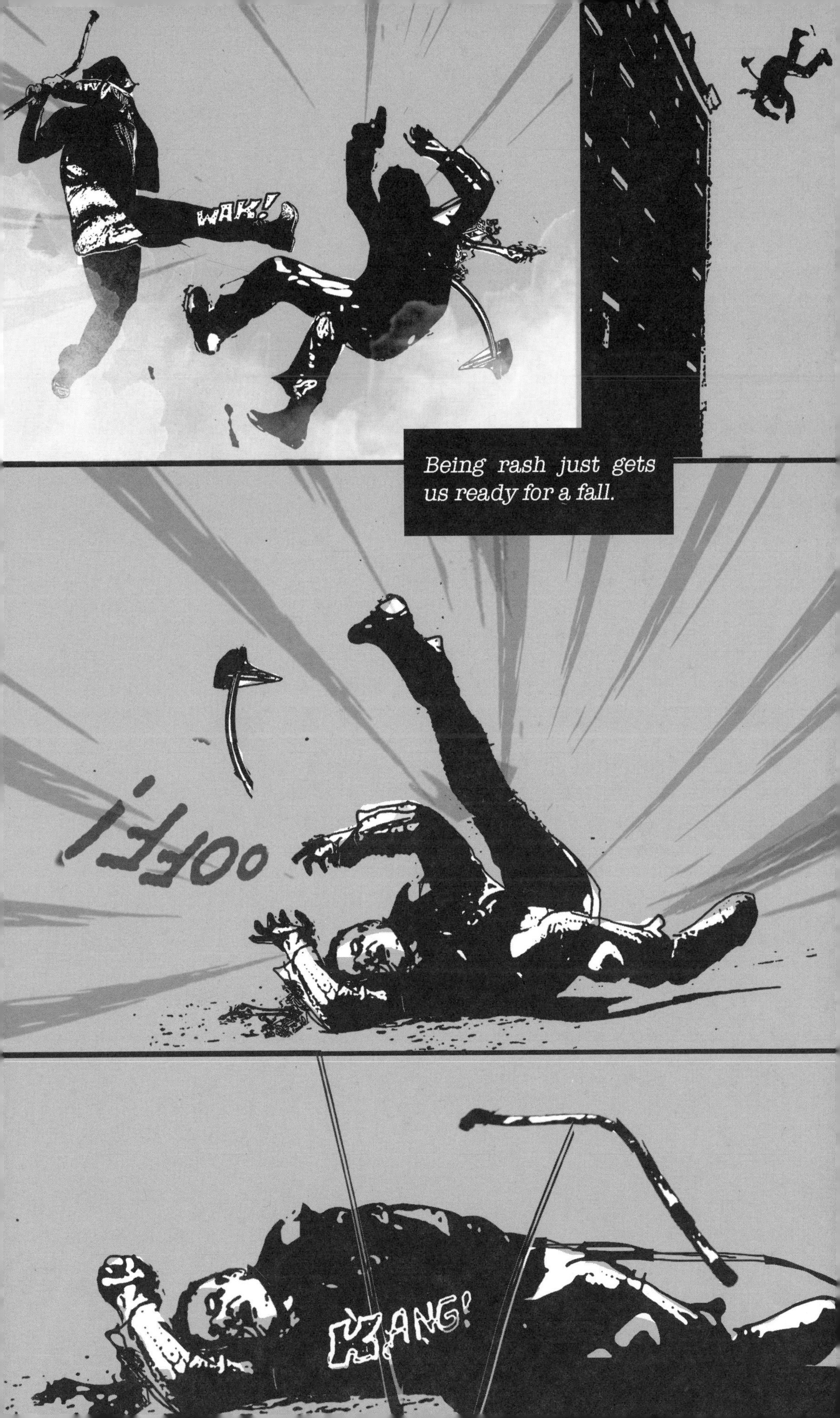
WAK!
Being rash just gets us ready for a fall.
OOF!
KANG!

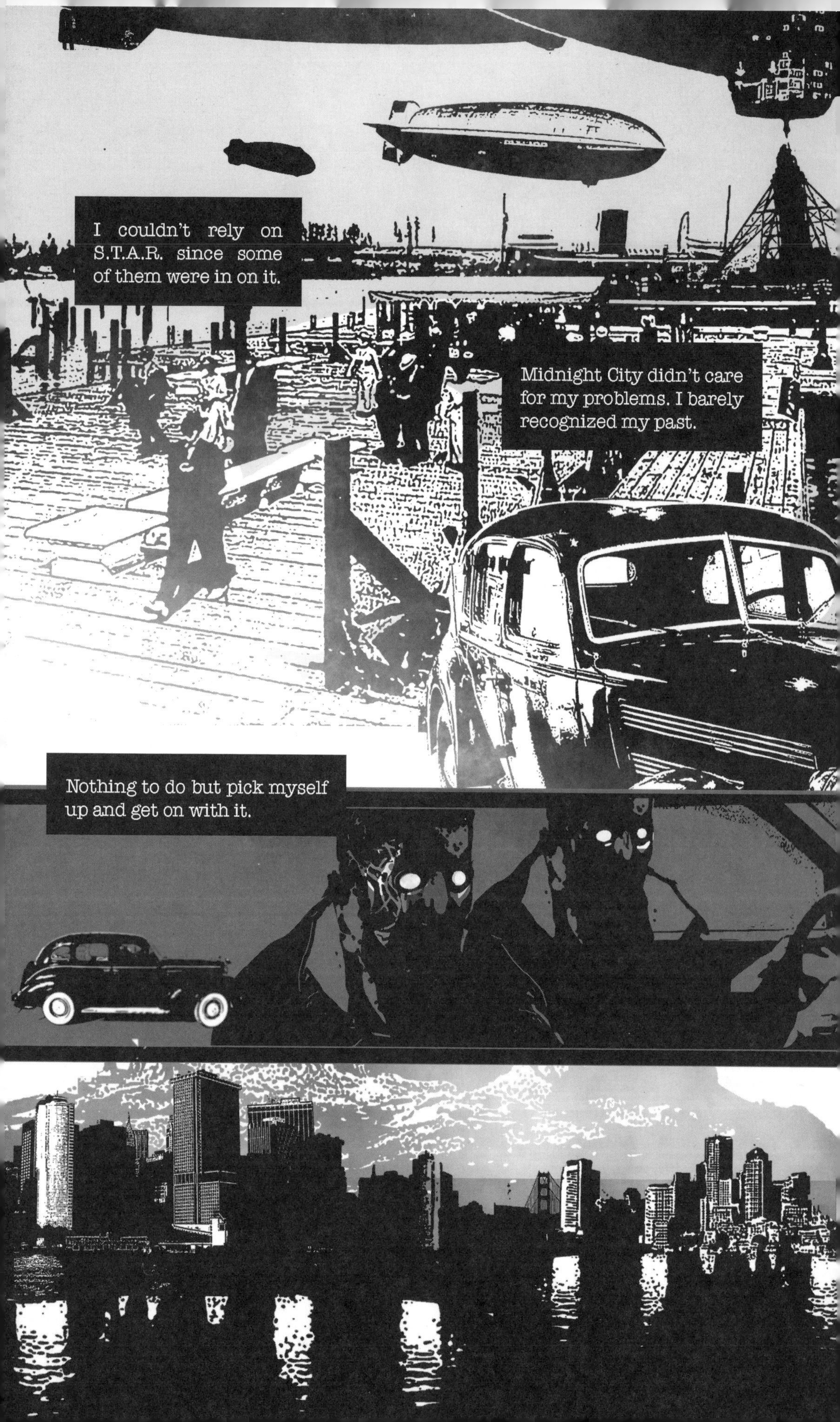
I couldn't rely on S.T.A.R. since some of them were in on it.
Midnight City didn't care for my problems. I barely recognized my past.
Nothing to do but pick myself up and get on with it.

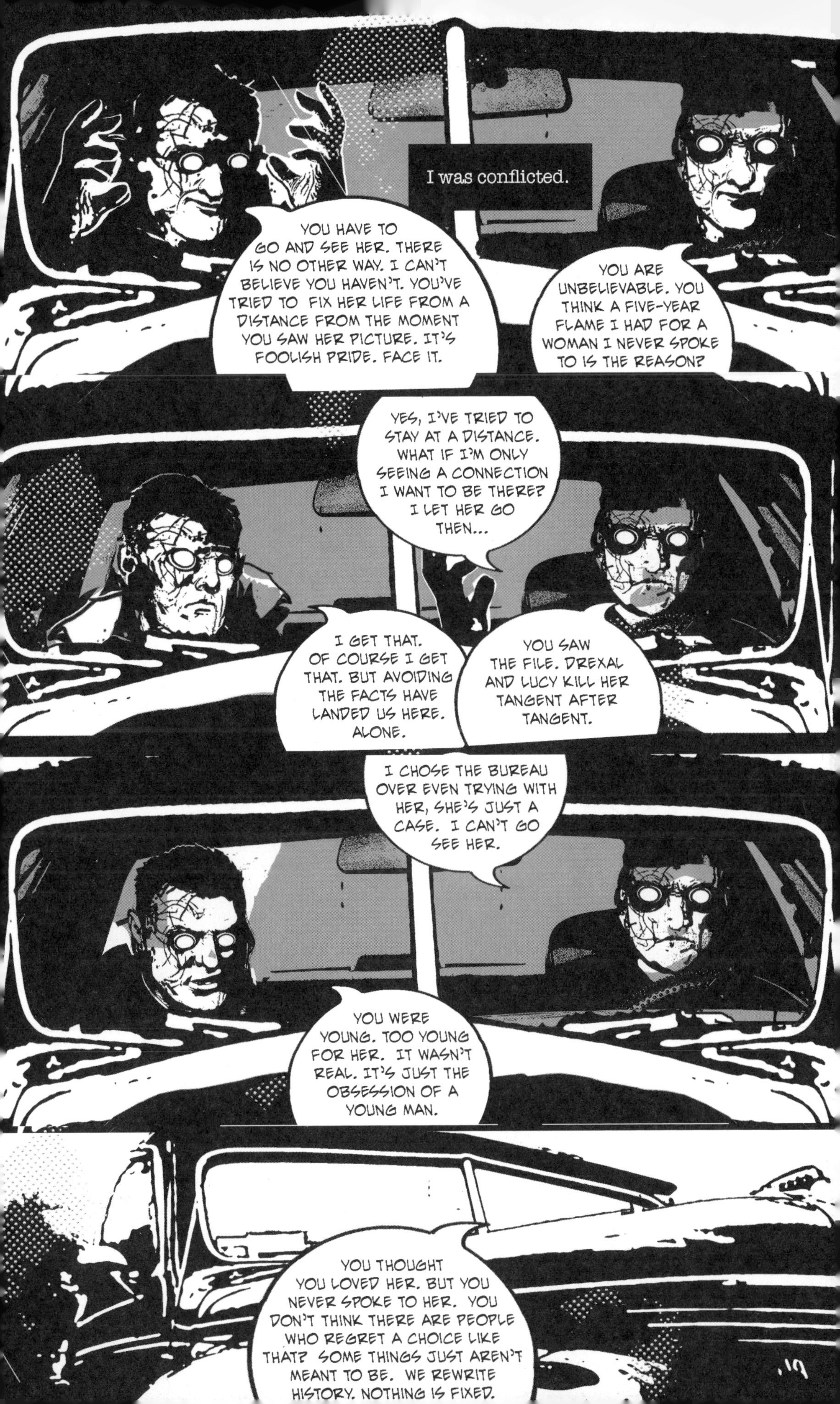
I was conflicted.
YOU HAVE TO GO AND SEE HER. THERE IS NO OTHER WAY. I CAN'T BELIEVE YOU HAVEN'T. YOU'VE TRIED TO FIX HER LIFE FROM A DISTANCE FROM THE MOMENT YOU SAW HER PICTURE. IT'S FOOLISH PRIDE. FACE IT.
YOU ARE UNBELIEVABLE. YOU THINK A FIVE-YEAR FLAME I HAD FOR A WOMAN I NEVER SPOKE TO IS THE REASON?
YES, I'VE TRIED TO STAY AT A DISTANCE. WHAT IF I'M ONLY SEEING A CONNECTION I WANT TO BE THERE? I LET HER GO THEN...
I GET THAT. OF COURSE I GET THAT. BUT AVOIDING THE FACTS HAVE LANDED US HERE. ALONE.
YOU SAW THE FILE. DREXAL AND LUCY KILL HER TANGENT AFTER TANGENT.
I CHOSE THE BUREAU OVER EVEN TRYING WITH HER, SHE'S JUST A CASE. I CAN'T GO SEE HER.
YOU WERE YOUNG. TOO YOUNG FOR HER. IT WASN'T REAL. IT'S JUST THE OBSESSION OF A YOUNG MAN.
YOU THOUGHT YOU LOVED HER. BUT YOU NEVER SPOKE TO HER. YOU DON'T THINK THERE ARE PEOPLE WHO REGRET A CHOICE LIKE THAT? SOME THINGS JUST AREN'T MEANT TO BE. WE REWRITE HISTORY. NOTHING IS FIXED.

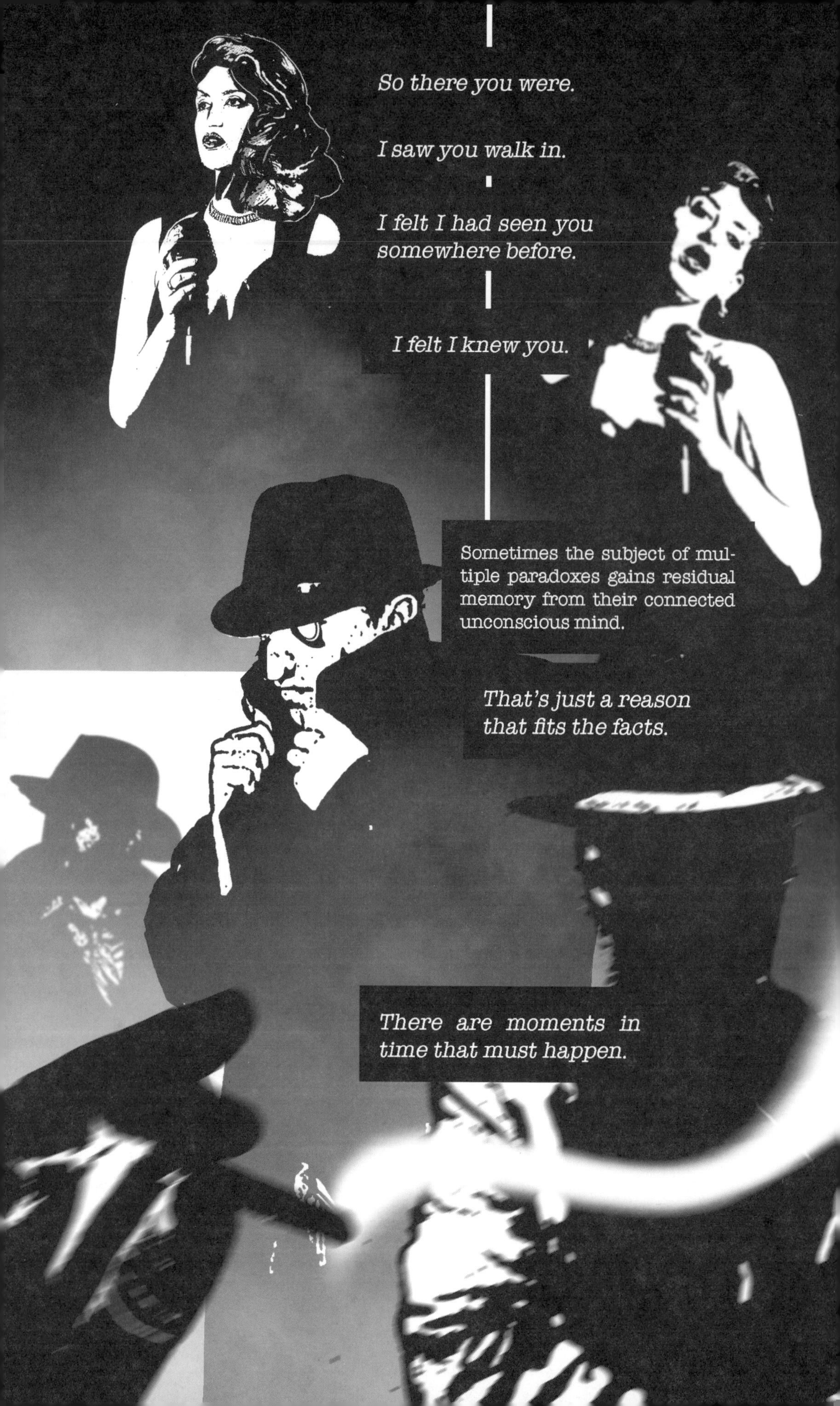
So there you were.
I saw you walk in.
I felt I had seen you somewhere before.
I felt I knew you.
Sometimes the subject of multiple paradoxes gains residual memory from their connected unconscious mind.
That's just a reason that fits the facts.
There are moments in time that must happen.

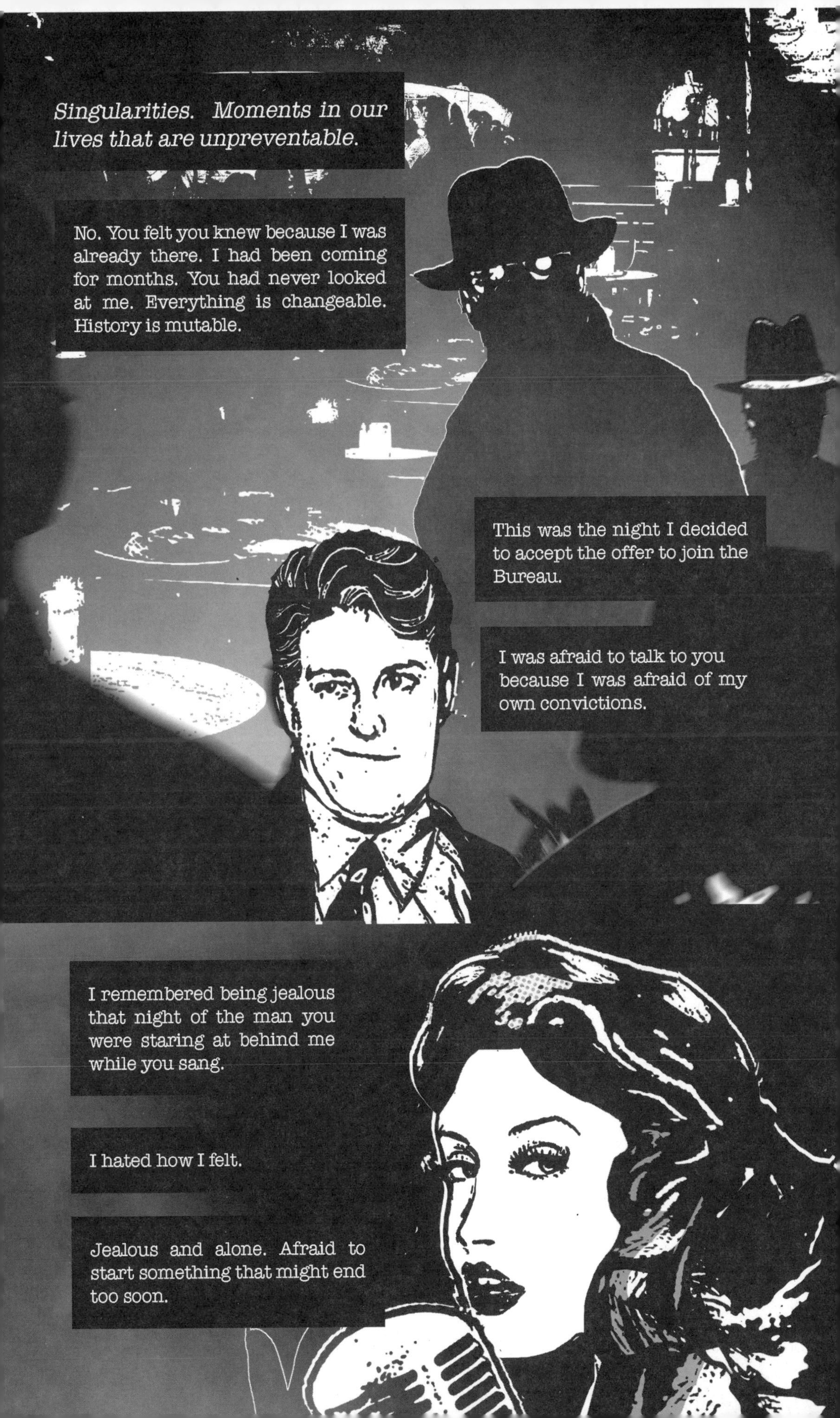

Singularities. Moments in our lives that are unpreventable.
No. You felt you knew because I was already there. I had been coming for months. You had never looked at me. Everything is changeable. History is mutable.
This was the night I decided to accept the offer to join the Bureau.
I was afraid to talk to you because I was afraid of my own convictions.
I remembered being jealous that night of the man you were staring at behind me while you sang.
I hated how I felt.
Jealous and alone. Afraid to start something that might end too soon.

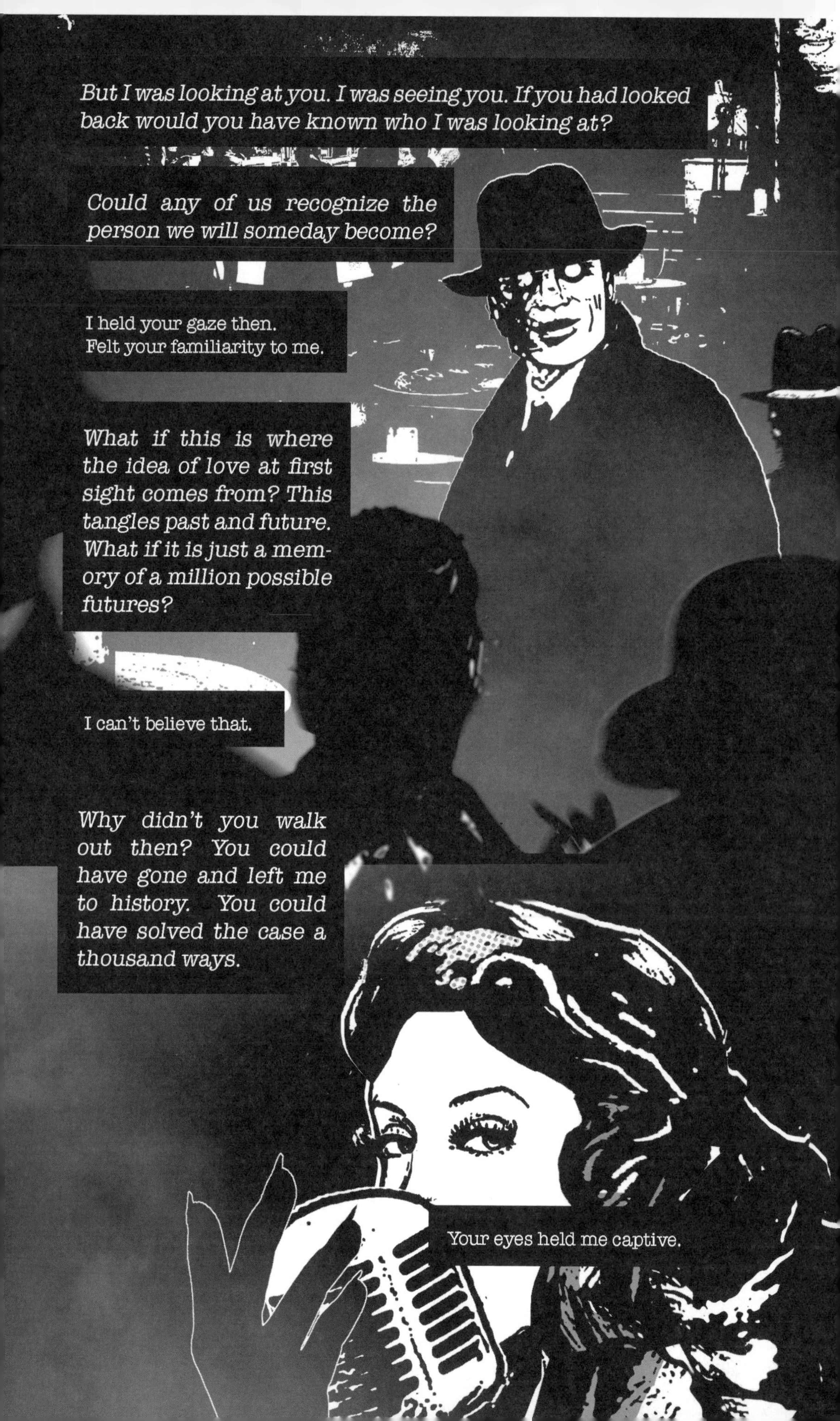
But I was looking at you. I was seeing you. If you had looked back would you have known who I was looking at?
Could any of us recognize the person we will someday become?
I held your gaze then. Felt your familiarity to me.
What if this is where the idea of love at first sight comes from? This tangles past and future. What if it is just a memory of a million possible futures?
I can't believe that.
Why didn't you walk out then? You could have gone and left me to history. You could have solved the case a thousand ways.
Your eyes held me captive.

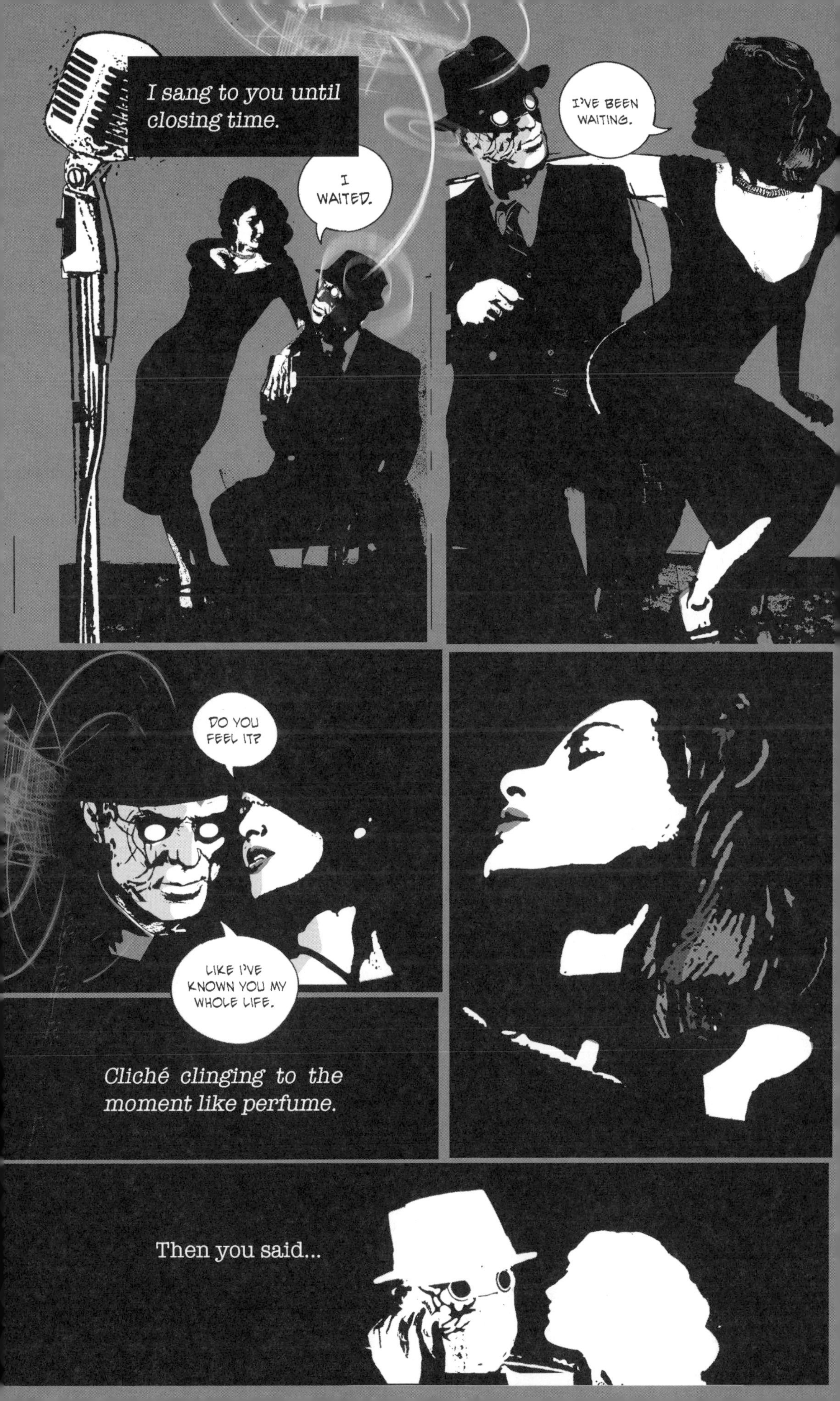

I sang to you until closing time.
I WAITED.
I'VE BEEN WAITING.
DO YOU FEEL IT?
LIKE I'VE KNOWN YOU MY WHOLE LIFE.
Cliché clinging to the moment like perfume.
Then you said...

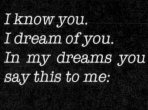

I know you.
I dream of you.
In my dreams you
say this to me:

Look at the smoke. It
must rise upwards.

Time goes on like
this. We can swirl
it around but it still
corresponds to the
laws of nature.

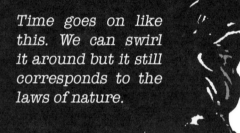

It goes up, it fades,
it dissipates. Close
to the source we can
seem to control it.

Up above is the
same cloud.

The Infinitum.

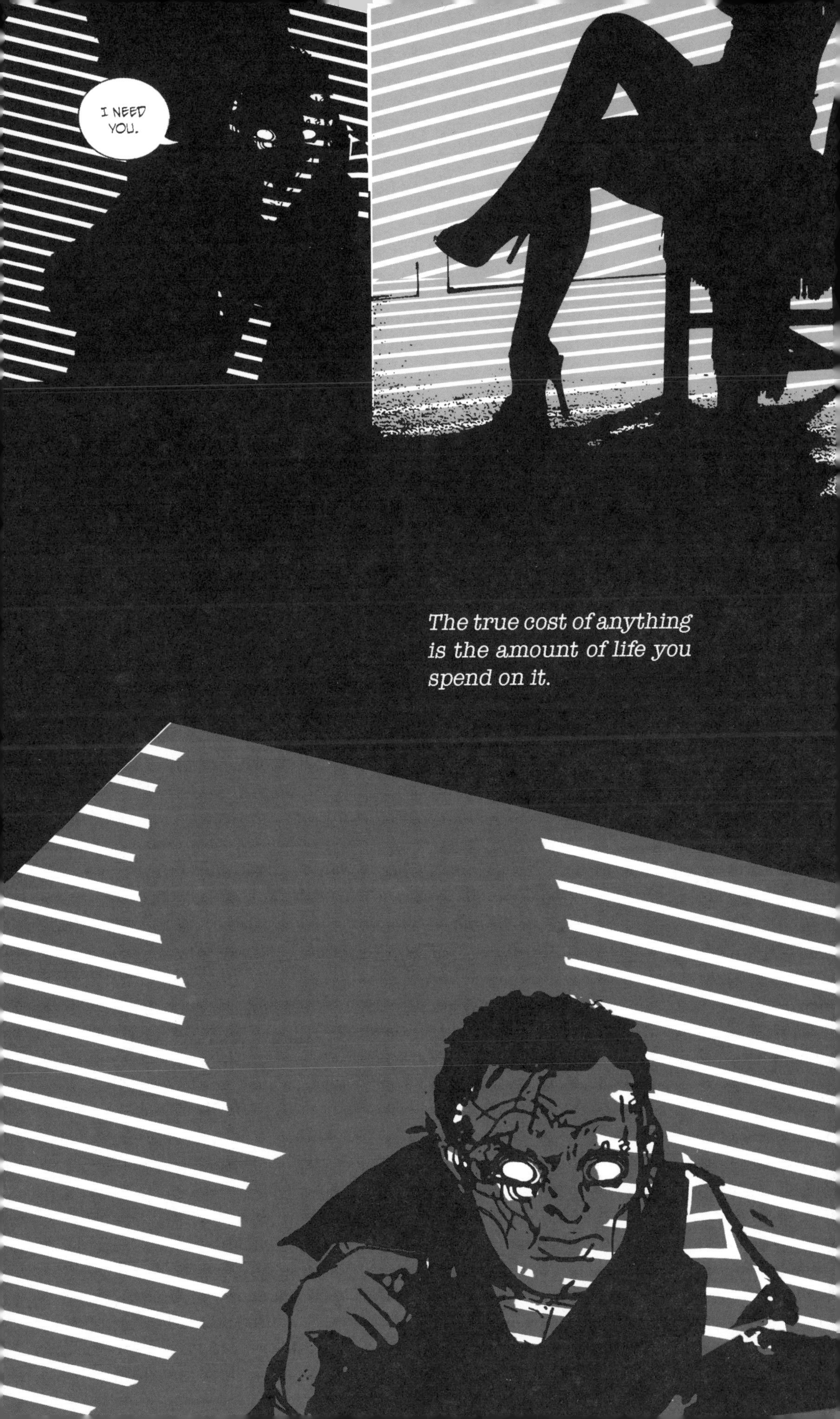
I NEED YOU.
The true cost of anything is the amount of life you spend on it.

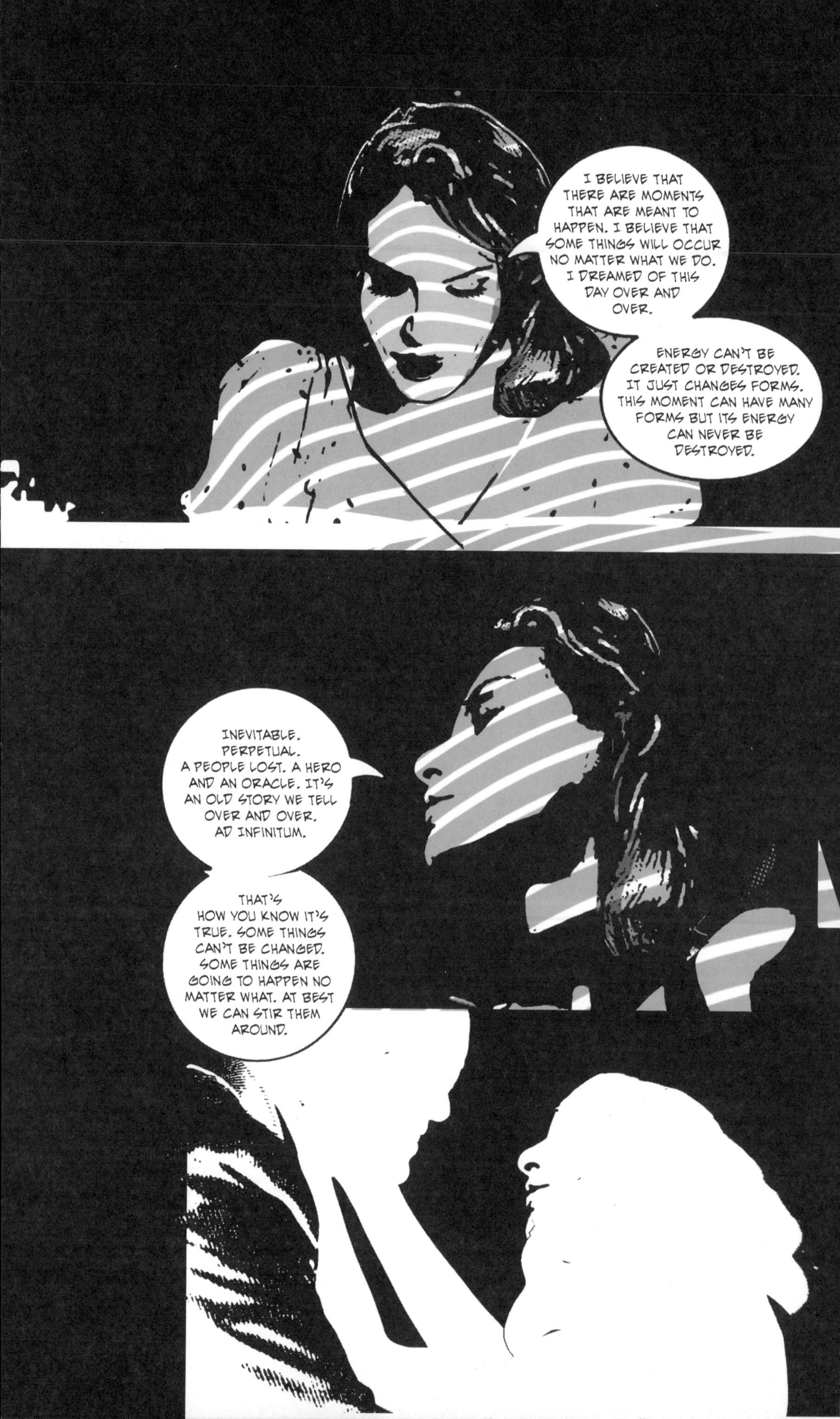
I BELIEVE THAT THERE ARE MOMENTS THAT ARE MEANT TO HAPPEN. I BELIEVE THAT SOME THINGS WILL OCCUR NO MATTER WHAT WE DO. I DREAMED OF THIS DAY OVER AND OVER.
ENERGY CAN'T BE CREATED OR DESTROYED. IT JUST CHANGES FORMS. THIS MOMENT CAN HAVE MANY FORMS BUT ITS ENERGY CAN NEVER BE DESTROYED.
INEVITABLE. PERPETUAL. A PEOPLE LOST. A HERO AND AN ORACLE. IT'S AN OLD STORY WE TELL OVER AND OVER. AD INFINITUM.
THAT'S HOW YOU KNOW IT'S TRUE. SOME THINGS CAN'T BE CHANGED. SOME THINGS ARE GOING TO HAPPEN NO MATTER WHAT. AT BEST WE CAN STIR THEM AROUND.

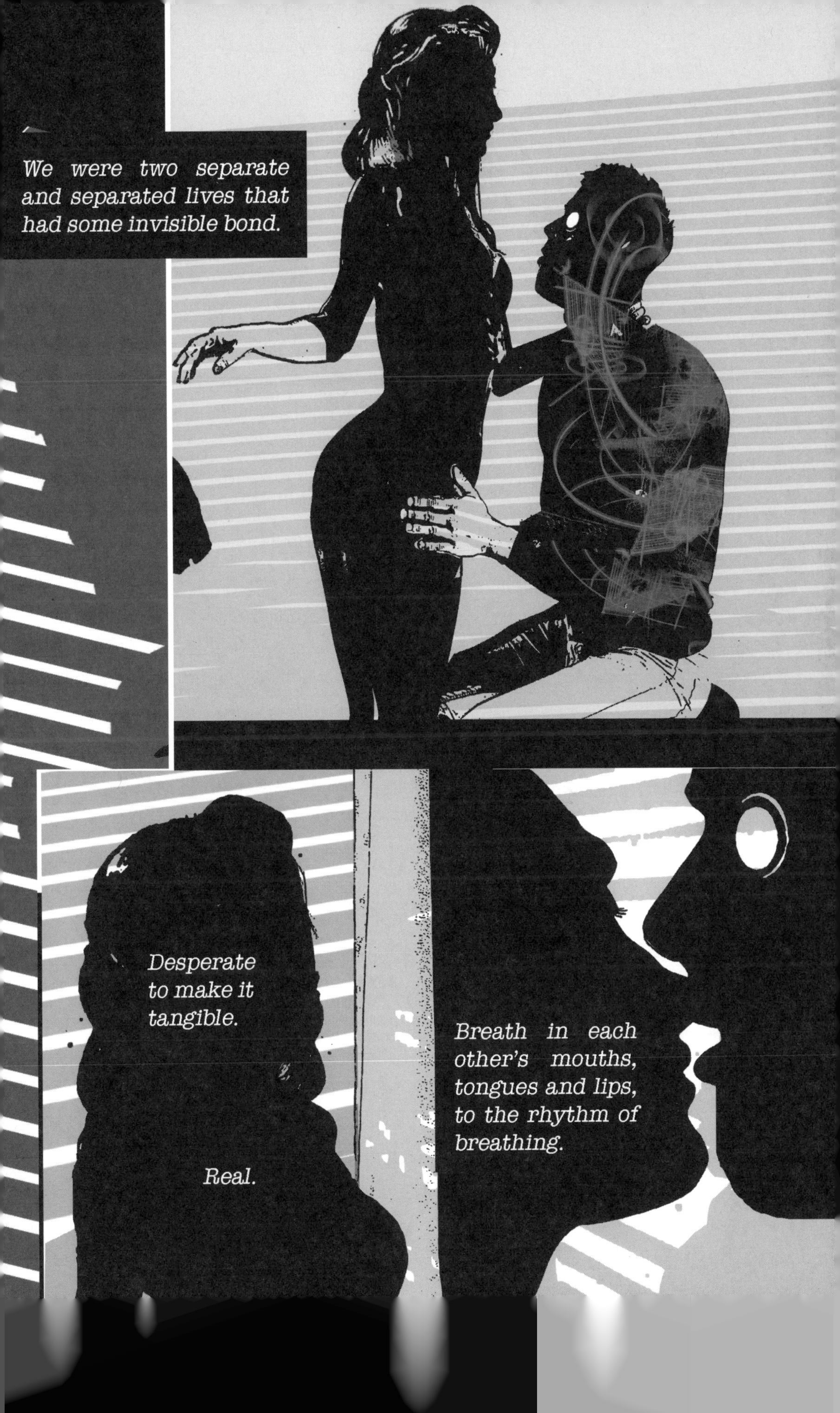
We were two separate and separated lives that had some invisible bond.
Desperate to make it tangible.
Real.
Breath in each other's mouths, tongues and lips, to the rhythm of breathing.

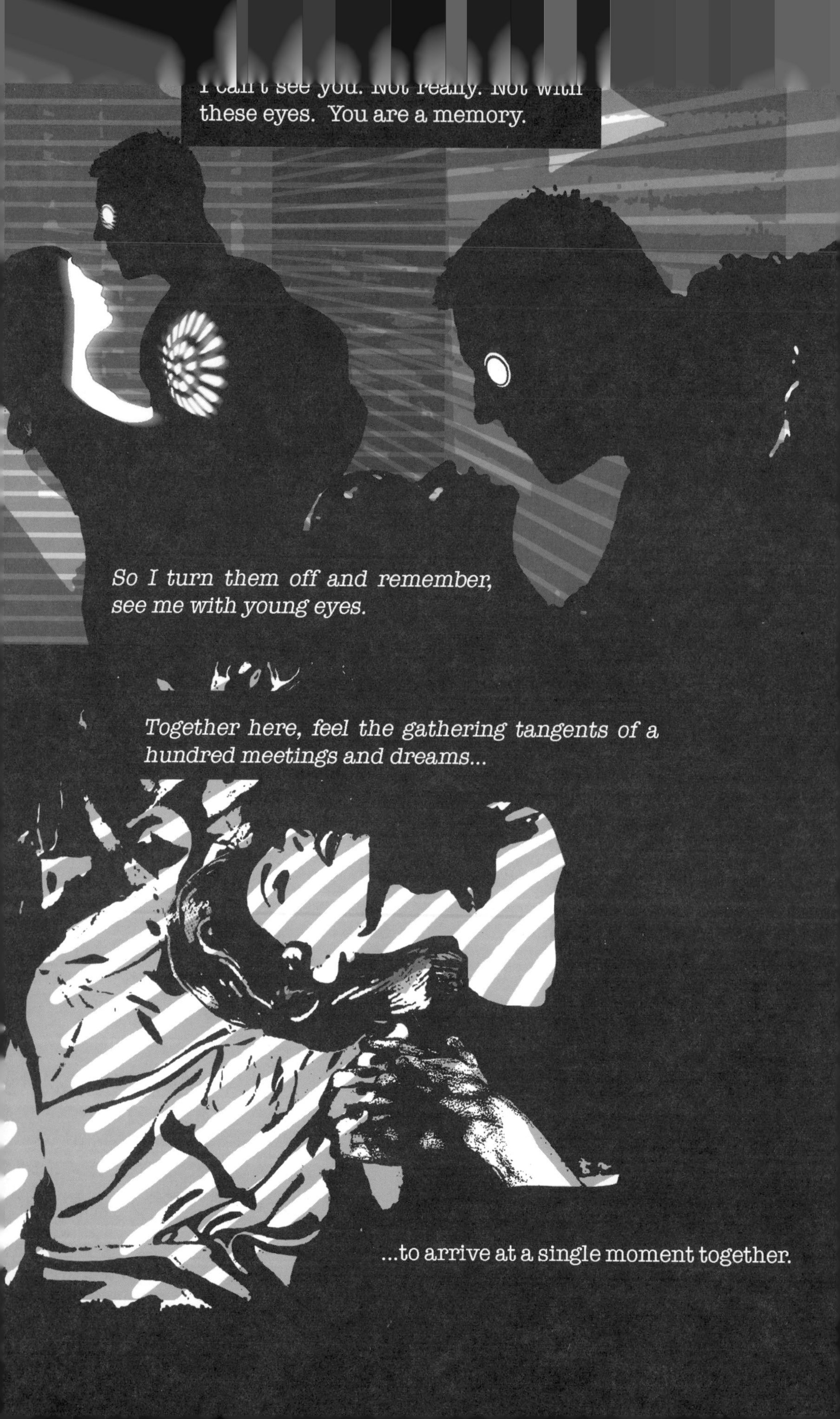
I can't see you. Not really. Not with these eyes. You are a memory.
So I turn them off and remember, see me with young eyes.
Together here, feel the gathering tangents of a hundred meetings and dreams...
...to arrive at a single moment together.

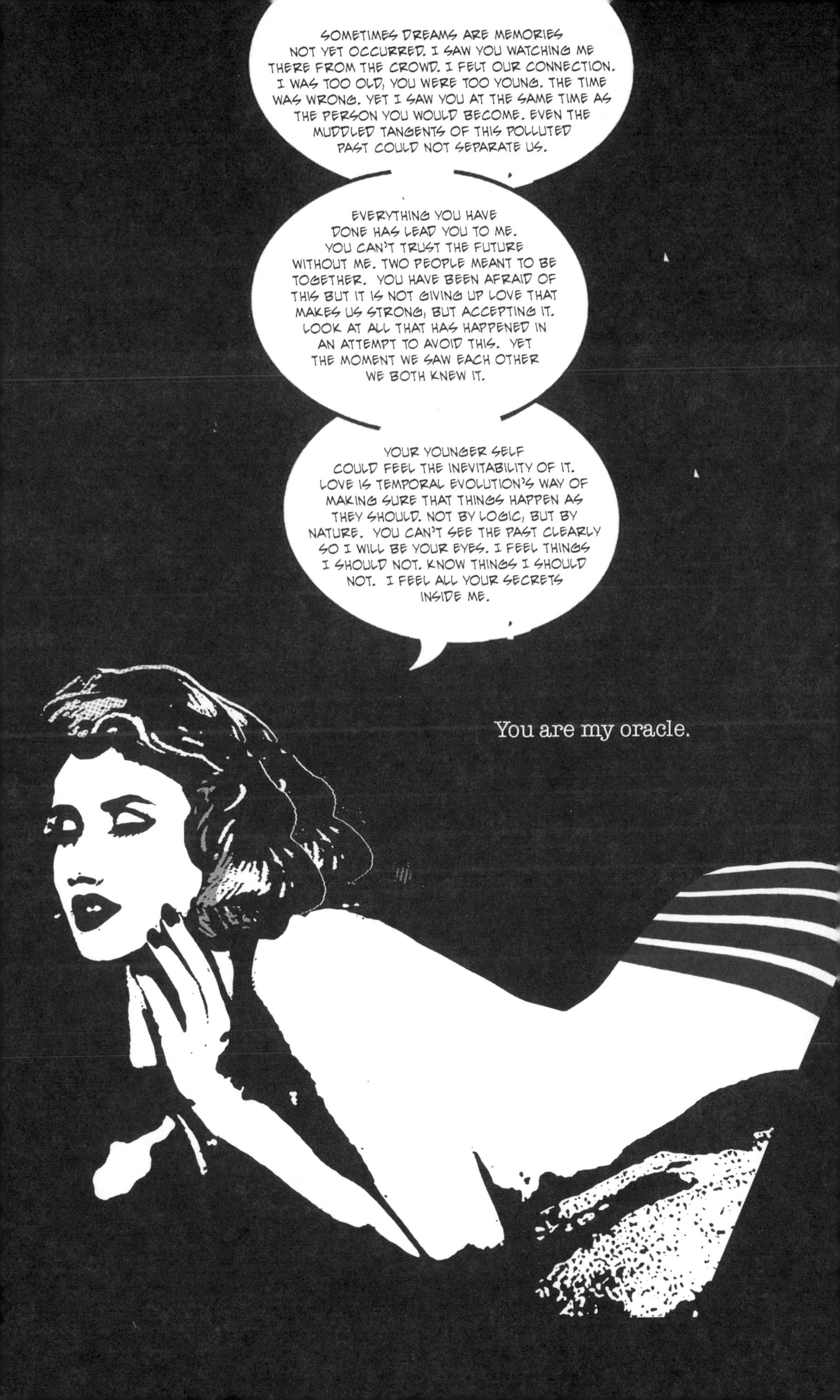
SOMETIMES DREAMS ARE MEMORIES NOT YET OCCURRED. I SAW YOU WATCHING ME THERE FROM THE CROWD. I FELT OUR CONNECTION. I WAS TOO OLD, YOU WERE TOO YOUNG. THE TIME WAS WRONG. YET I SAW YOU AT THE SAME TIME AS THE PERSON YOU WOULD BECOME. EVEN THE MUDDLED TANGENTS OF THIS POLLUTED PAST COULD NOT SEPARATE US.
EVERYTHING YOU HAVE DONE HAS LEAD YOU TO ME. YOU CAN'T TRUST THE FUTURE WITHOUT ME. TWO PEOPLE MEANT TO BE TOGETHER. YOU HAVE BEEN AFRAID OF THIS BUT IT IS NOT GIVING UP LOVE THAT MAKES US STRONG, BUT ACCEPTING IT. LOOK AT ALL THAT HAS HAPPENED IN AN ATTEMPT TO AVOID THIS. YET THE MOMENT WE SAW EACH OTHER WE BOTH KNEW IT.
YOUR YOUNGER SELF COULD FEEL THE INEVITABILITY OF IT. LOVE IS TEMPORAL EVOLUTION'S WAY OF MAKING SURE THAT THINGS HAPPEN AS THEY SHOULD. NOT BY LOGIC, BUT BY NATURE. YOU CAN'T SEE THE PAST CLEARLY SO I WILL BE YOUR EYES. I FEEL THINGS I SHOULD NOT. KNOW THINGS I SHOULD NOT. I FEEL ALL YOUR SECRETS INSIDE ME.
You are my oracle.

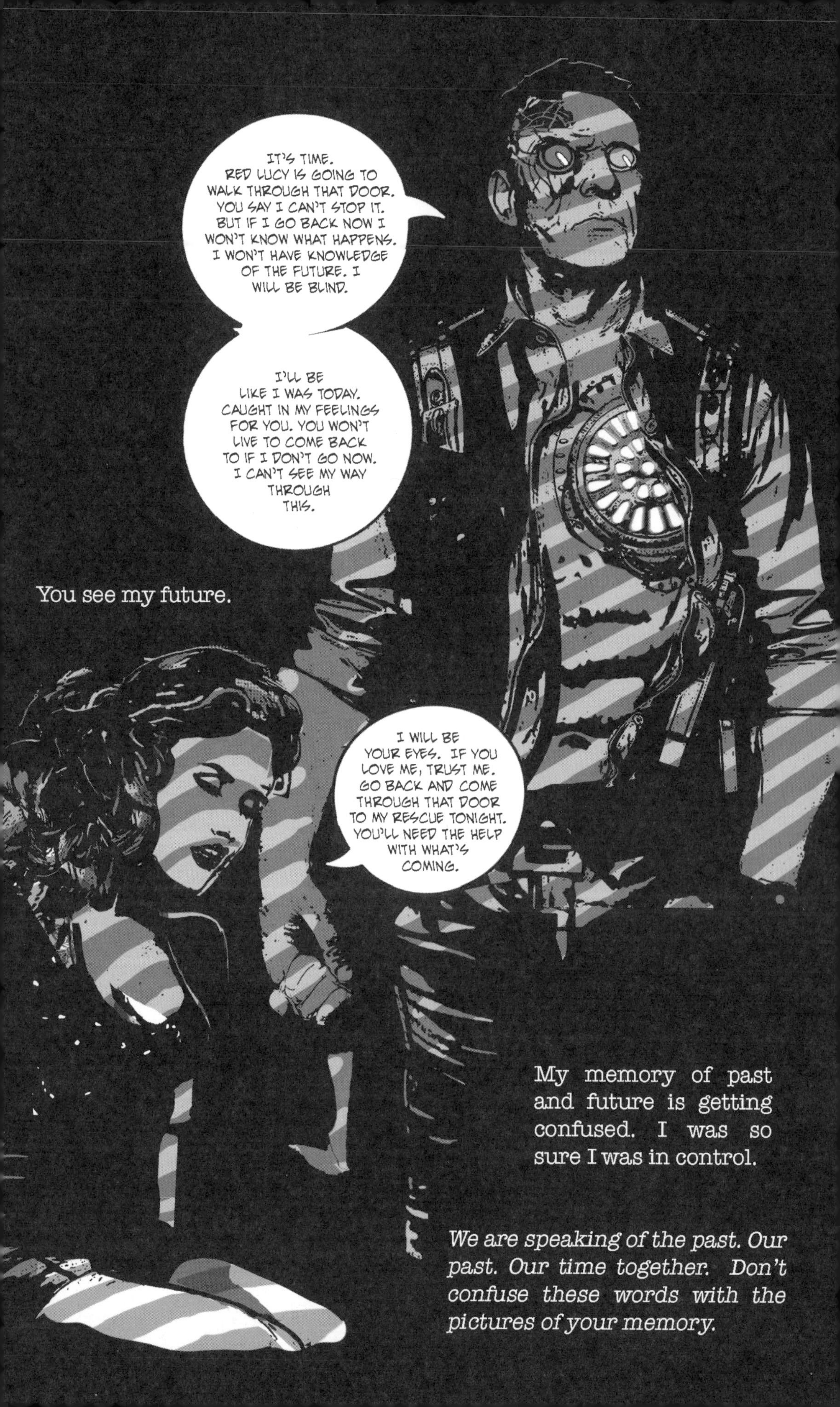
IT'S TIME. RED LUCY IS GOING TO WALK THROUGH THAT DOOR. YOU SAY I CAN'T STOP IT. BUT IF I GO BACK NOW I WON'T KNOW WHAT HAPPENS. I WON'T HAVE KNOWLEDGE OF THE FUTURE. I WILL BE BLIND.
I'LL BE LIKE I WAS TODAY. CAUGHT IN MY FEELINGS FOR YOU. YOU WON'T LIVE TO COME BACK TO IF I DON'T GO NOW. I CAN'T SEE MY WAY THROUGH THIS.
You see my future.
I WILL BE YOUR EYES. IF YOU LOVE ME, TRUST ME. GO BACK AND COME THROUGH THAT DOOR TO MY RESCUE TONIGHT. YOU'LL NEED THE HELP WITH WHAT'S COMING.
My memory of past and future is getting confused. I was so sure I was in control.
We are speaking of the past. Our past. Our time together. Don't confuse these words with the pictures of your memory.

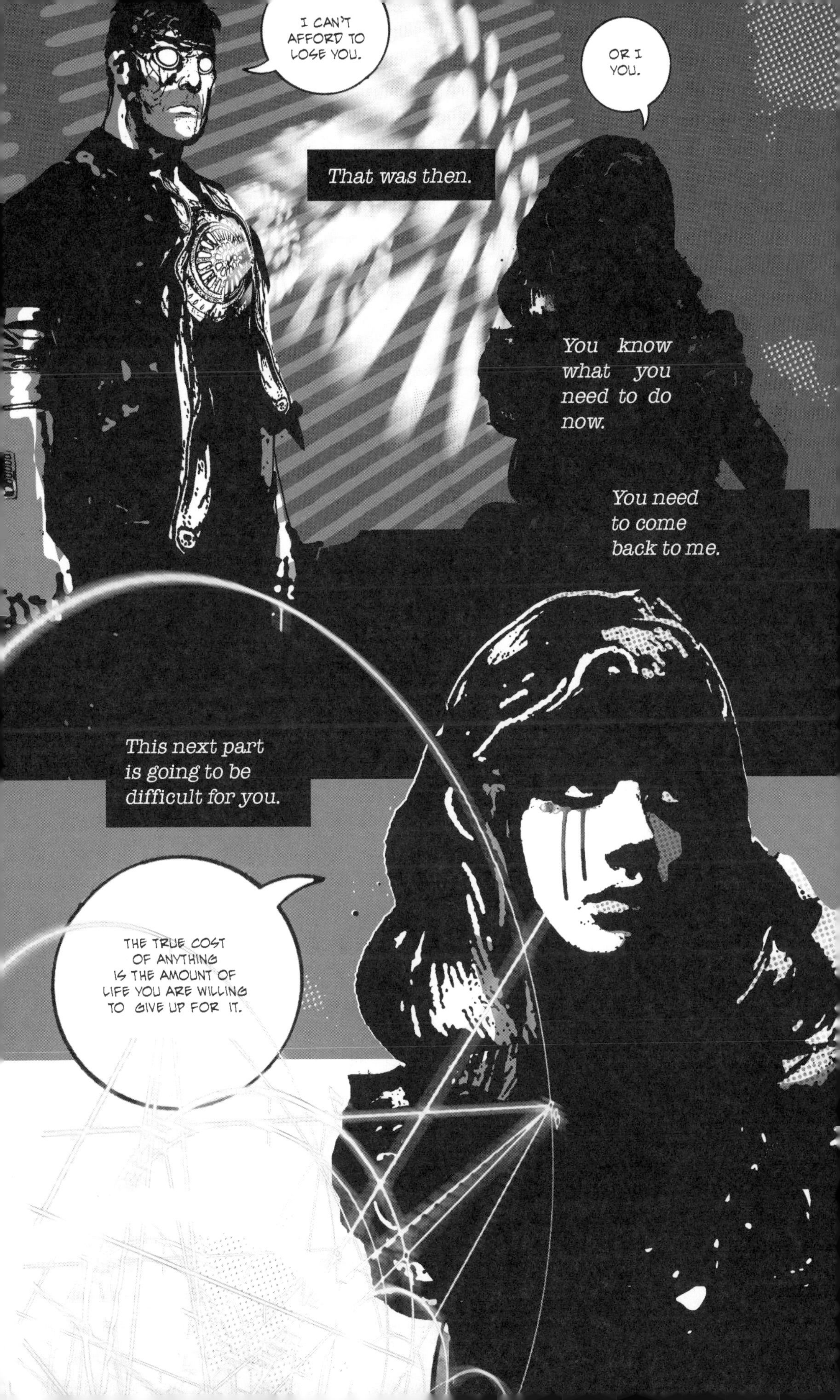

I CAN'T AFFORD TO LOSE YOU.
OR I YOU.
That was then.
You know what you need to do now.
You need to come back to me.
This next part is going to be difficult for you.
THE TRUE COST OF ANYTHING IS THE AMOUNT OF LIFE YOU ARE WILLING TO GIVE UP FOR IT.

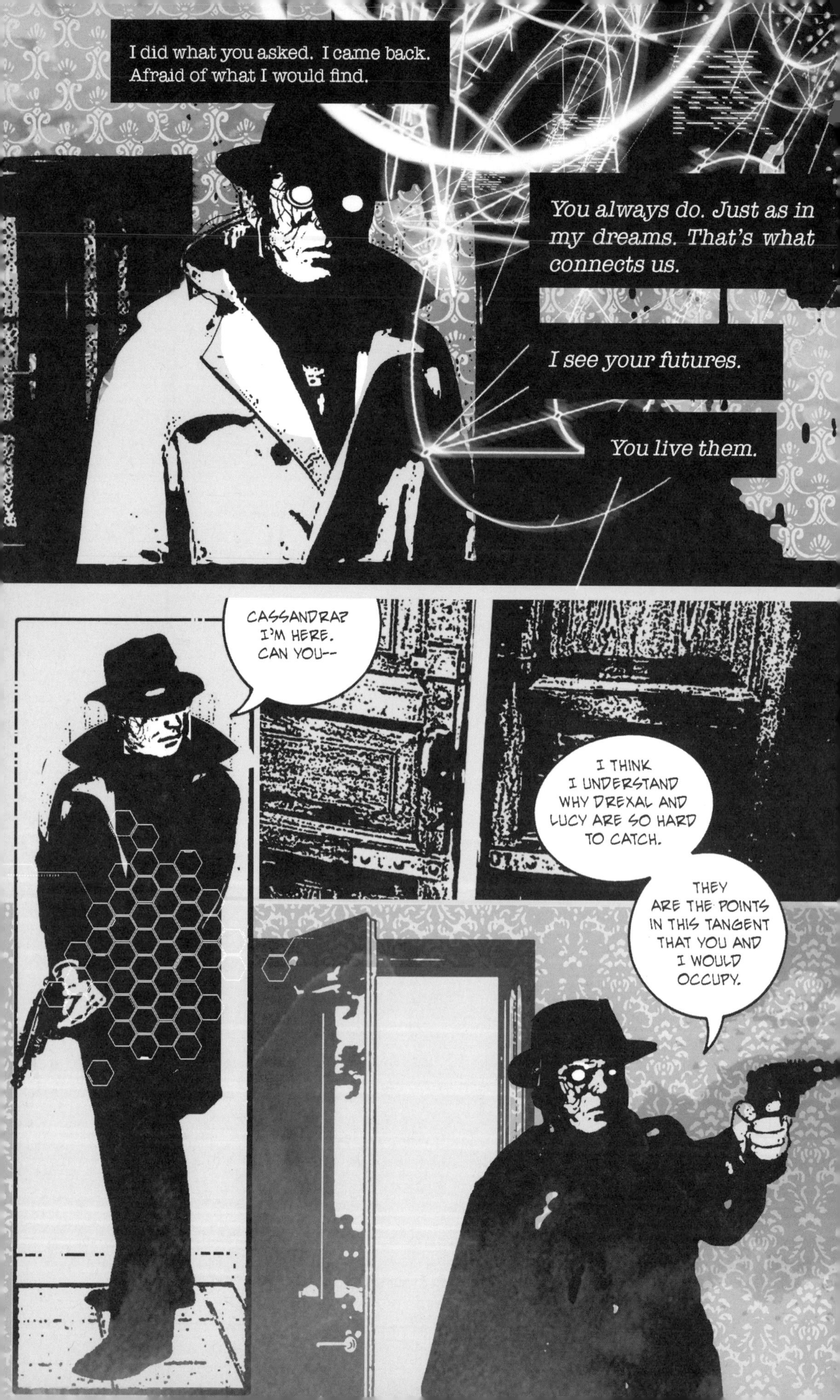
I did what you asked. I came back. Afraid of what I would find.
You always do. Just as in my dreams. That's what connects us.
I see your futures.
You live them.
CASSANDRA? I'M HERE. CAN YOU--
I THINK I UNDERSTAND WHY DREXAL AND LUCY ARE SO HARD TO CATCH.
THEY ARE THE POINTS IN THIS TANGENT THAT YOU AND I WOULD OCCUPY.

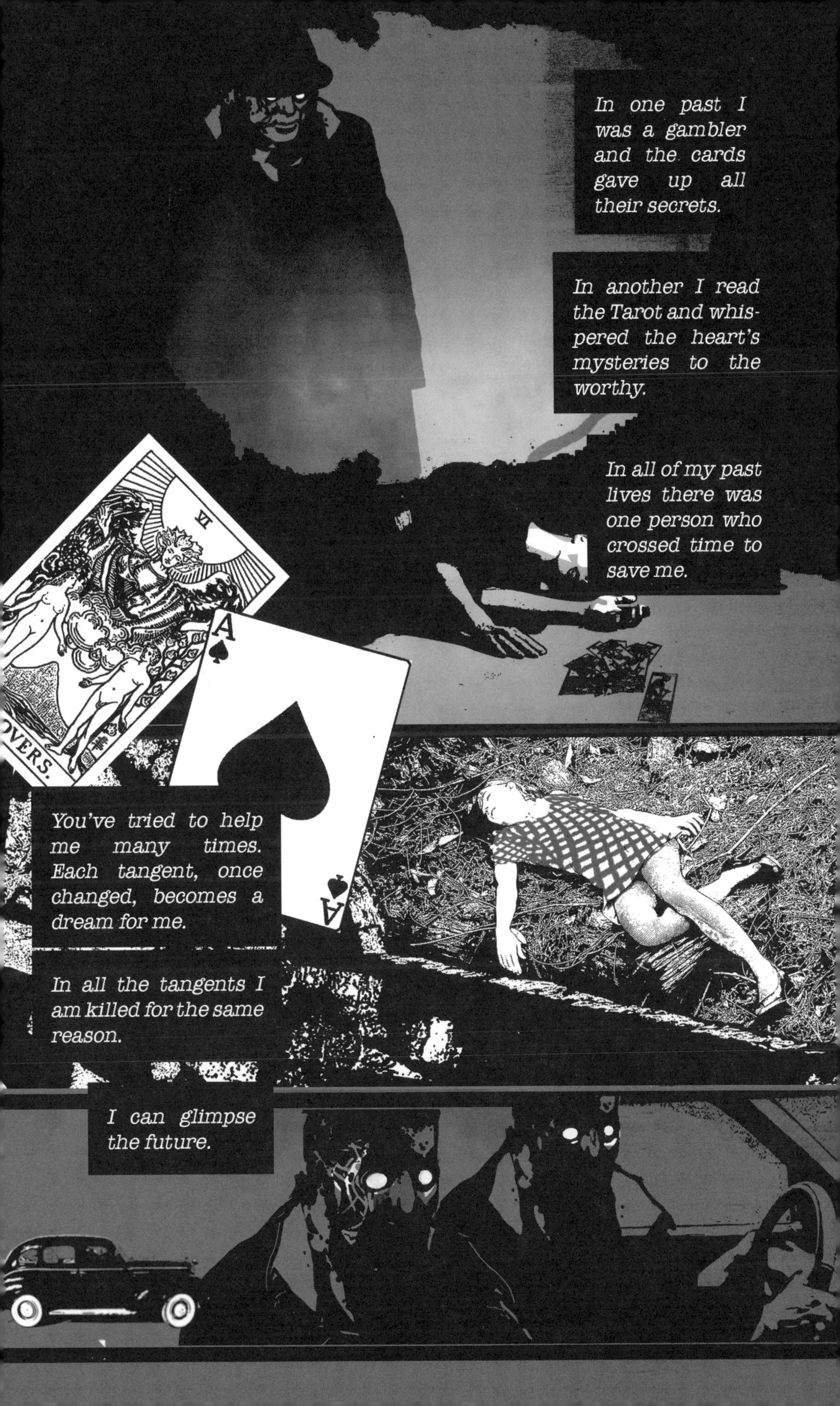

In one past I was a gambler and the cards gave up all their secrets.
In another I read the Tarot and whispered the heart's mysteries to the worthy.
In all of my past lives there was one person who crossed time to save me.
VI
LOVERS.
A
A
You've tried to help me many times. Each tangent, once changed, becomes a dream for me.
In all the tangents I am killed for the same reason.
I can glimpse the future.

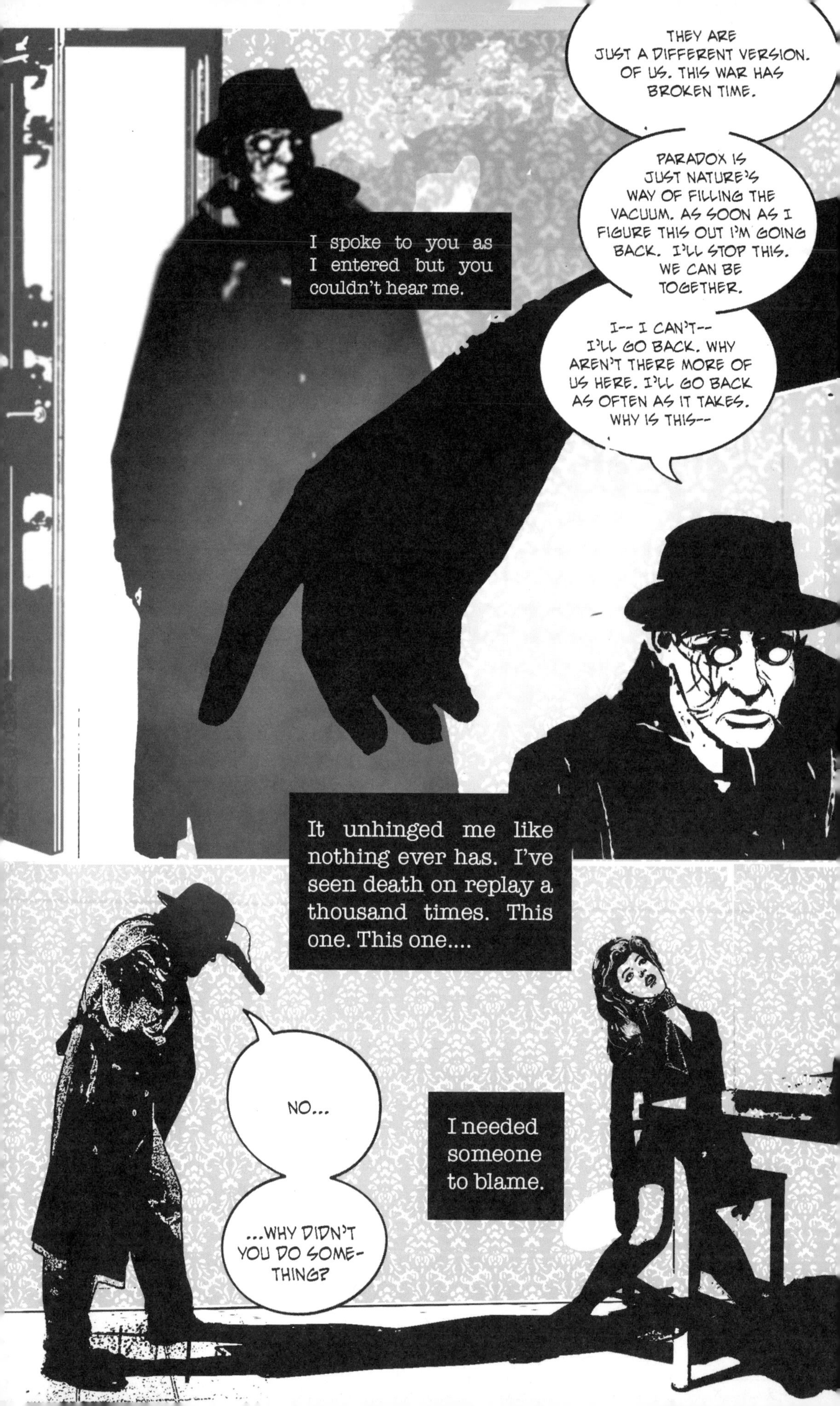

THEY ARE JUST A DIFFERENT VERSION. OF US. THIS WAR HAS BROKEN TIME.
PARADOX IS JUST NATURE'S WAY OF FILLING THE VACUUM. AS SOON AS I FIGURE THIS OUT I'M GOING BACK. I'LL STOP THIS. WE CAN BE TOGETHER.
I spoke to you as I entered but you couldn't hear me.
I-- I CAN'T-- I'LL GO BACK. WHY AREN'T THERE MORE OF US HERE. I'LL GO BACK AS OFTEN AS IT TAKES. WHY IS THIS--
It unhinged me like nothing ever has. I've seen death on replay a thousand times. This one. This one....
NO...
...WHY DIDN'T YOU DO SOME-THING?
I needed someone to blame.

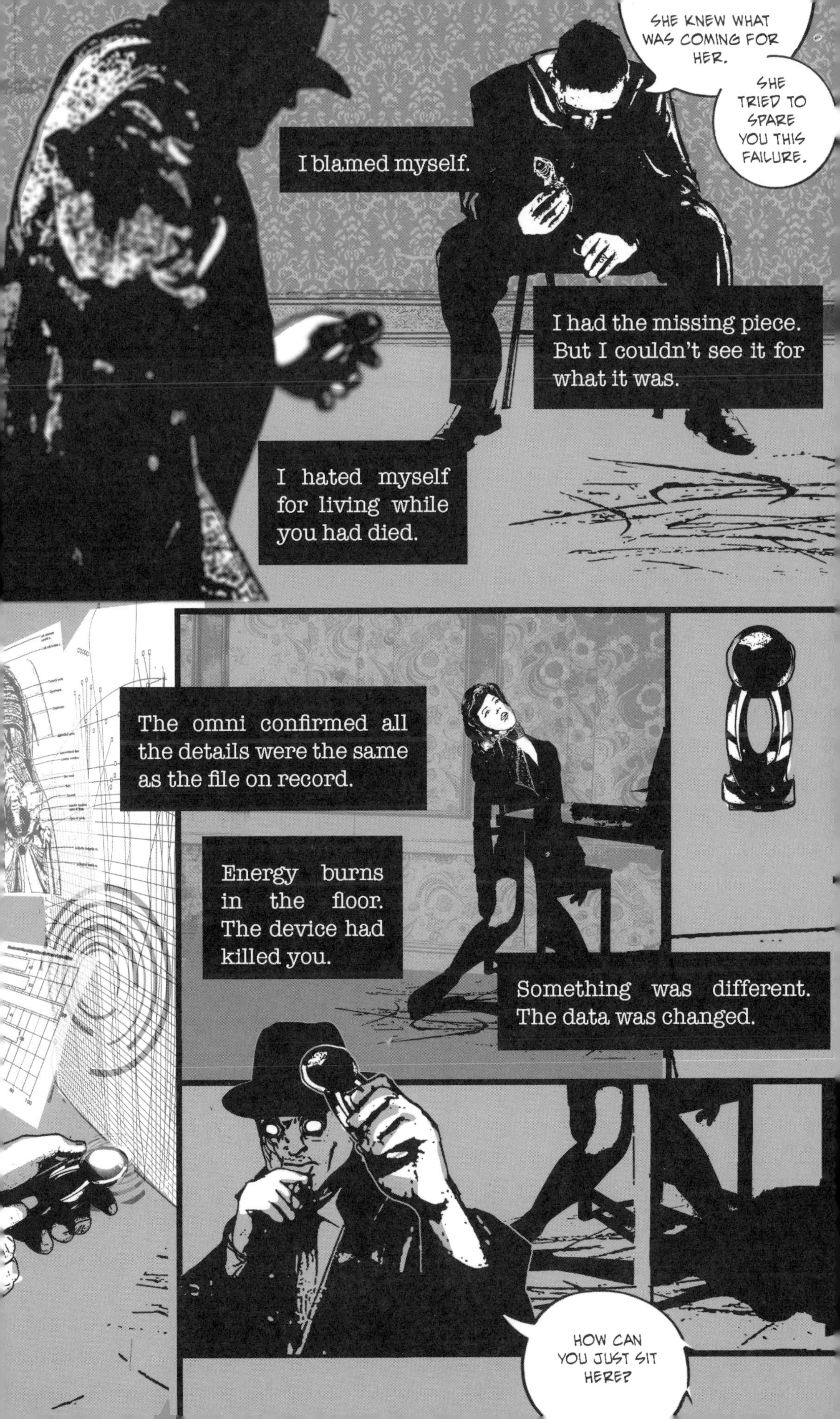
SHE KNEW WHAT WAS COMING FOR HER.
SHE TRIED TO SPARE YOU THIS FAILURE.
I blamed myself.
I had the missing piece. But I couldn't see it for what it was.
I hated myself for living while you had died.
The omni confirmed all the details were the same as the file on record.
Energy burns in the floor. The device had killed you.
Something was different. The data was changed.
HOW CAN YOU JUST SIT HERE?

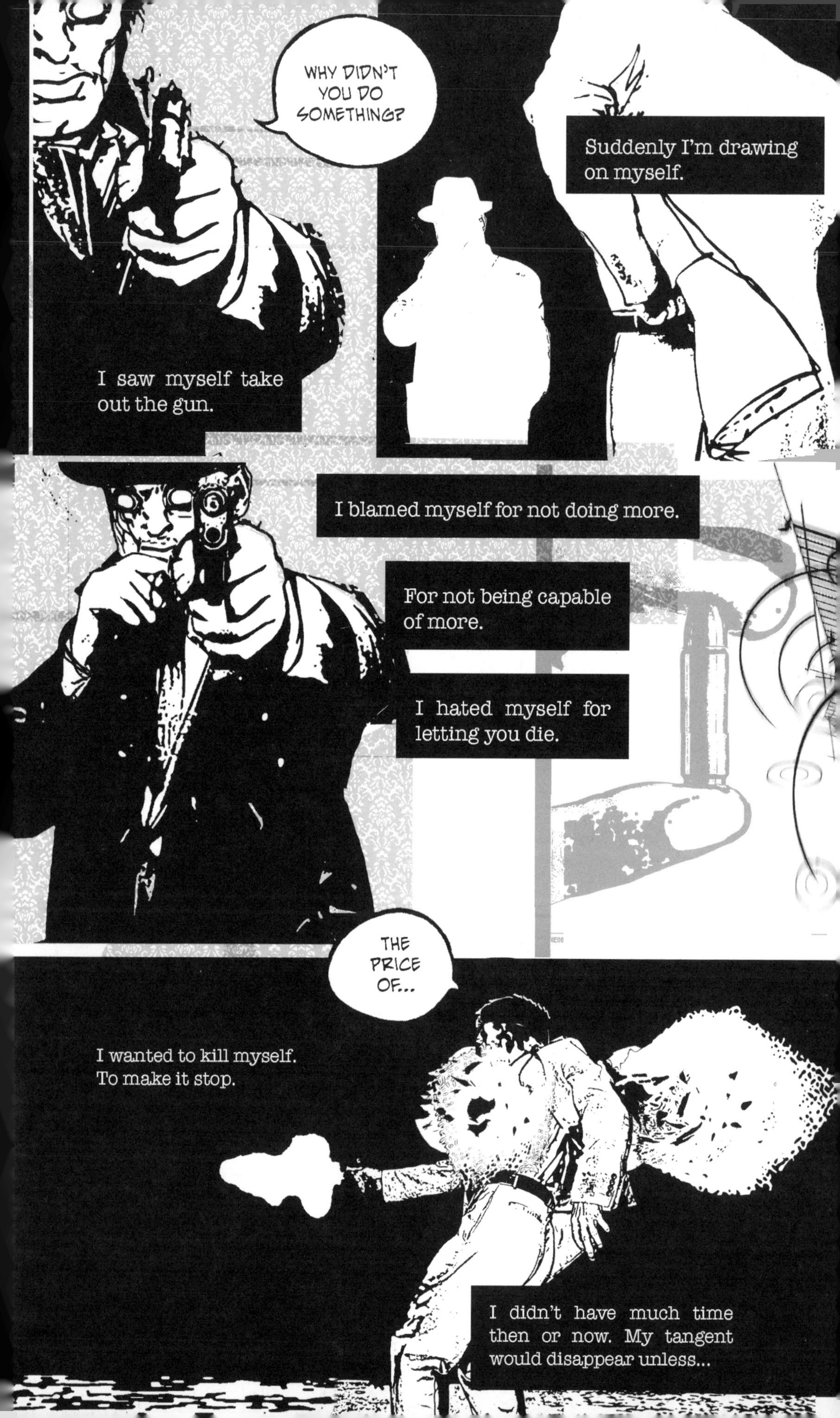
WHY DIDN'T YOU DO SOMETHING?
I saw myself take out the gun.
Suddenly I'm drawing on myself.
I blamed myself for not doing more.
For not being capable of more.
I hated myself for letting you die.
THE PRICE OF...
I wanted to kill myself. To make it stop.
I didn't have much time then or now. My tangent would disappear unless...

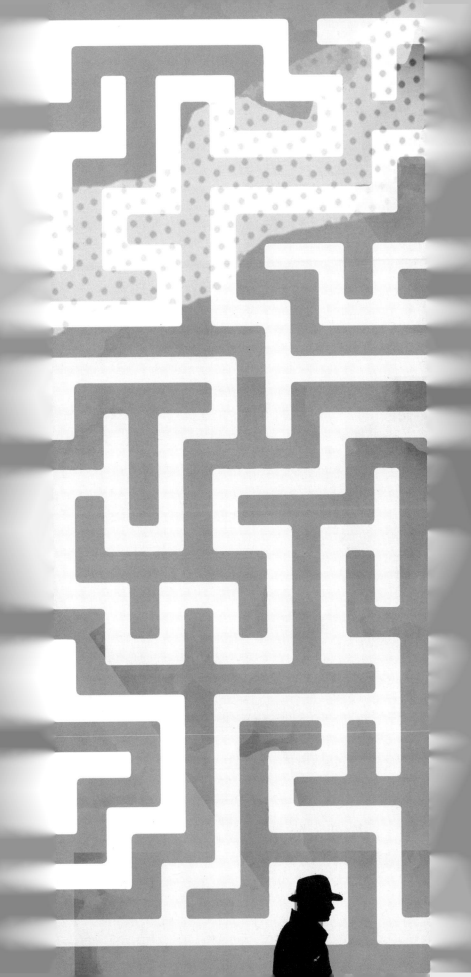

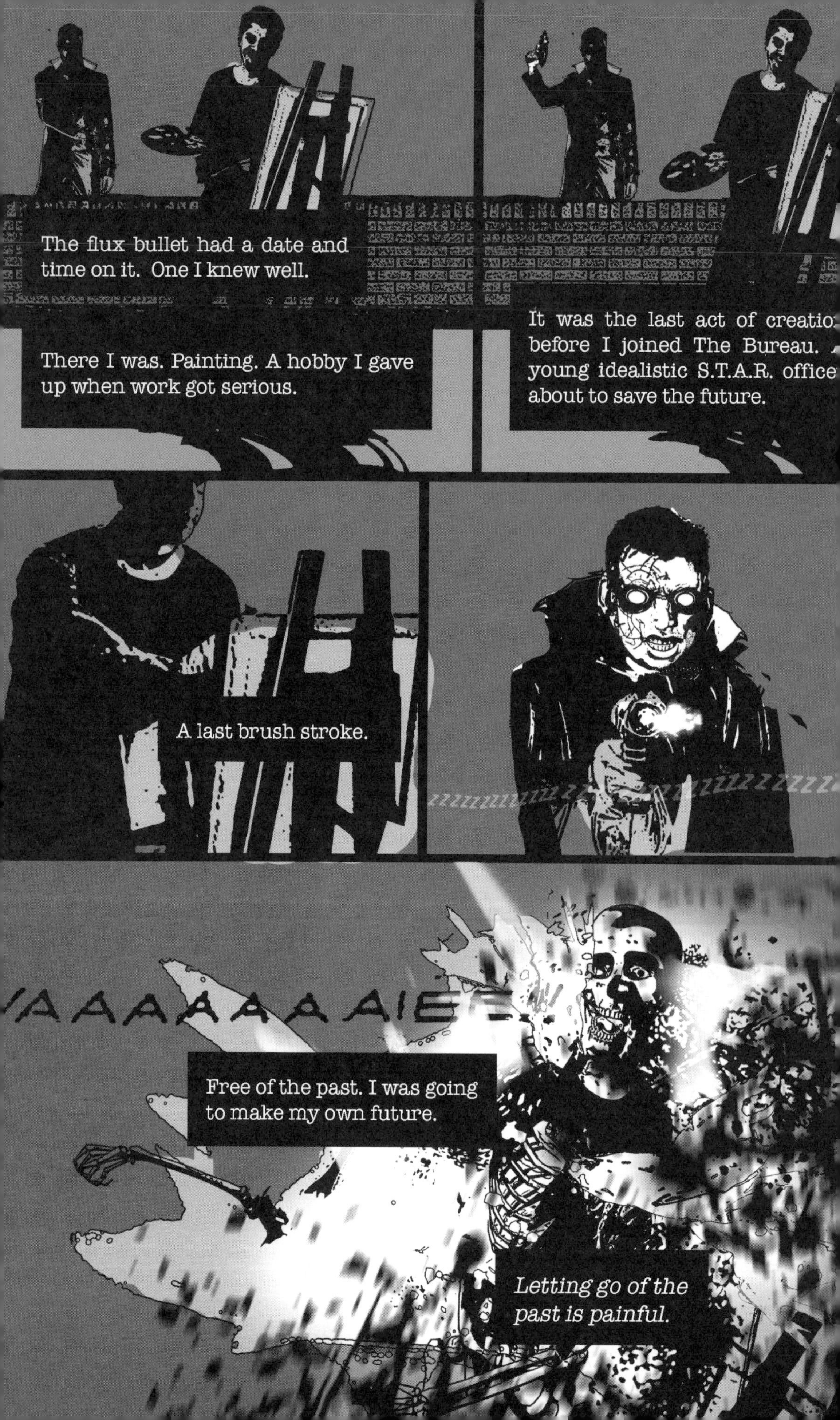

The flux bullet had a date and time on it. One I knew well.
There I was. Painting. A hobby I gave up when work got serious.
It was the last act of creatio before I joined The Bureau. young idealistic S.T.A.R. office about to save the future.
A last brush stroke.
zzzzzzzzzzzzzzzzzzzzzzzzzzzz
AAAAAAAAIE
Free of the past. I was going to make my own future.
Letting go of the past is painful.

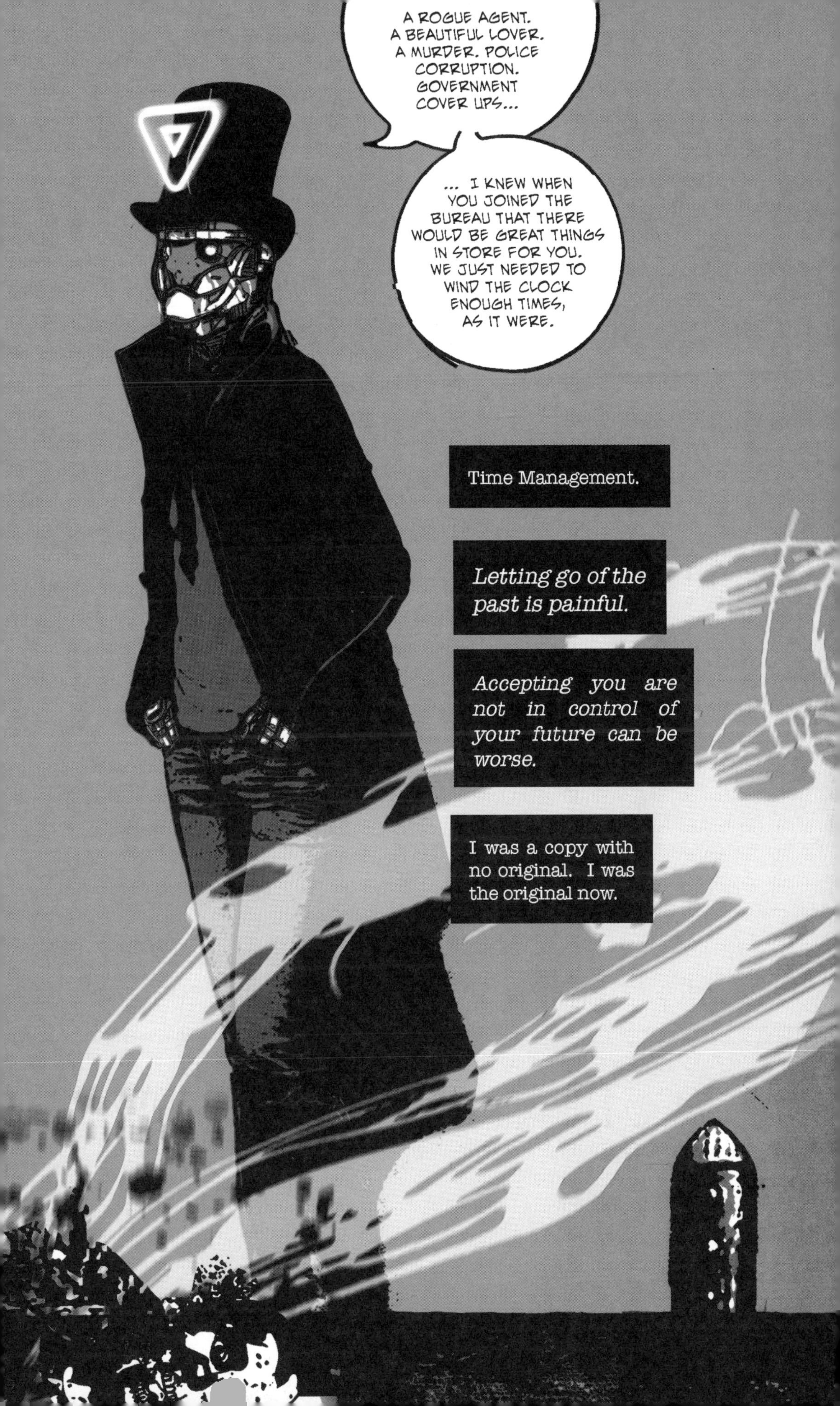
A ROGUE AGENT. A BEAUTIFUL LOVER. A MURDER. POLICE CORRUPTION. GOVERNMENT COVER UPS...
... I KNEW WHEN YOU JOINED THE BUREAU THAT THERE WOULD BE GREAT THINGS IN STORE FOR YOU. WE JUST NEEDED TO WIND THE CLOCK ENOUGH TIMES, AS IT WERE.
Time Management.
Letting go of the past is painful.
Accepting you are not in control of your future can be worse.
I was a copy with no original. I was the original now.

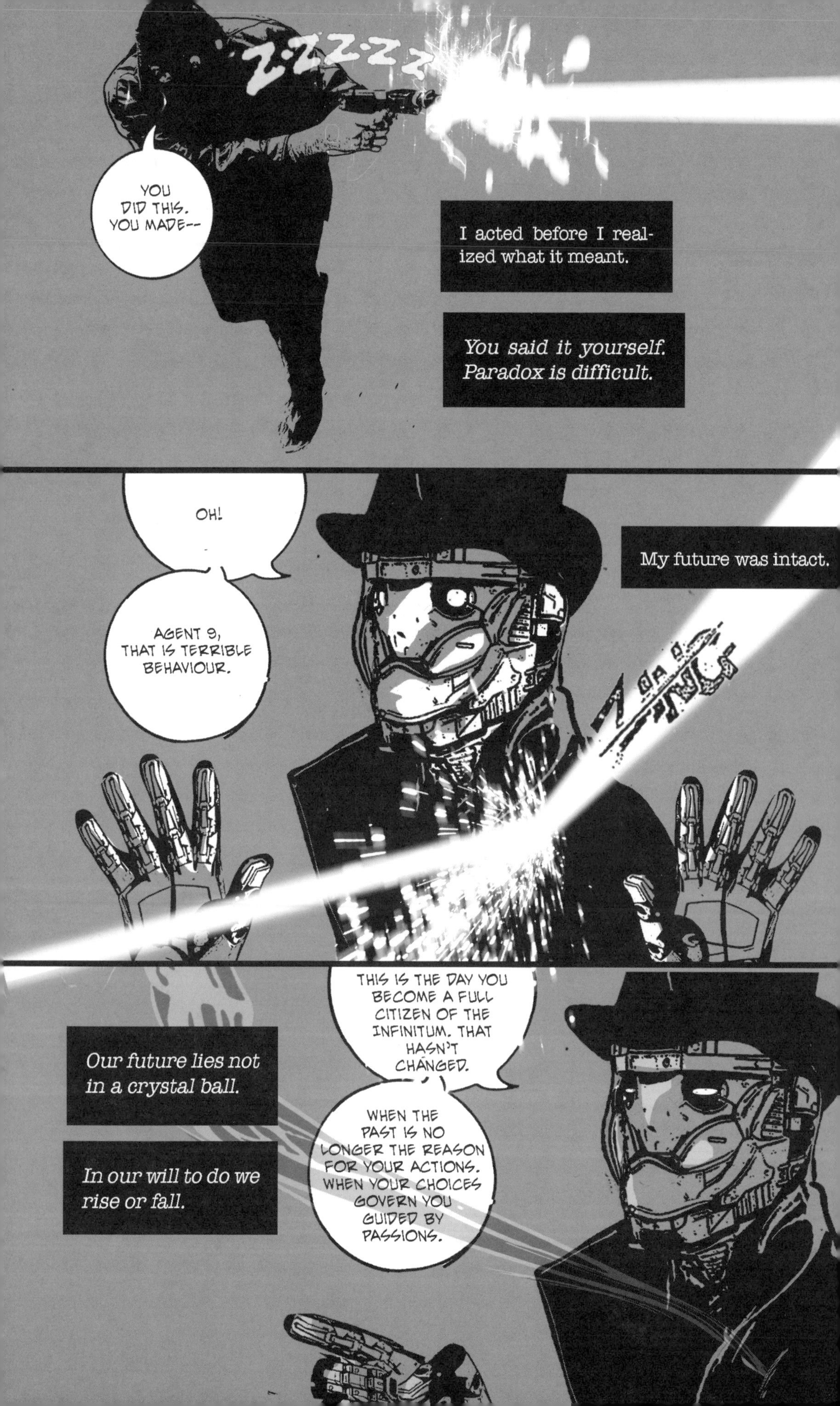

Z-Z-Z-Z-Z
YOU DID THIS. YOU MADE--
I acted before I realized what it meant.
You said it yourself. Paradox is difficult.
OH!
AGENT 9, THAT IS TERRIBLE BEHAVIOUR.
My future was intact.
THIS IS THE DAY YOU BECOME A FULL CITIZEN OF THE INFINITUM. THAT HASN'T CHANGED.
WHEN THE PAST IS NO LONGER THE REASON FOR YOUR ACTIONS. WHEN YOUR CHOICES GOVERN YOU GUIDED BY PASSIONS.
Our future lies not in a crystal ball.
In our will to do we rise or fall.

I went back to Beiko's.

I waited until 6 and I left.

Looking back, like pages in a book. When the S.T.A.R. officers
ambushed me there was one face I couldn't remember from the
Drexal bust, but one I knew. One I knew where to find.

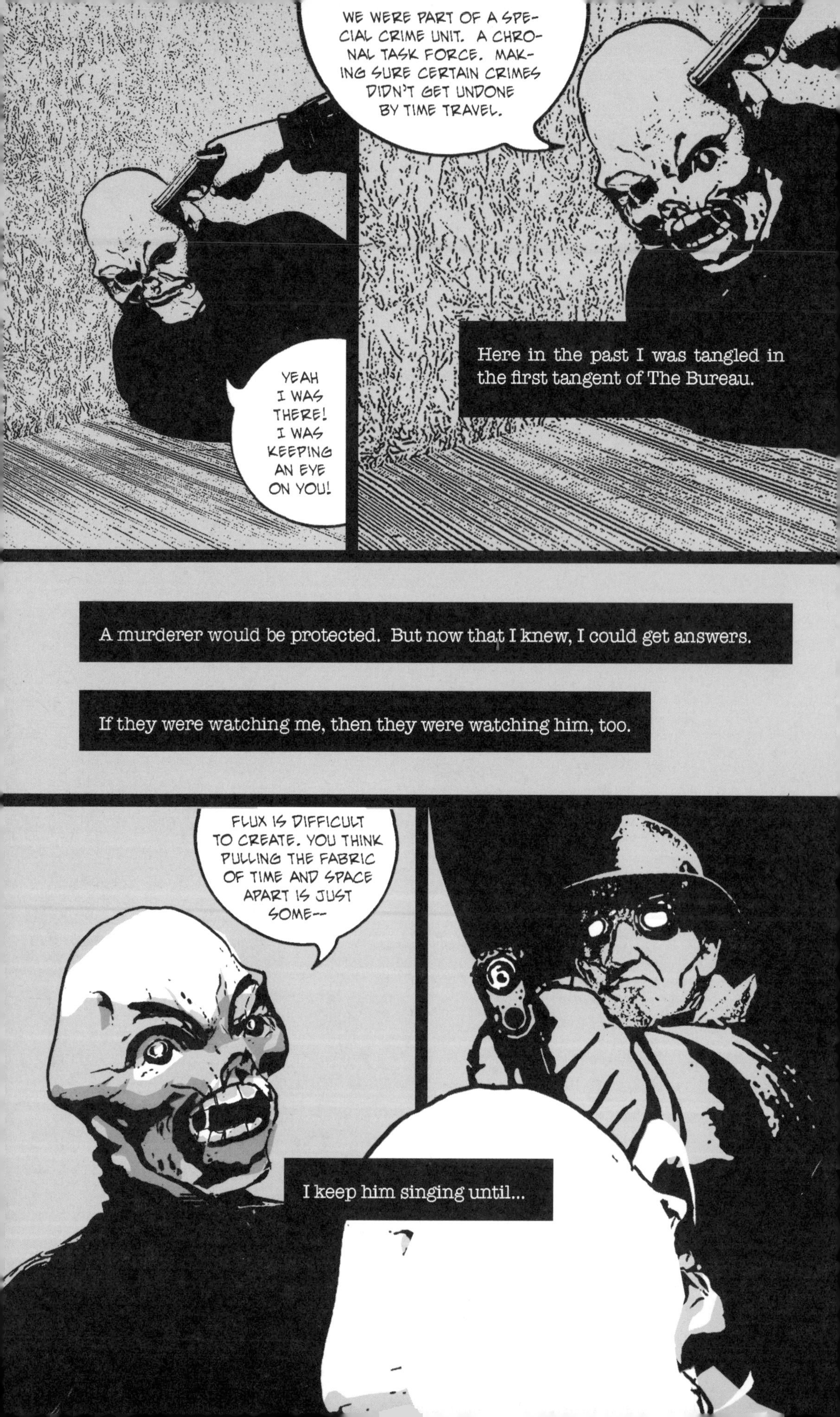
WE WERE PART OF A SPECIAL CRIME UNIT. A CHRONAL TASK FORCE. MAKING SURE CERTAIN CRIMES DIDN'T GET UNDONE BY TIME TRAVEL.
YEAH I WAS THERE! I WAS KEEPING AN EYE ON YOU!
Here in the past I was tangled in the first tangent of The Bureau.
A murderer would be protected. But now that I knew, I could get answers.
If they were watching me, then they were watching him, too.
FLUX IS DIFFICULT TO CREATE. YOU THINK PULLING THE FABRIC OF TIME AND SPACE APART IS JUST SOME--
I keep him singing until...

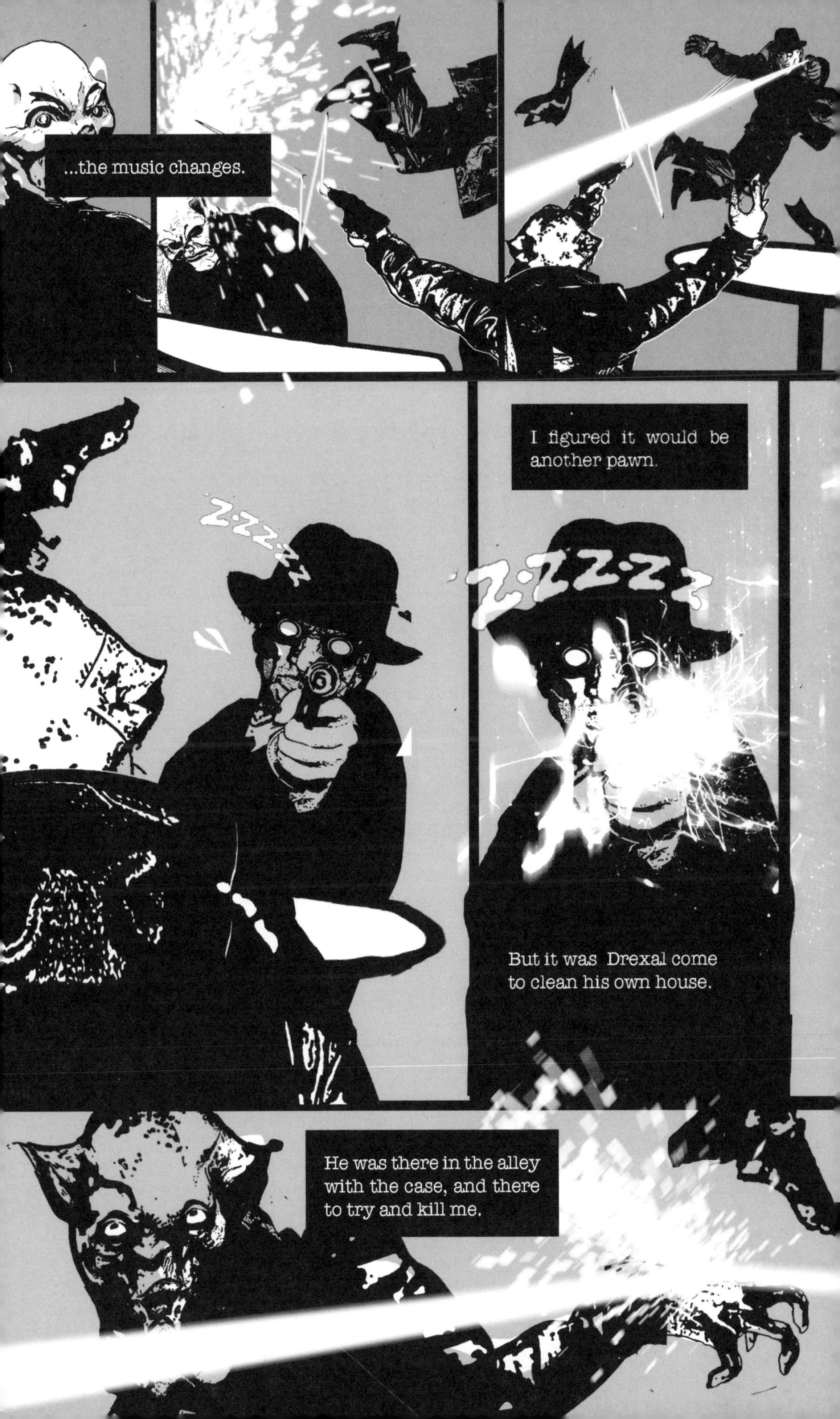
...the music changes.
I figured it would be another pawn.
Z-Z-Z-Z
Z-Z-Z-Z-Z
But it was Drexal come to clean his own house.
He was there in the alley with the case, and there to try and kill me.

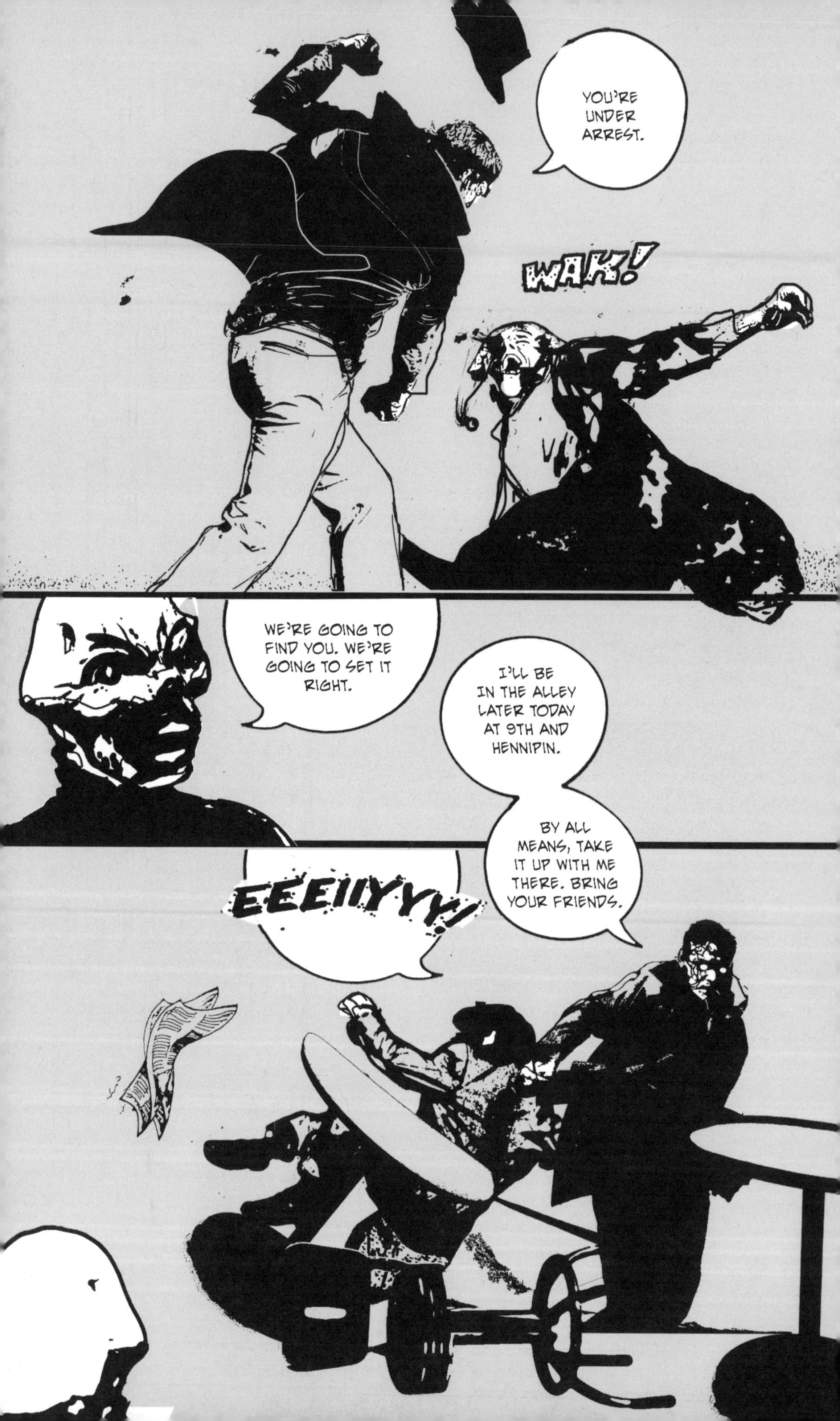

YOU'RE UNDER ARREST.
WAK!
WE'RE GOING TO FIND YOU. WE'RE GOING TO SET IT RIGHT.
I'LL BE IN THE ALLEY LATER TODAY AT 9TH AND HENNIPIN.
BY ALL MEANS, TAKE IT UP WITH ME THERE. BRING YOUR FRIENDS.
EEEIIYYY!

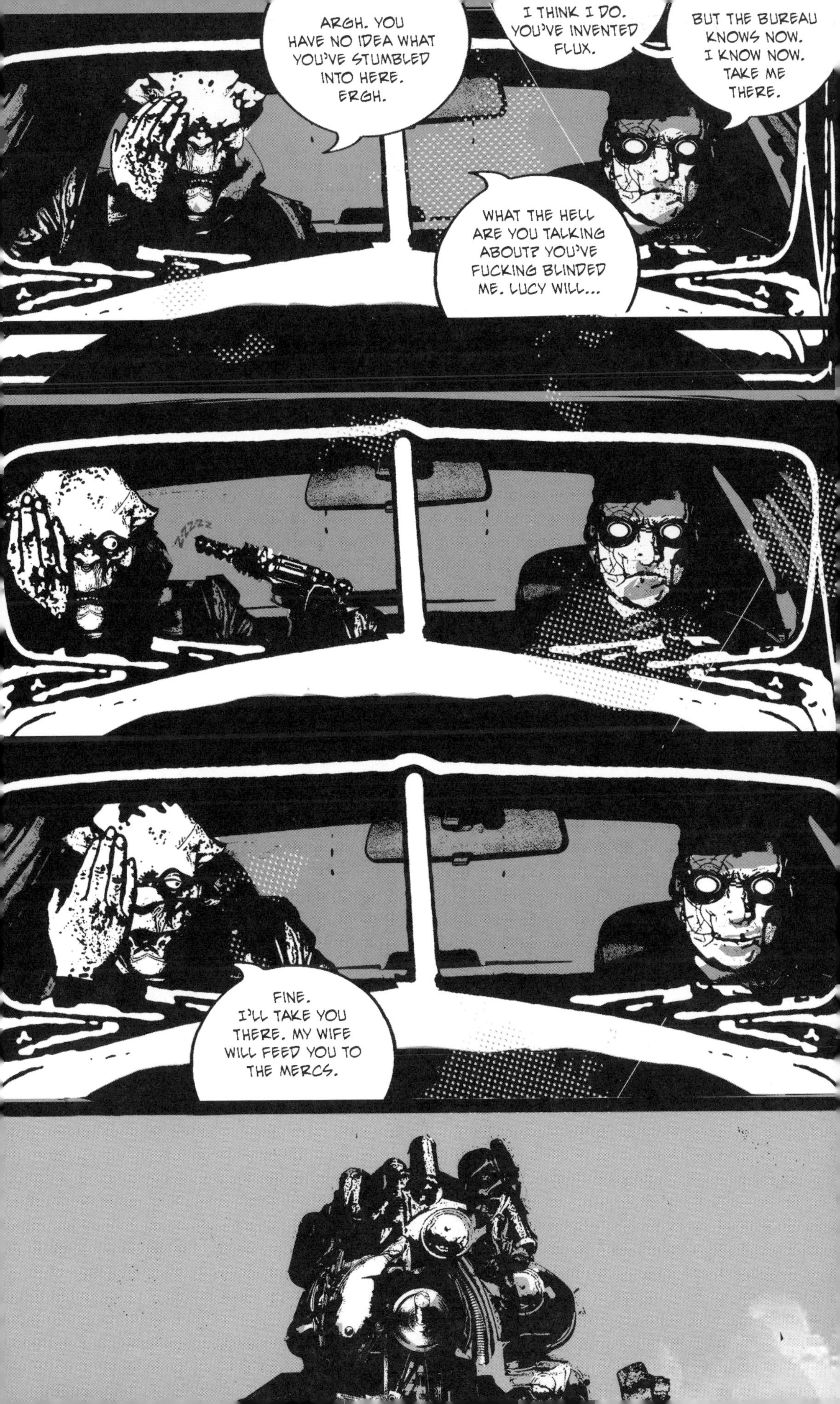
ARGH. YOU HAVE NO IDEA WHAT YOU'VE STUMBLED INTO HERE. ERGH.
I THINK I DO. YOU'VE INVENTED FLUX.
BUT THE BUREAU KNOWS NOW. I KNOW NOW. TAKE ME THERE.
WHAT THE HELL ARE YOU TALKING ABOUT? YOU'VE FUCKING BLINDED ME. LUCY WILL...
ZZZZZ
FINE. I'LL TAKE YOU THERE. MY WIFE WILL FEED YOU TO THE MERCS.

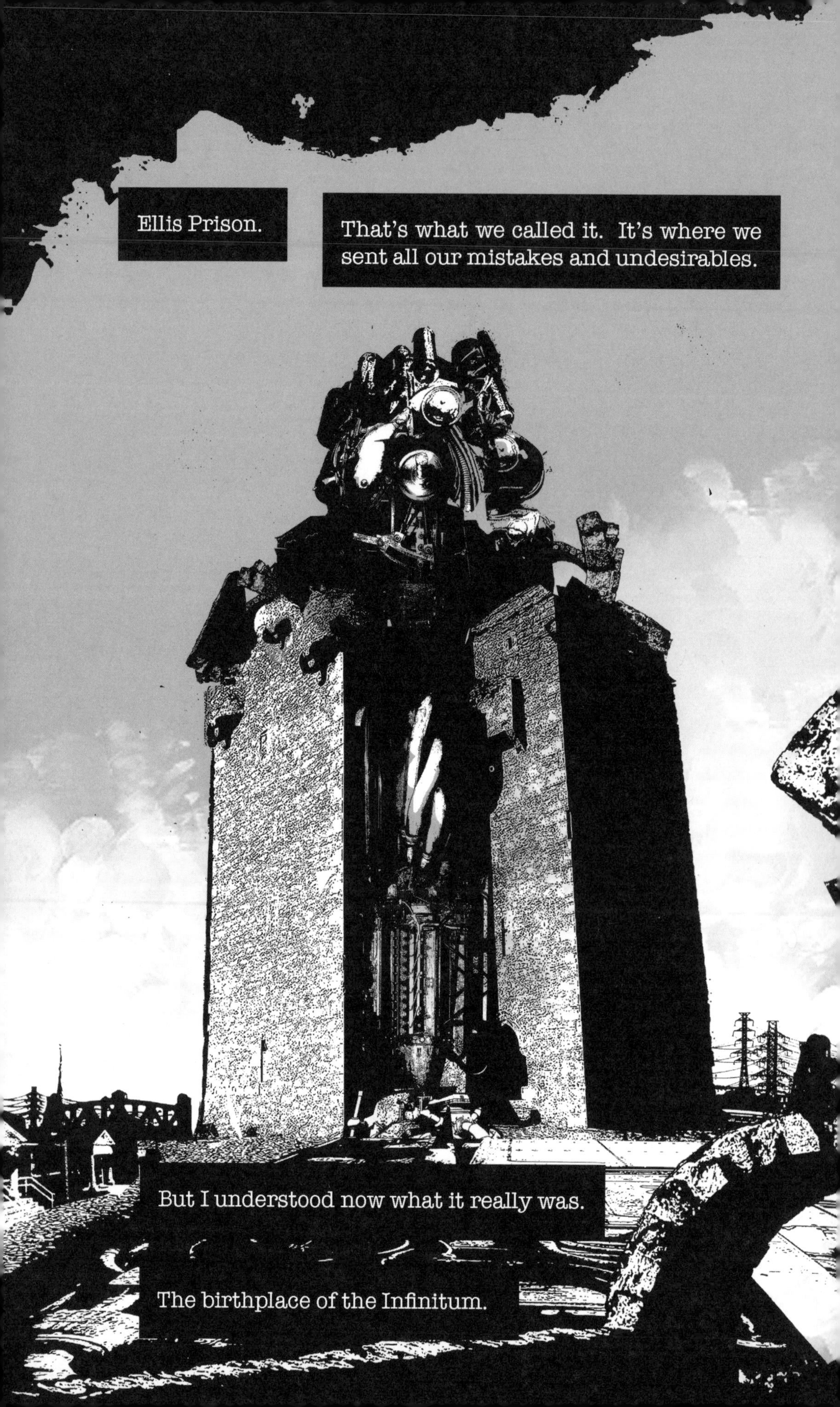
Ellis Prison.
That's what we called it. It's where we sent all our mistakes and undesirables.
But I understood now what it really was.
The birthplace of the Infinitum.

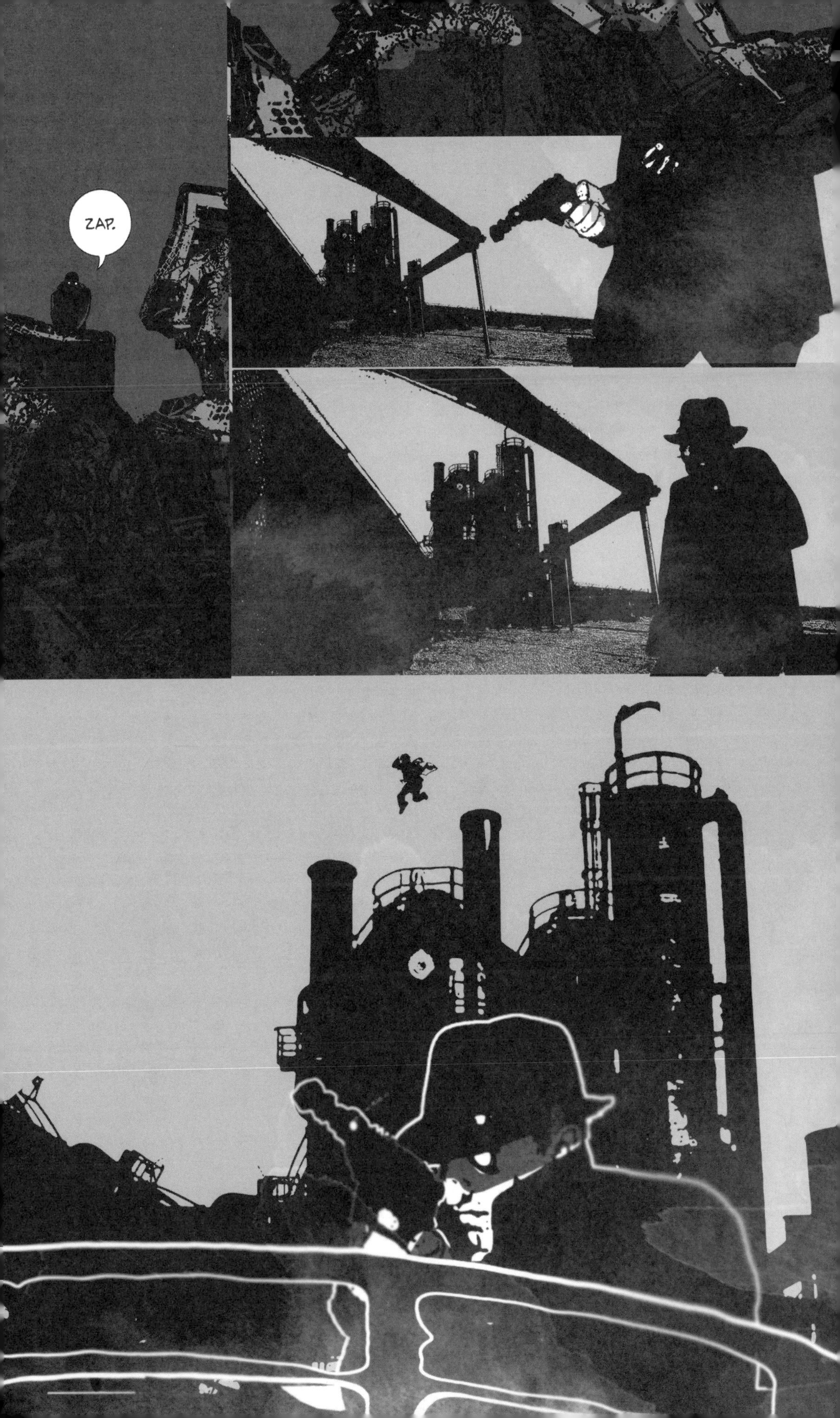
ZAP.

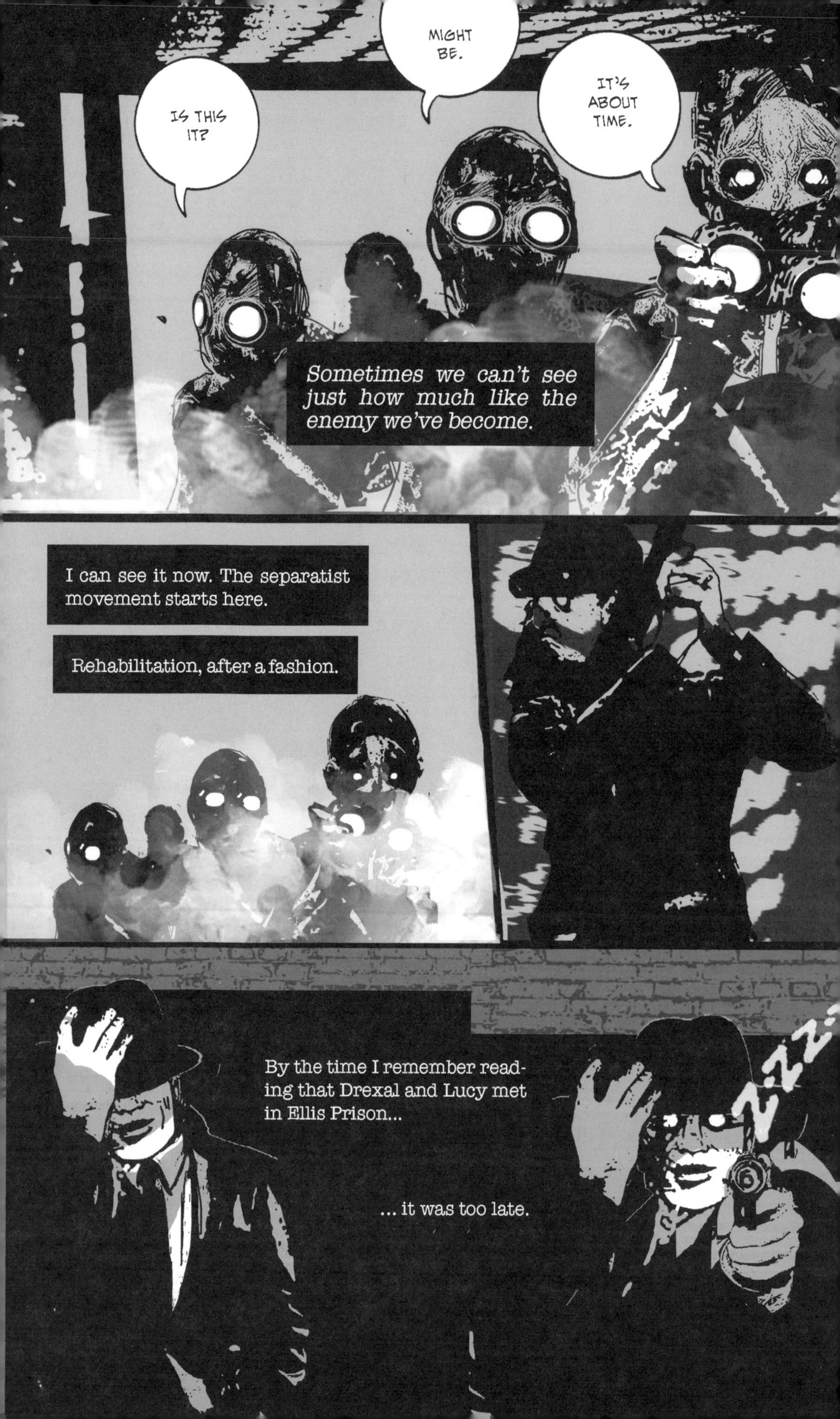
IS THIS IT?
MIGHT BE.
IT'S ABOUT TIME.
Sometimes we can't see just how much like the enemy we've become.
I can see it now. The separatist movement starts here.
Rehabilitation, after a fashion.
By the time I remember reading that Drexal and Lucy met in Ellis Prison...
... it was too late.
ZZZ

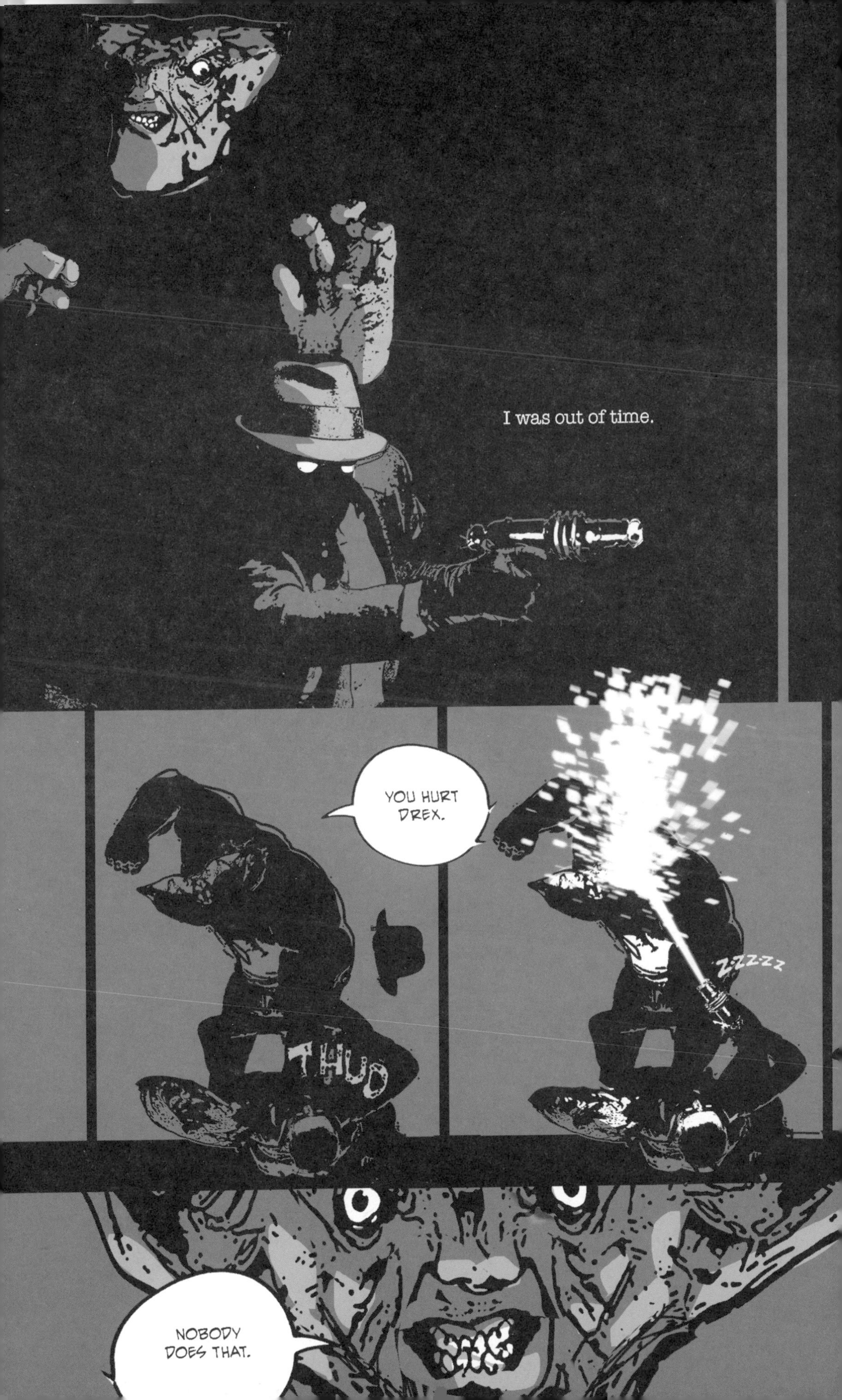
I was out of time.
YOU HURT DREX.
THUD
Z-Z-Z-Z-Z
NOBODY DOES THAT.

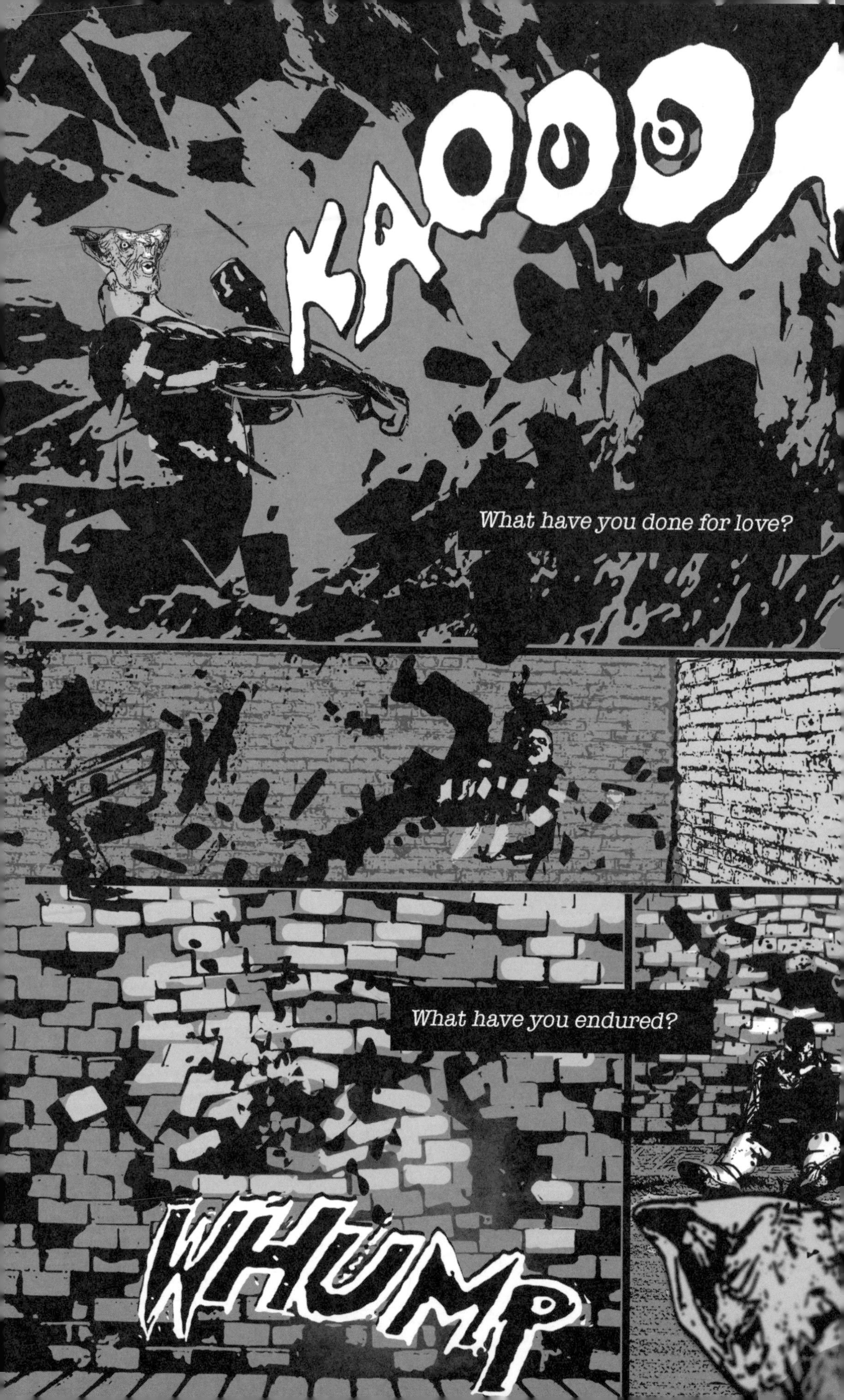
KAOOOM
What have you done for love?
What have you endured?
WHUMP

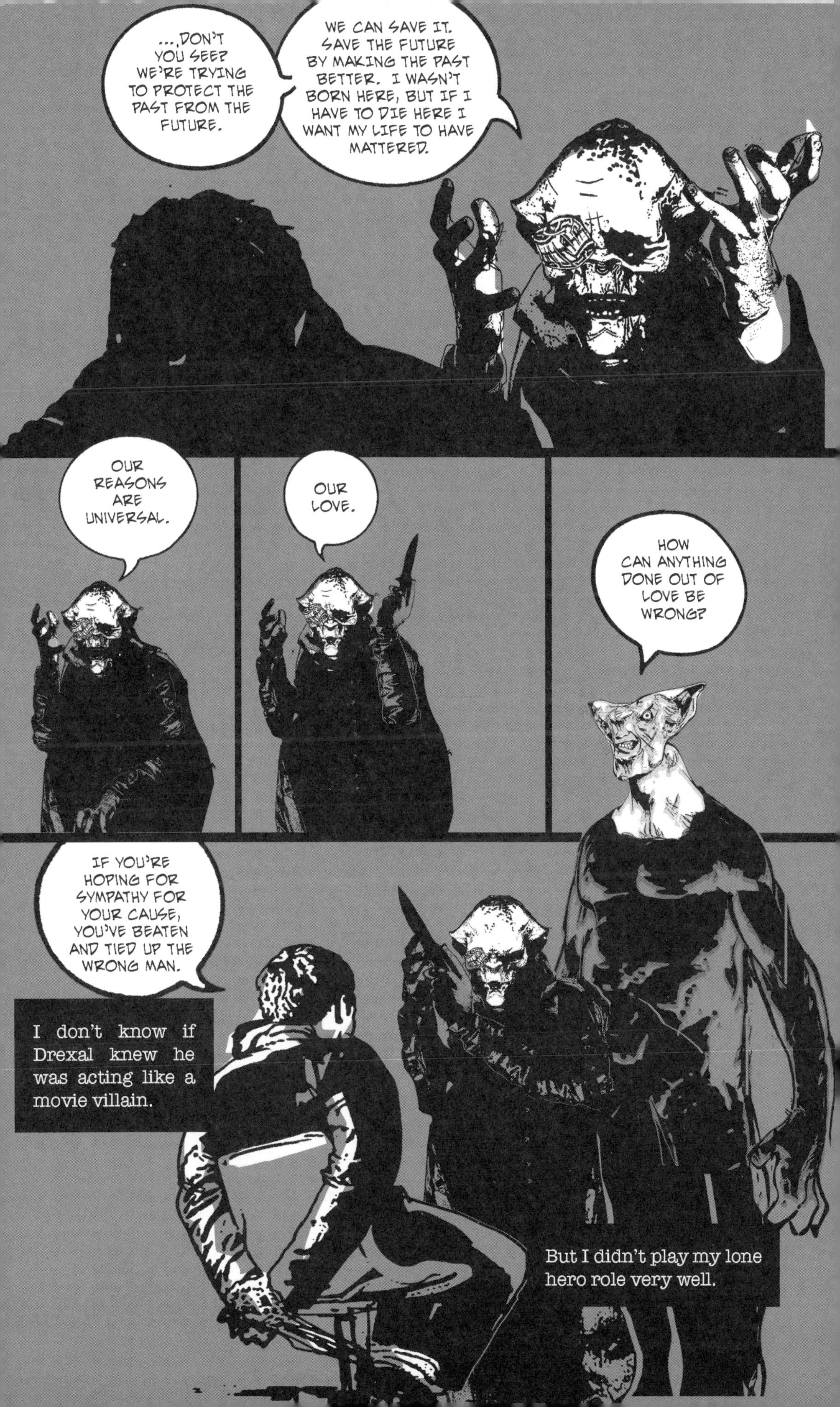

...,DON'T YOU SEE? WE'RE TRYING TO PROTECT THE PAST FROM THE FUTURE.
WE CAN SAVE IT. SAVE THE FUTURE BY MAKING THE PAST BETTER. I WASN'T BORN HERE, BUT IF I HAVE TO DIE HERE I WANT MY LIFE TO HAVE MATTERED.
OUR REASONS ARE UNIVERSAL.
OUR LOVE.
HOW CAN ANYTHING DONE OUT OF LOVE BE WRONG?
IF YOU'RE HOPING FOR SYMPATHY FOR YOUR CAUSE, YOU'VE BEATEN AND TIED UP THE WRONG MAN.
I don't know if Drexal knew he was acting like a movie villain.
But I didn't play my lone hero role very well.

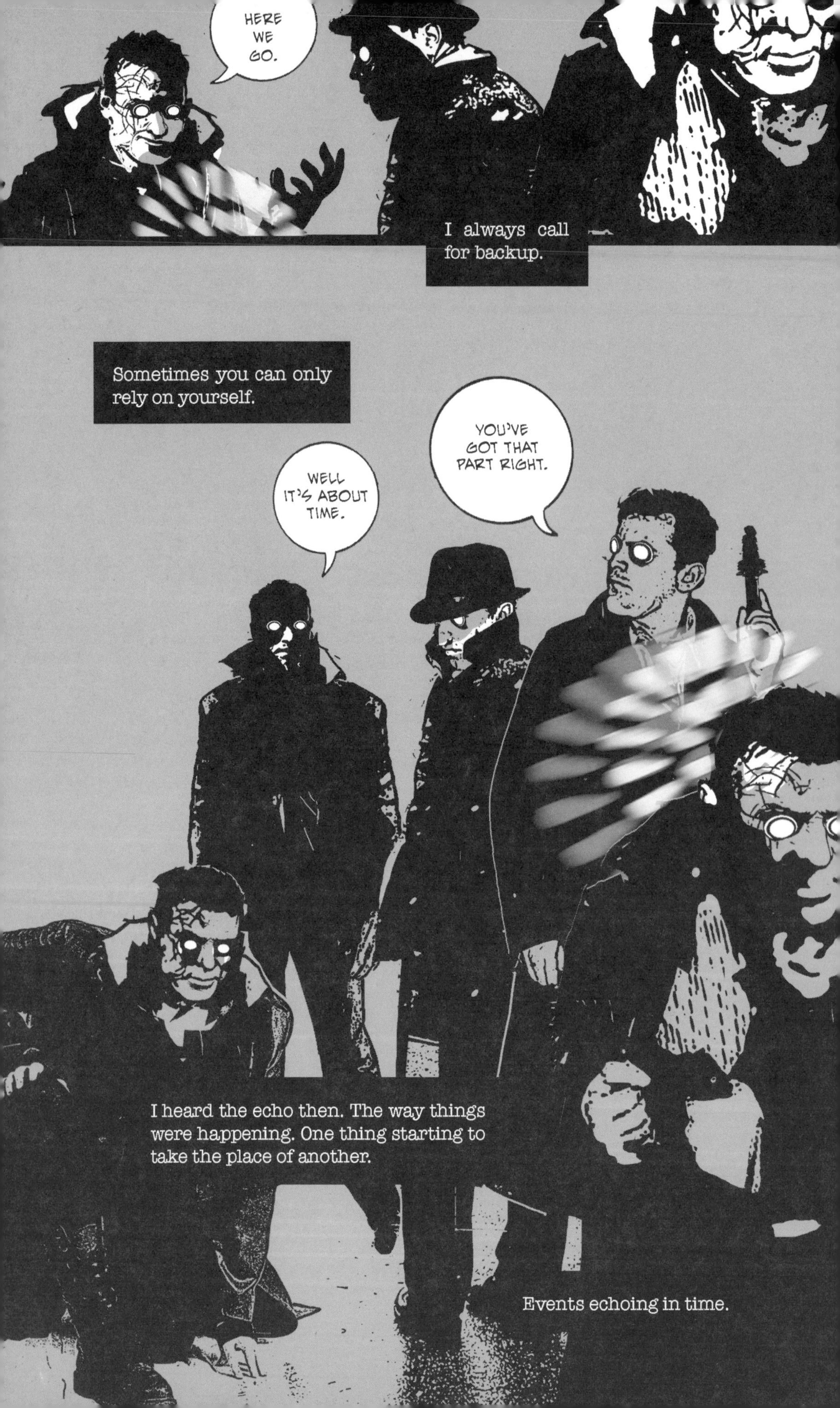
HERE WE GO.
I always call for backup.
Sometimes you can only rely on yourself.
WELL IT'S ABOUT TIME.
YOU'VE GOT THAT PART RIGHT.
I heard the echo then. The way things were happening. One thing starting to take the place of another.
Events echoing in time.

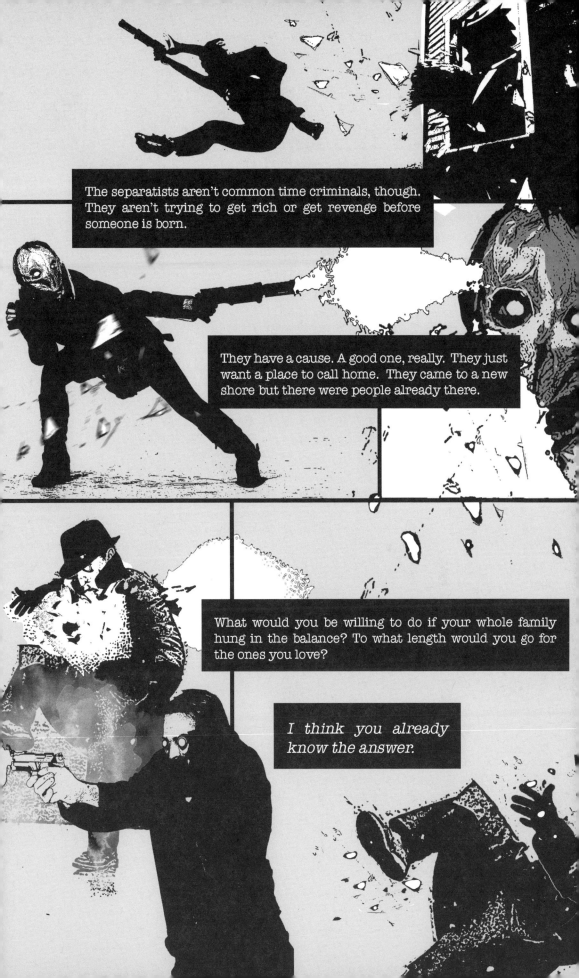

The separatists aren't common time criminals, though. They aren't trying to get rich or get revenge before someone is born.

They have a cause. A good one, really. They just want a place to call home. They came to a new shore but there were people already there.

What would you be willing to do if your whole family hung in the balance? To what length would you go for the ones you love?

I think you already know the answer.

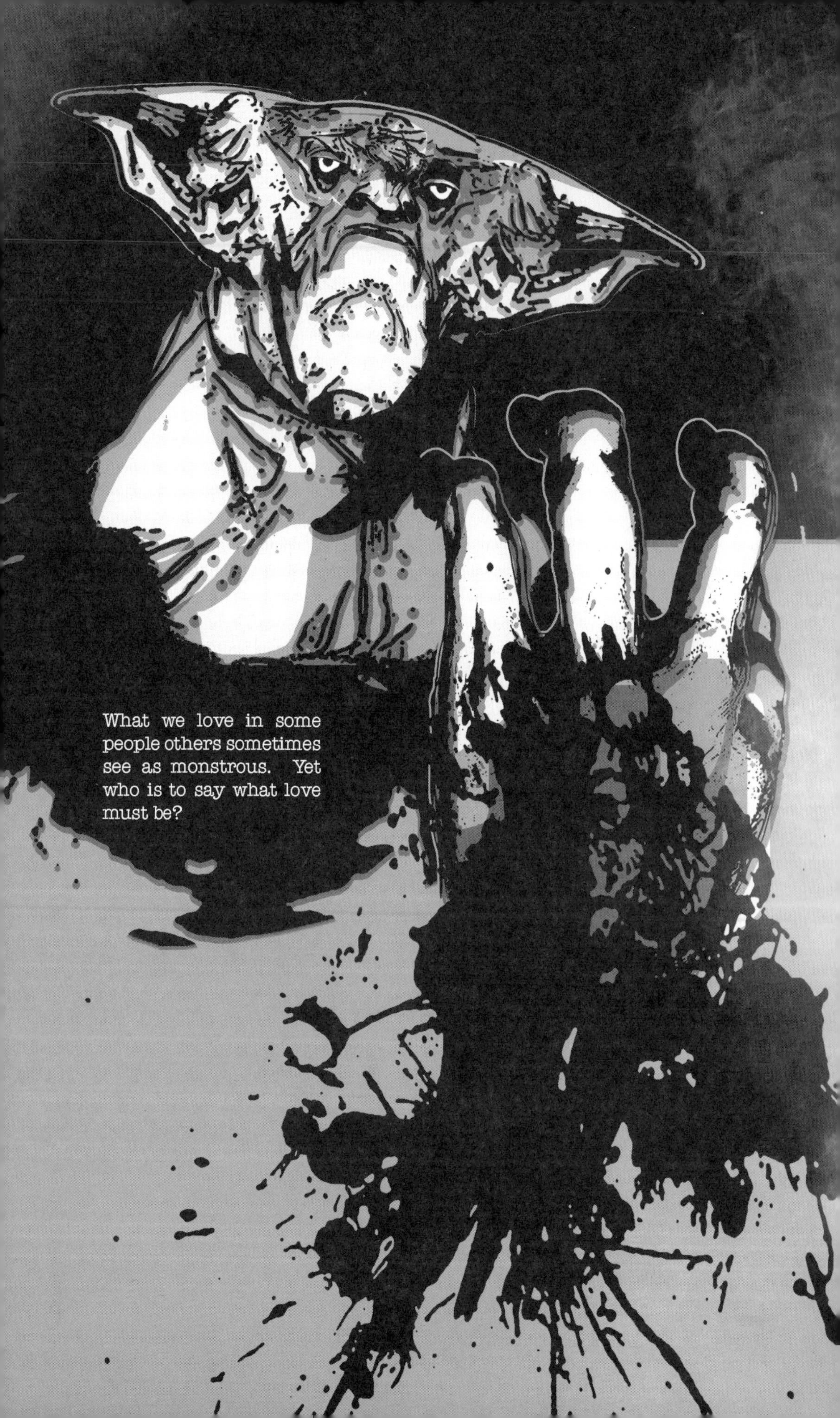
What we love in some people others sometimes see as monstrous. Yet who is to say what love must be?

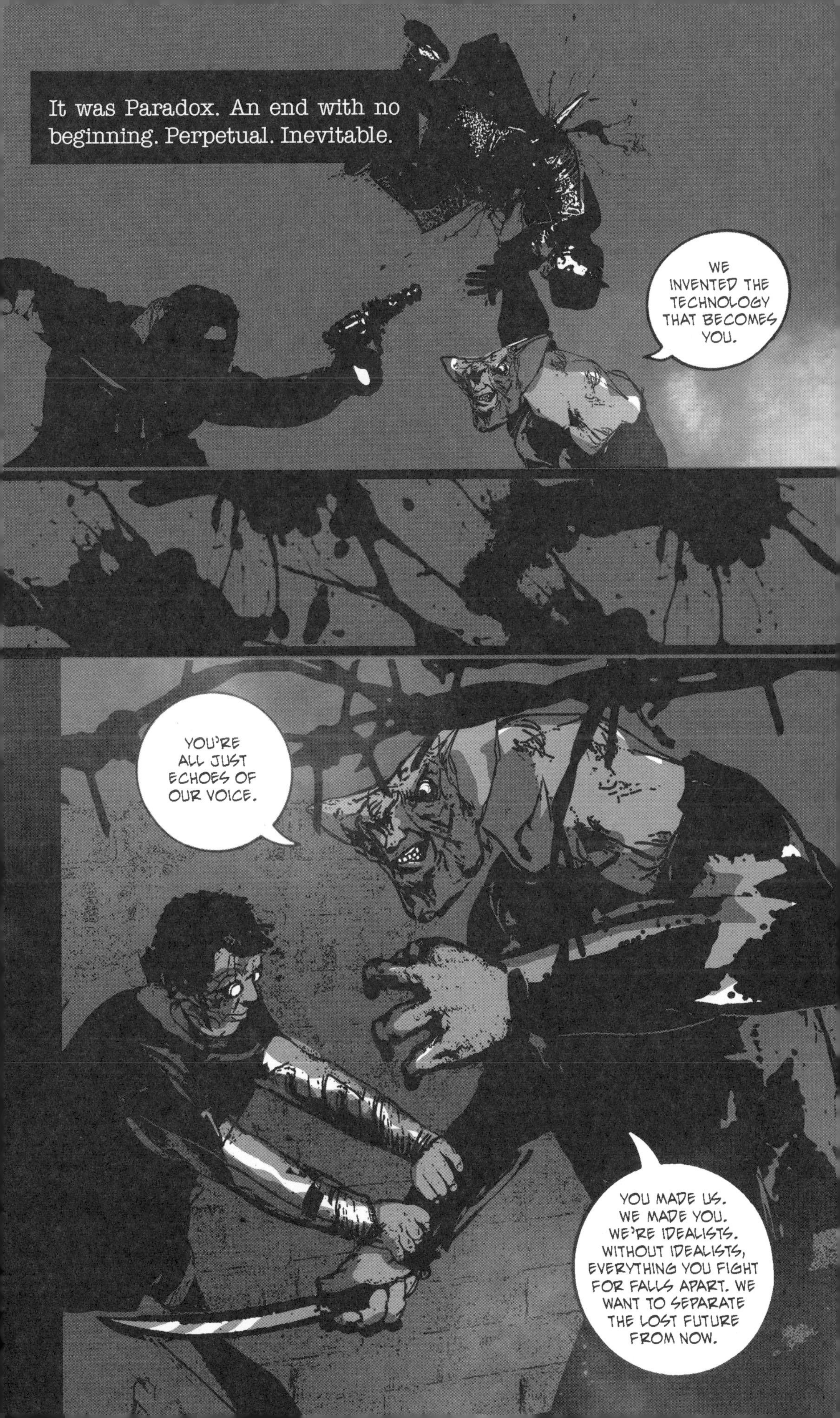
It was Paradox. An end with no beginning. Perpetual. Inevitable.
WE INVENTED THE TECHNOLOGY THAT BECOMES YOU.
YOU'RE ALL JUST ECHOES OF OUR VOICE.
YOU MADE US. WE MADE YOU. WE'RE IDEALISTS. WITHOUT IDEALISTS, EVERYTHING YOU FIGHT FOR FALLS APART. WE WANT TO SEPARATE THE LOST FUTURE FROM NOW.

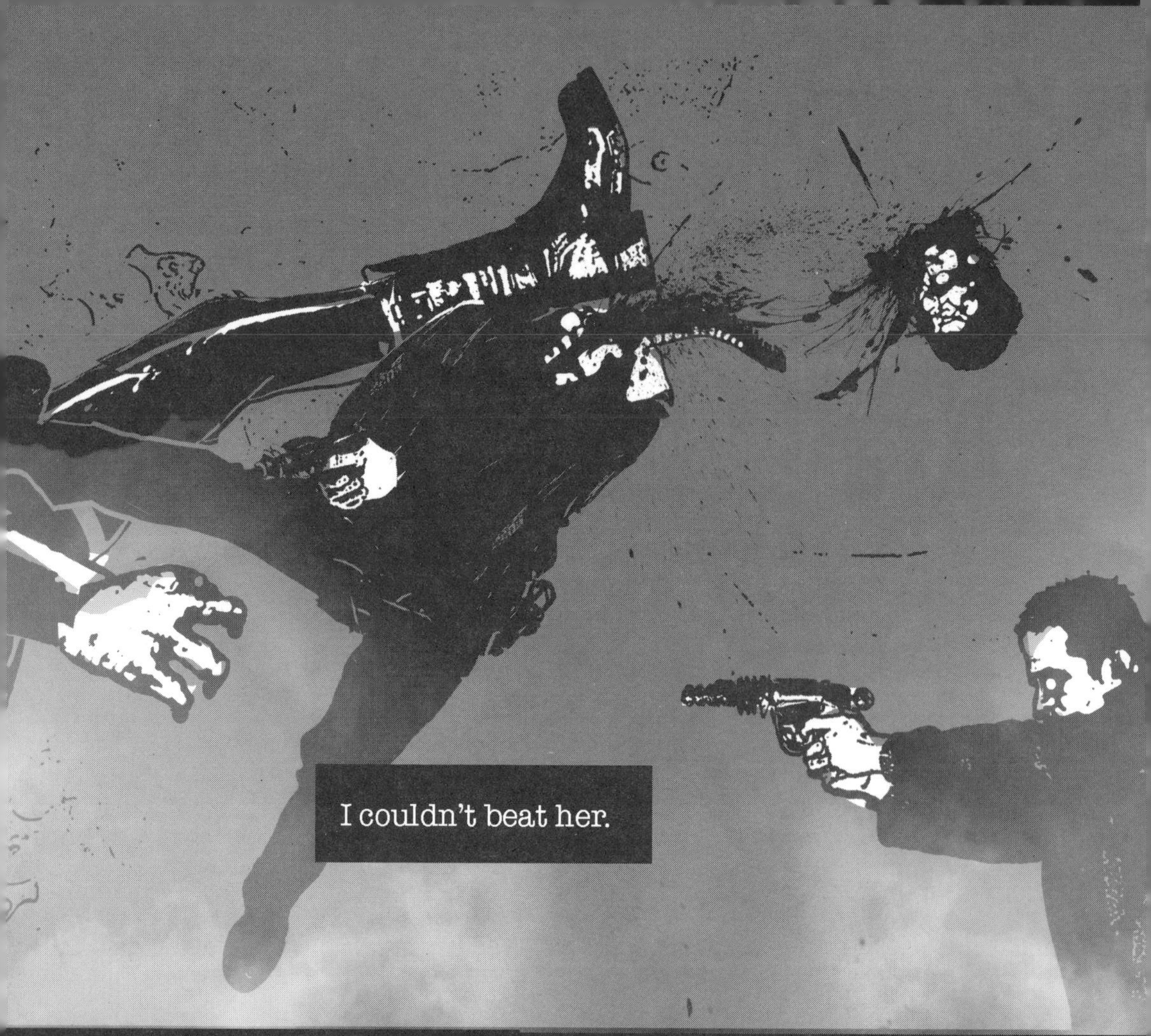
I couldn't beat her.

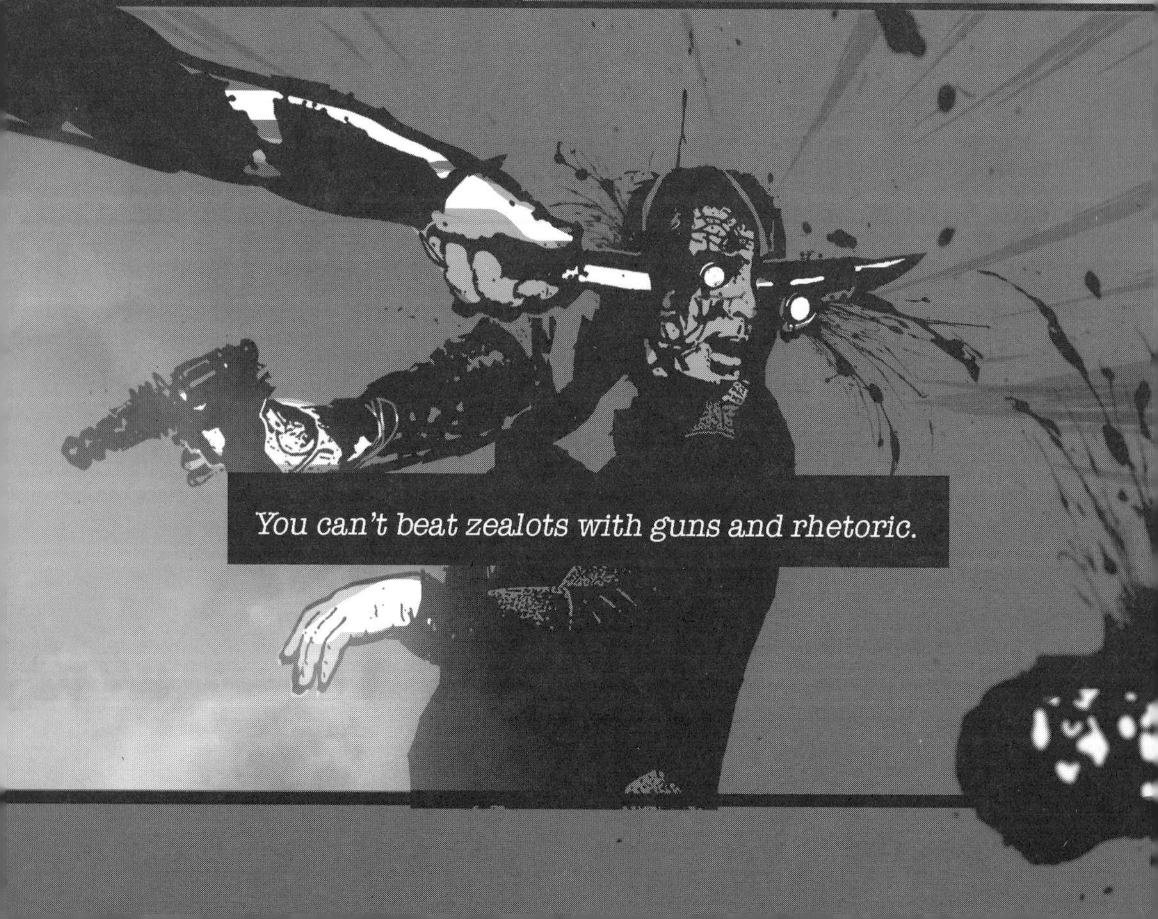
You can't beat zealots with guns and rhetoric.

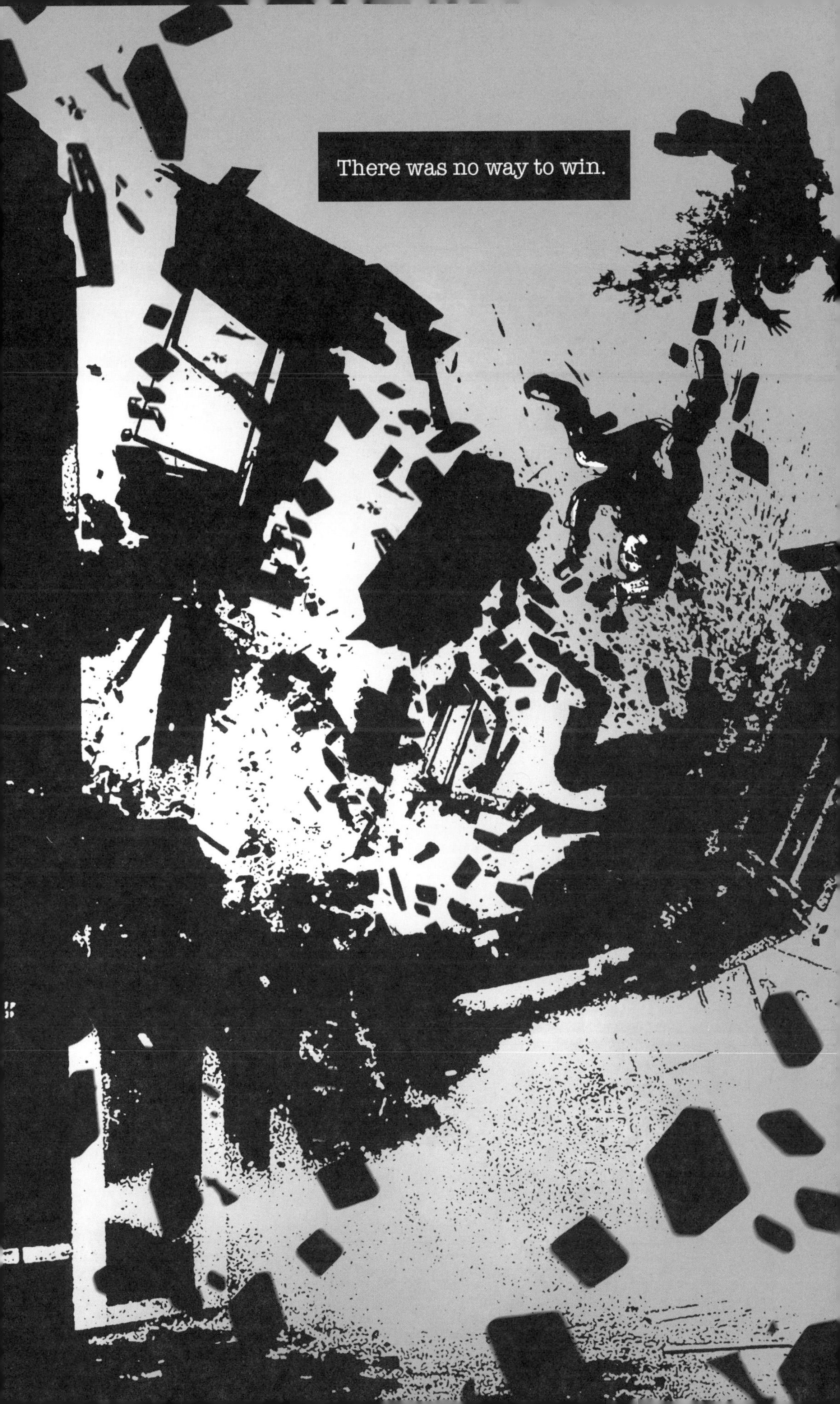
There was no way to win.

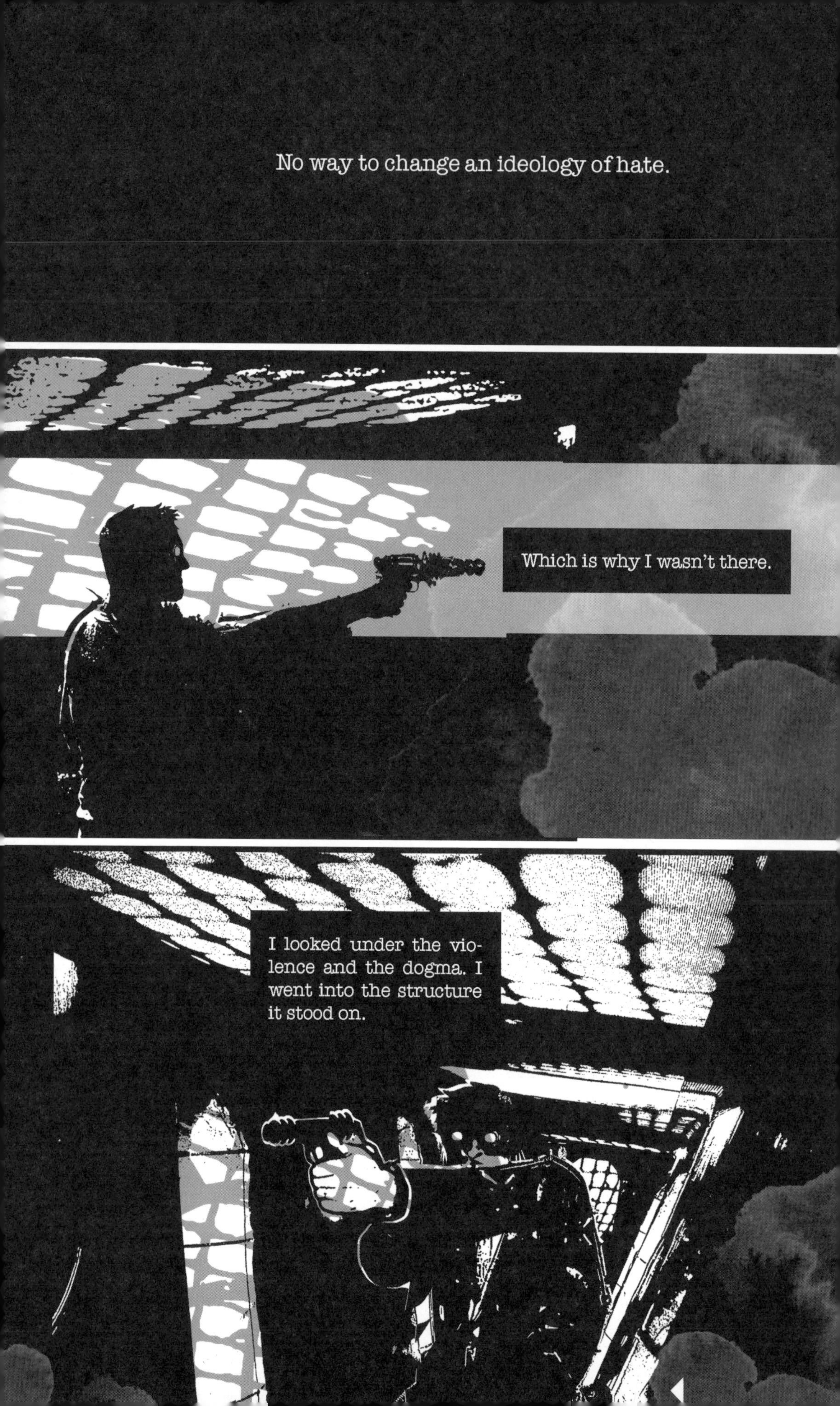
No way to change an ideology of hate.
Which is why I wasn't there.
I looked under the violence and the dogma. I went into the structure it stood on.

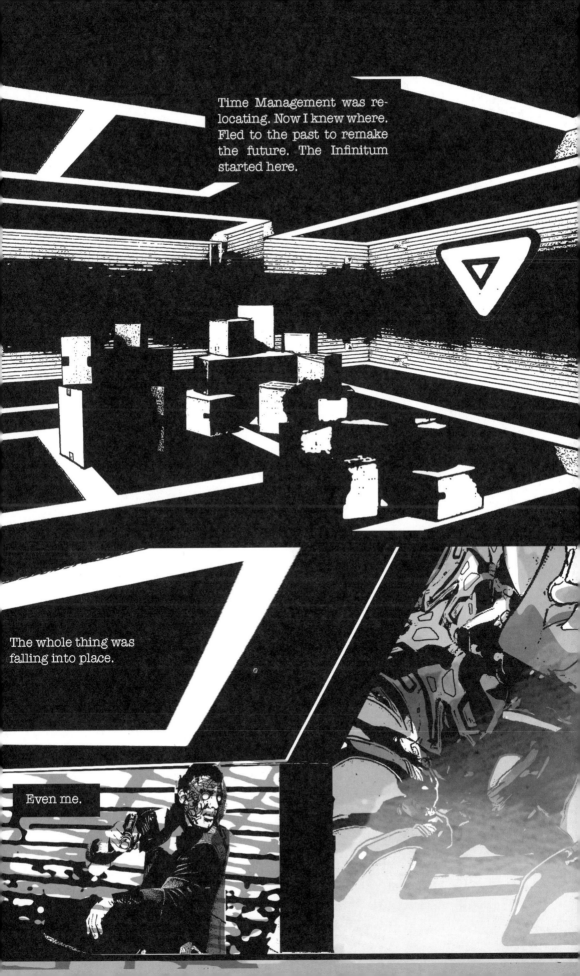

Time Management was re-locating. Now I knew where. Fled to the past to remake the future. The Infinitum started here.

The whole thing was falling into place.

Even me.

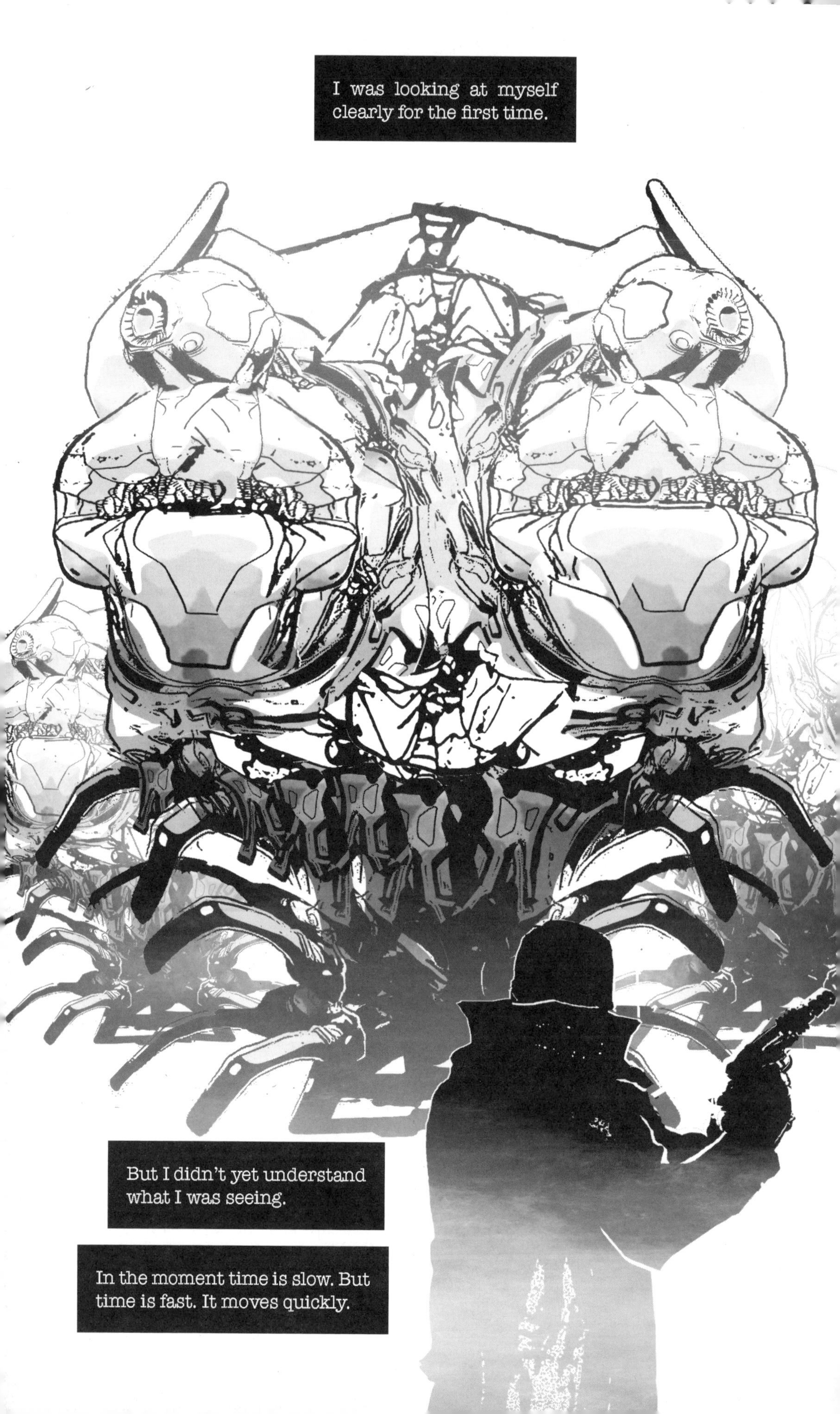
I was looking at myself clearly for the first time.
But I didn't yet understand what I was seeing.
In the moment time is slow. But time is fast. It moves quickly.

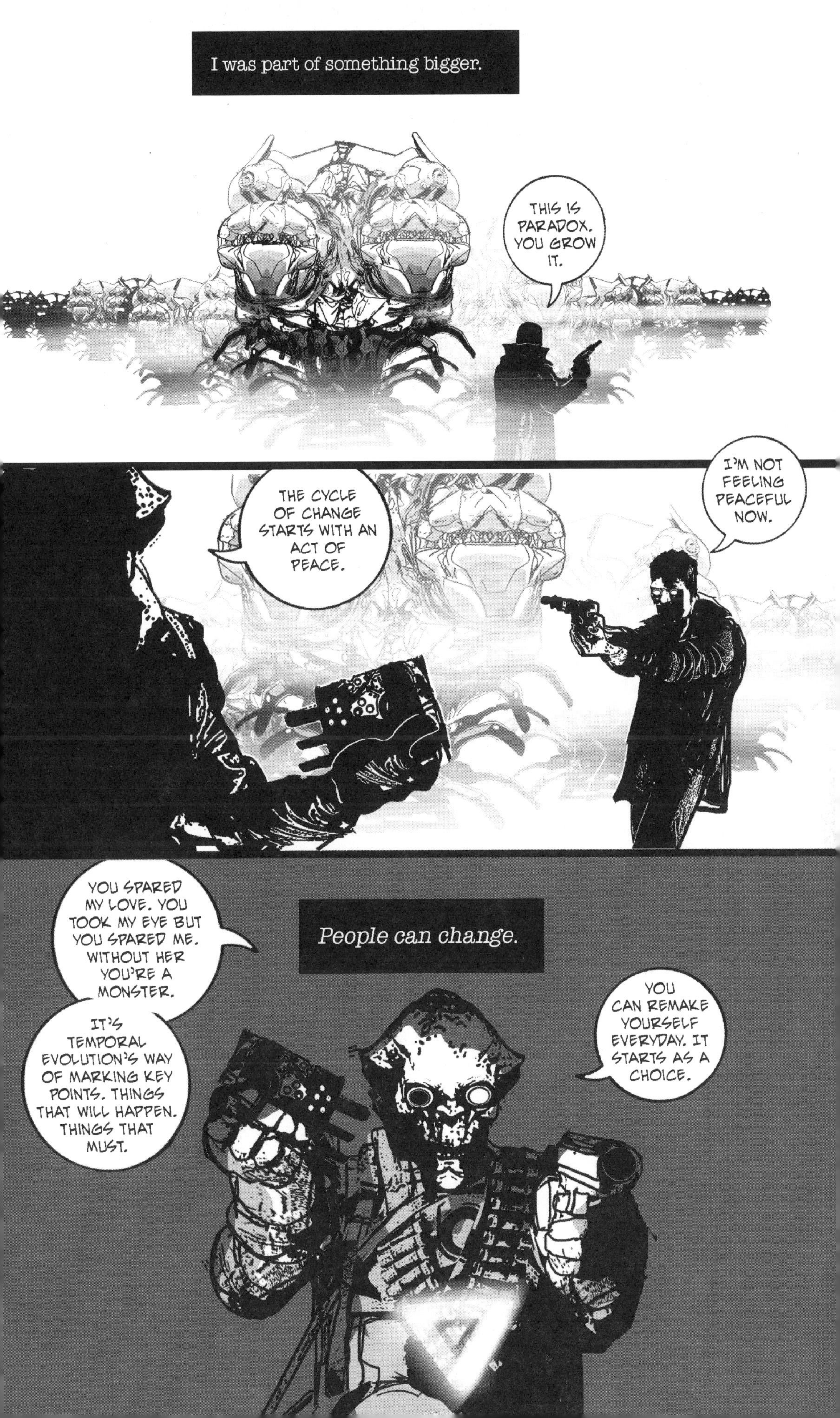
I was part of something bigger.
THIS IS PARADOX. YOU GROW IT.
THE CYCLE OF CHANGE STARTS WITH AN ACT OF PEACE.
I'M NOT FEELING PEACEFUL NOW.
YOU SPARED MY LOVE. YOU TOOK MY EYE BUT YOU SPARED ME. WITHOUT HER YOU'RE A MONSTER.
IT'S TEMPORAL EVOLUTION'S WAY OF MARKING KEY POINTS. THINGS THAT WILL HAPPEN. THINGS THAT MUST.
People can change.
YOU CAN REMAKE YOURSELF EVERYDAY. IT STARTS AS A CHOICE.

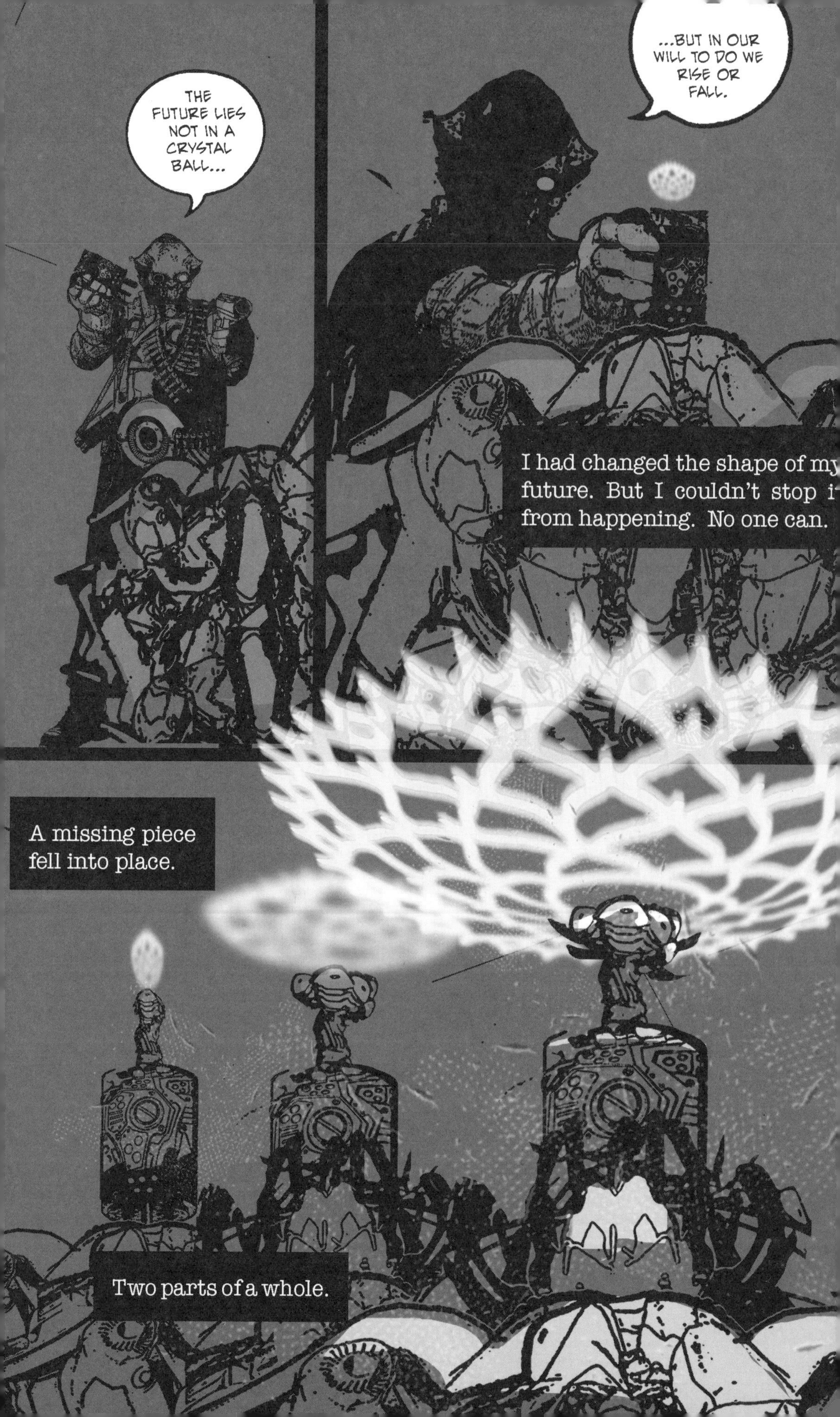
THE FUTURE LIES NOT IN A CRYSTAL BALL...
...BUT IN OUR WILL TO DO WE RISE OR FALL.
I had changed the shape of my future. But I couldn't stop it from happening. No one can.
A missing piece fell into place.
Two parts of a whole.

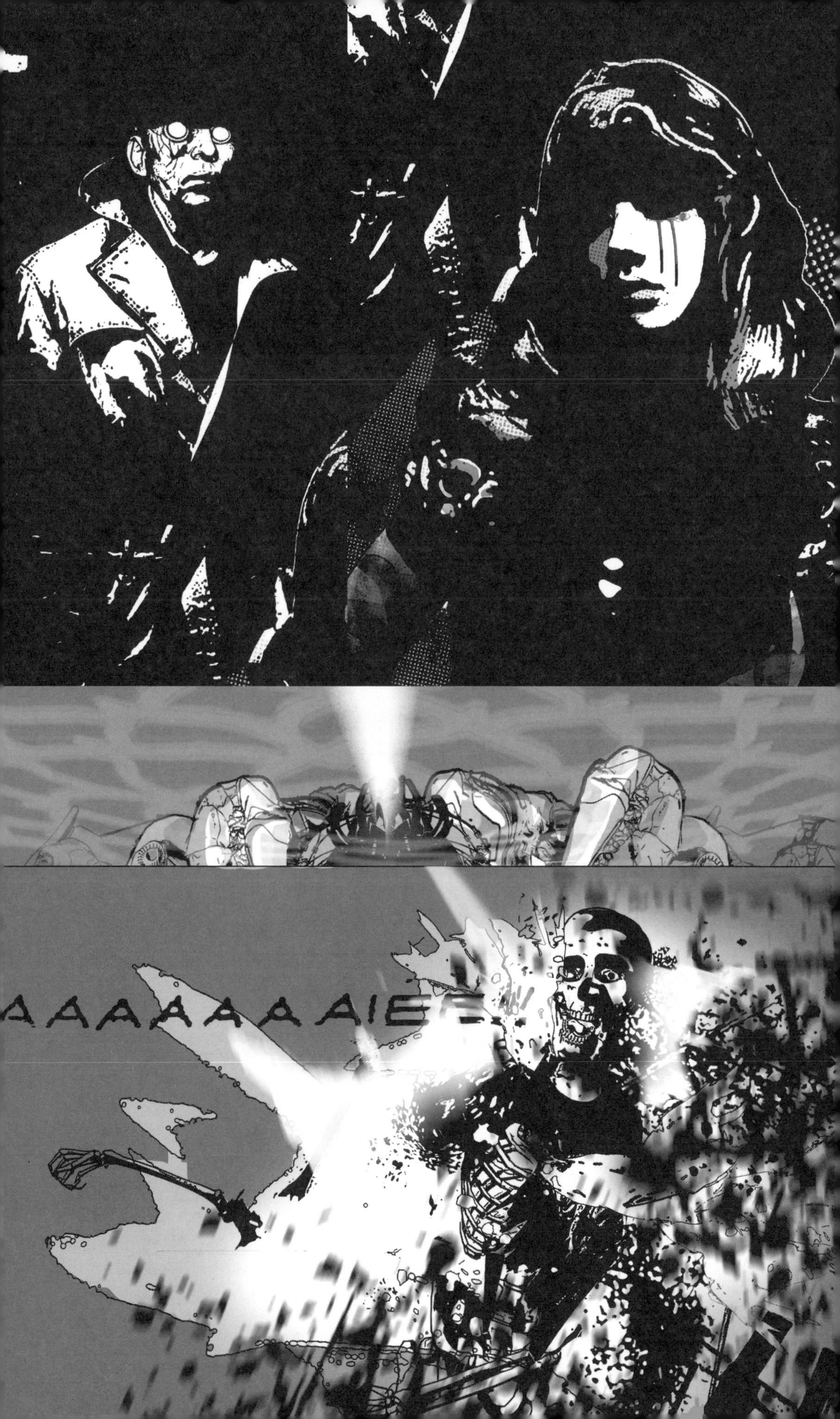

AAAAAAAIEE

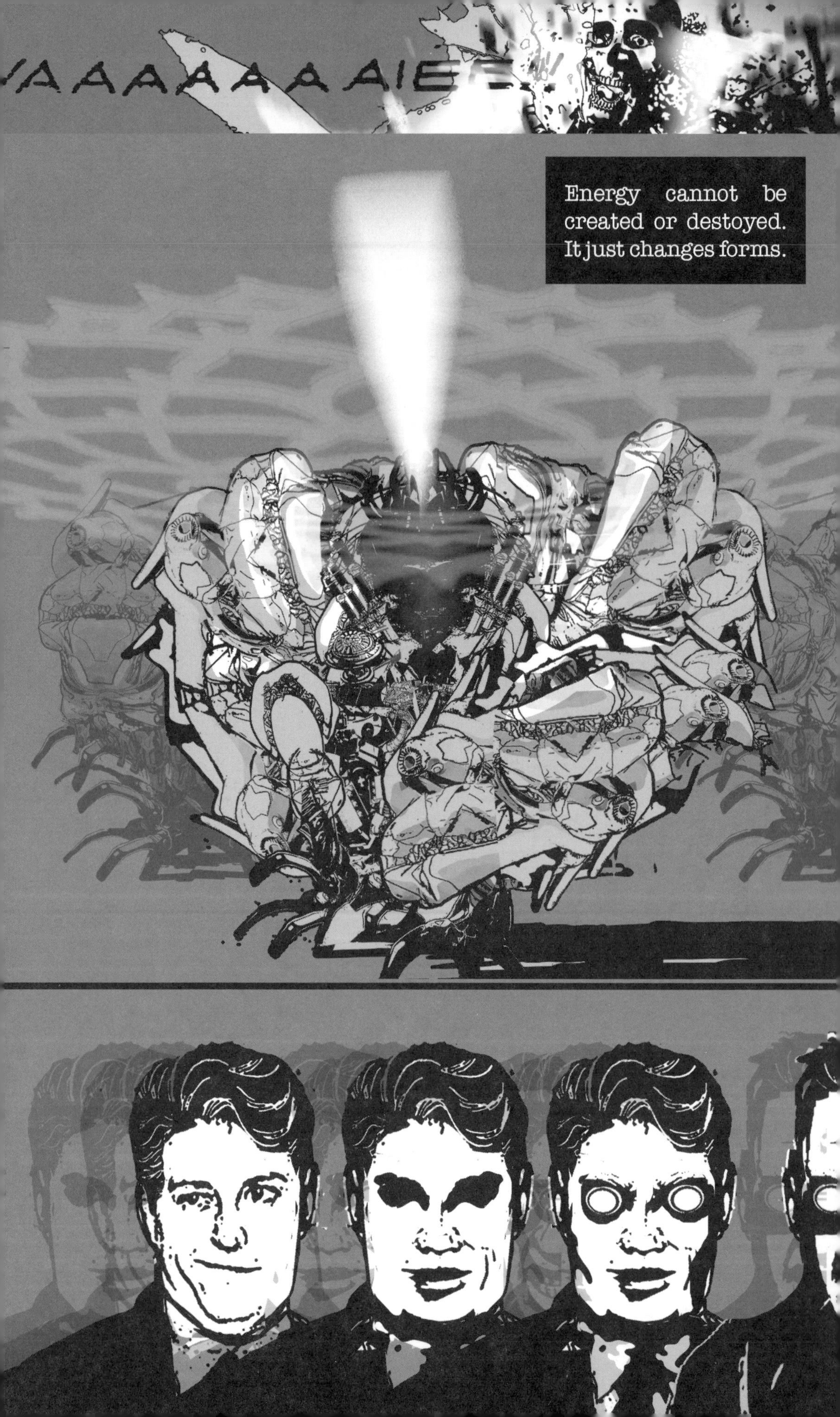
AAAAAAAAIEE
Energy cannot be created or destoyed. It just changes forms.

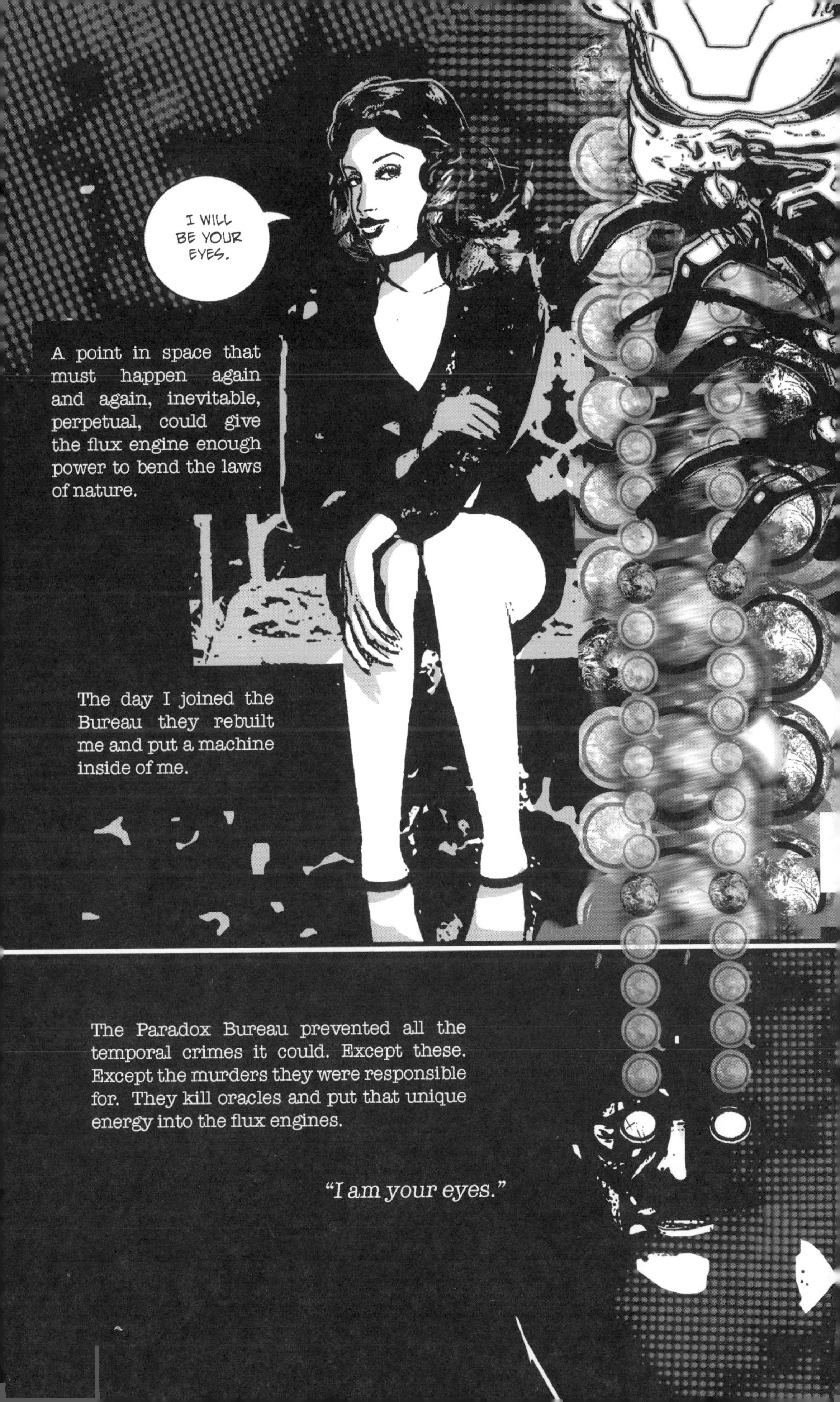
I WILL BE YOUR EYES.
A point in space that must happen again and again, inevitable, perpetual, could give the flux engine enough power to bend the laws of nature.
The day I joined the Bureau they rebuilt me and put a machine inside of me.
The Paradox Bureau prevented all the temporal crimes it could. Except these. Except the murders they were responsible for. They kill oracles and put that unique energy into the flux engines.
"I am your eyes."

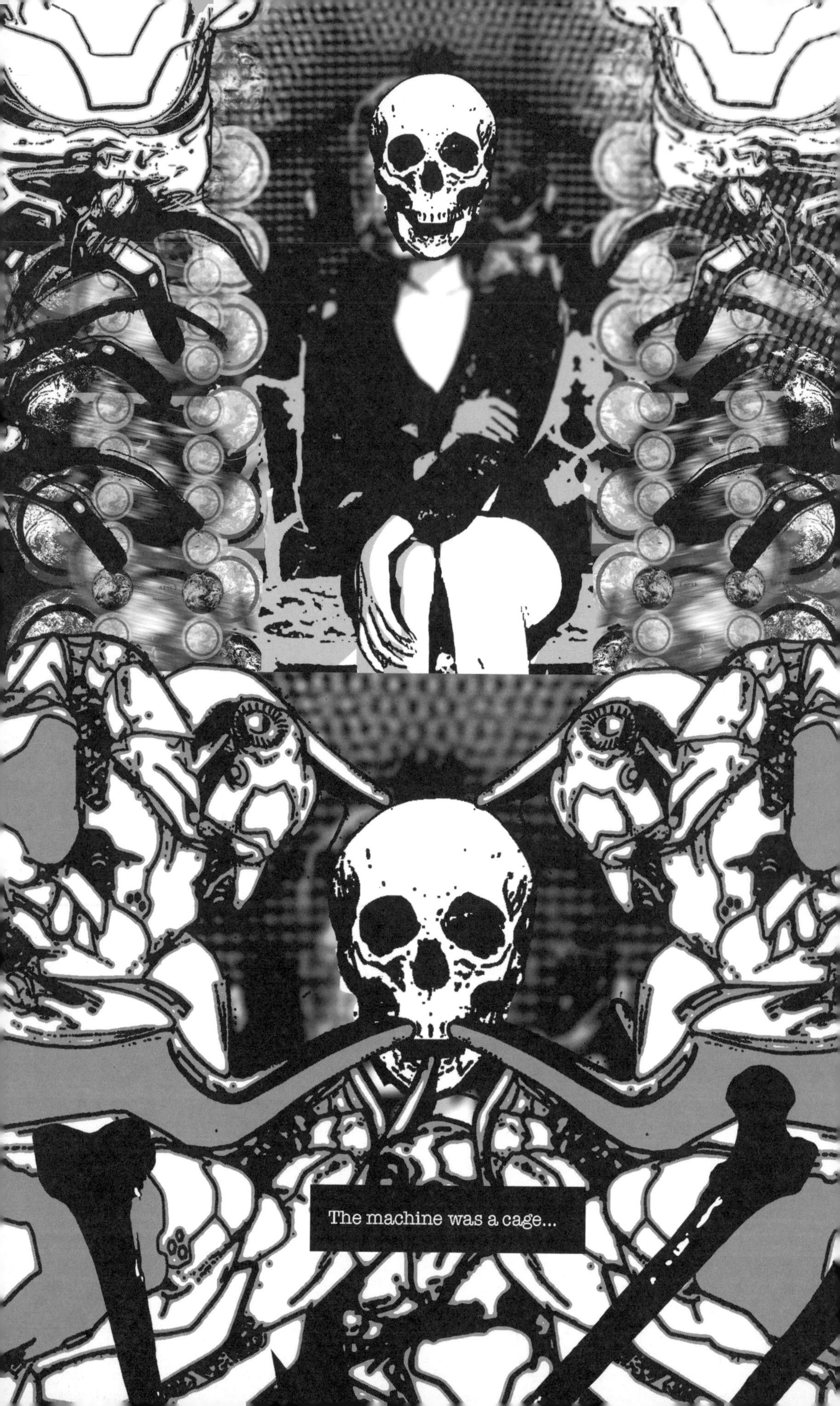
The machine was a cage...

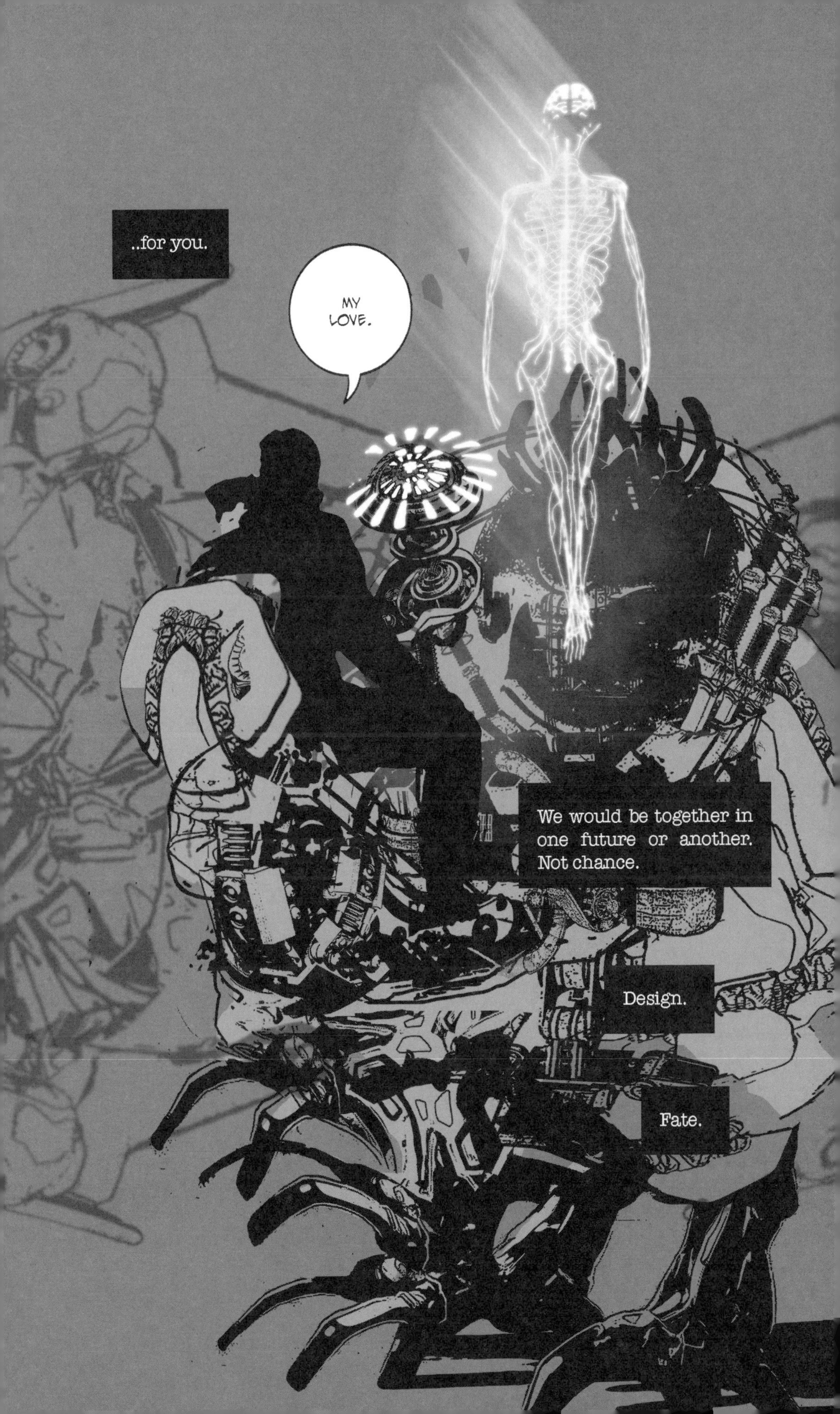
..for you.
MY LOVE.
We would be together in one future or another. Not chance.
Design.
Fate.

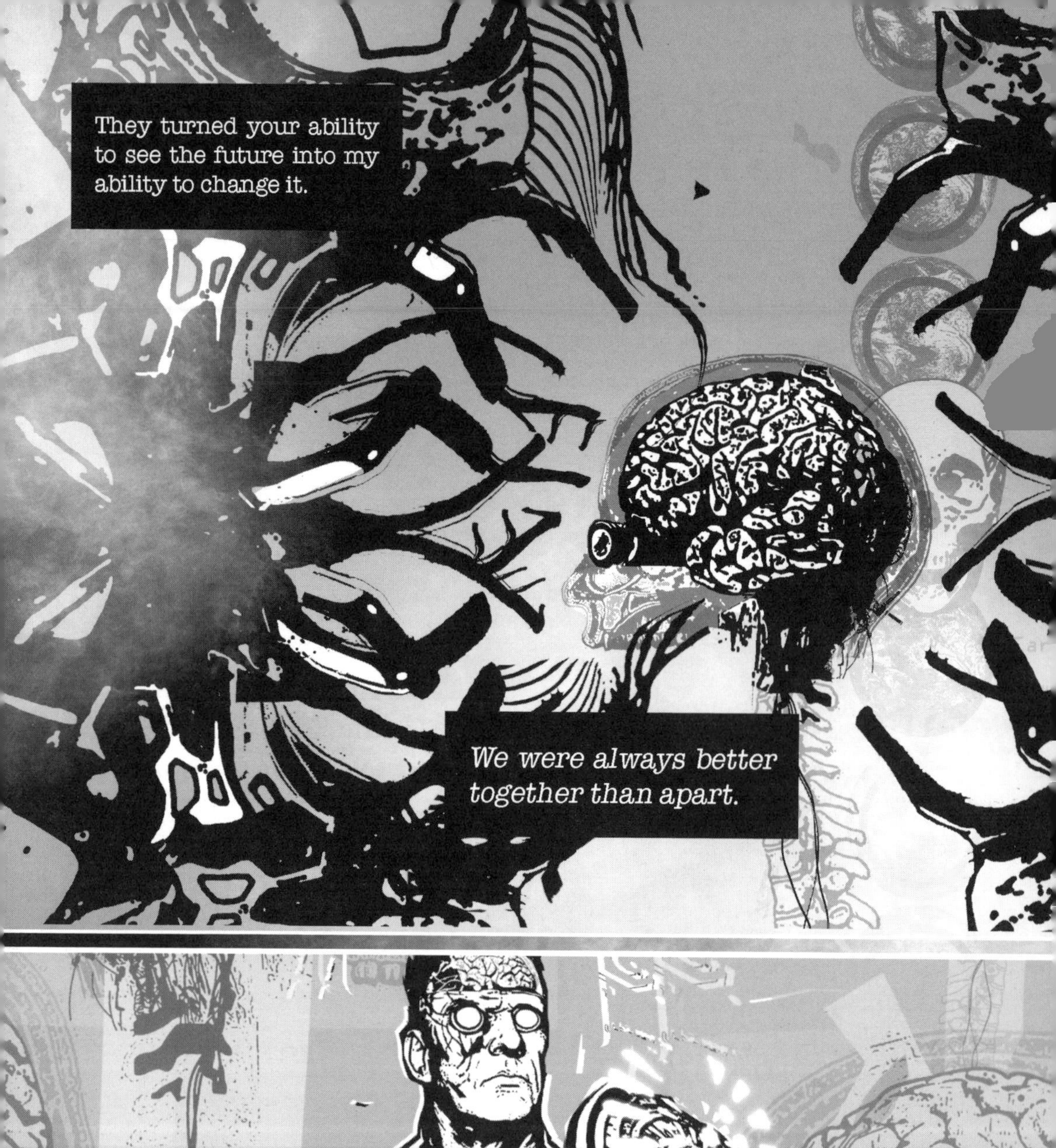
They turned your ability to see the future into my ability to change it.
We were always better together than apart.
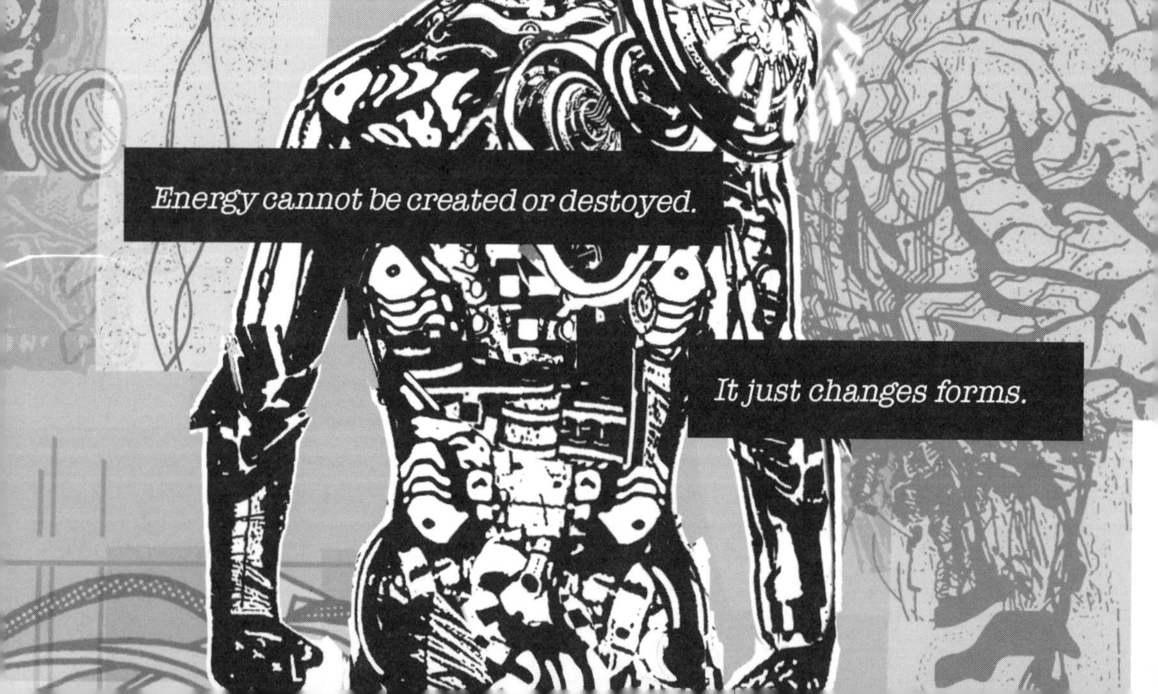
Energy cannot be created or destoyed.
It just changes forms.

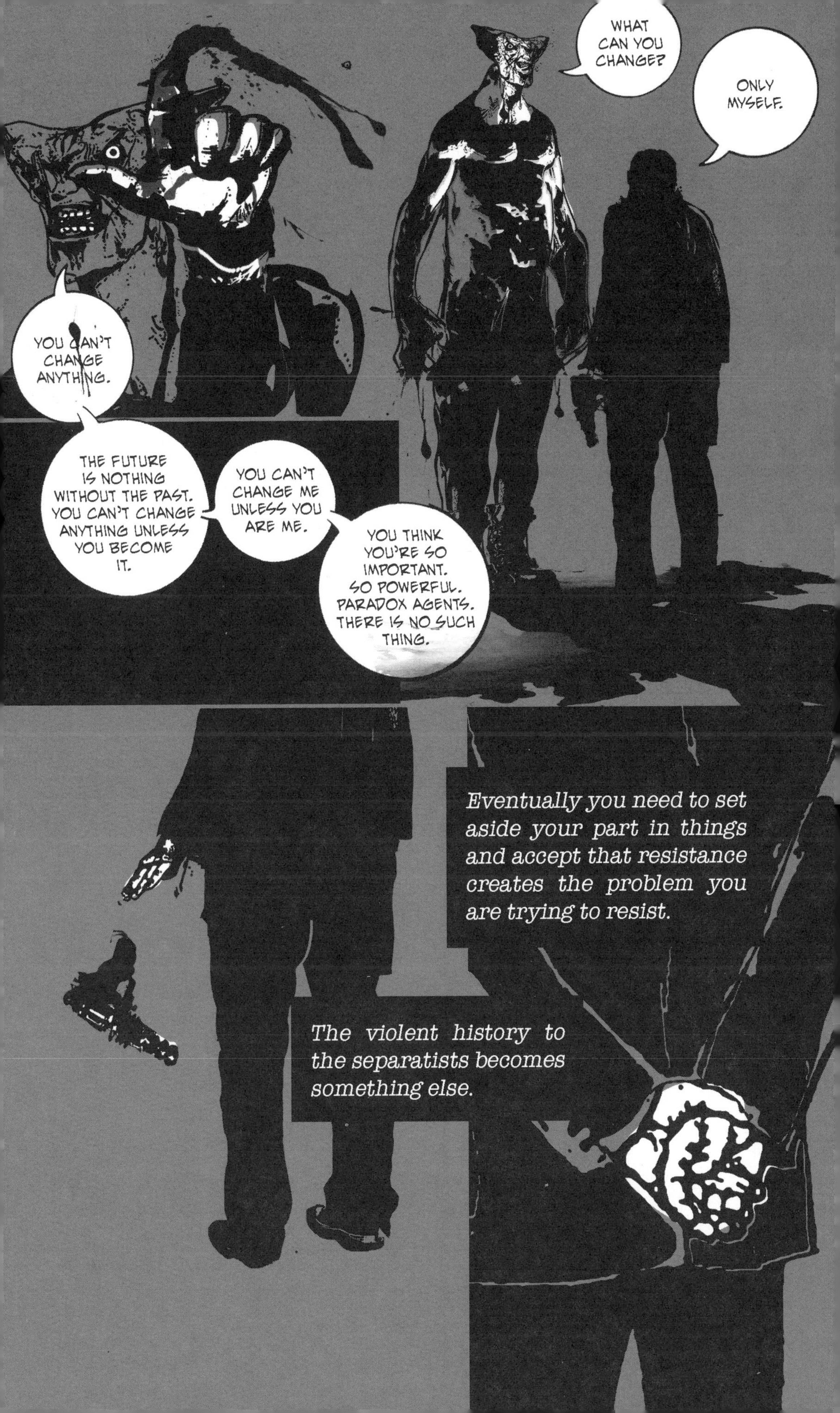
WHAT CAN YOU CHANGE?
ONLY MYSELF.
YOU CAN'T CHANGE ANYTHING.
THE FUTURE IS NOTHING WITHOUT THE PAST. YOU CAN'T CHANGE ANYTHING UNLESS YOU BECOME IT.
YOU CAN'T CHANGE ME UNLESS YOU ARE ME.
YOU THINK YOU'RE SO IMPORTANT. SO POWERFUL. PARADOX AGENTS. THERE IS NO SUCH THING.
Eventually you need to set aside your part in things and accept that resistance creates the problem you are trying to resist.
The violent history to the separatists becomes something else.

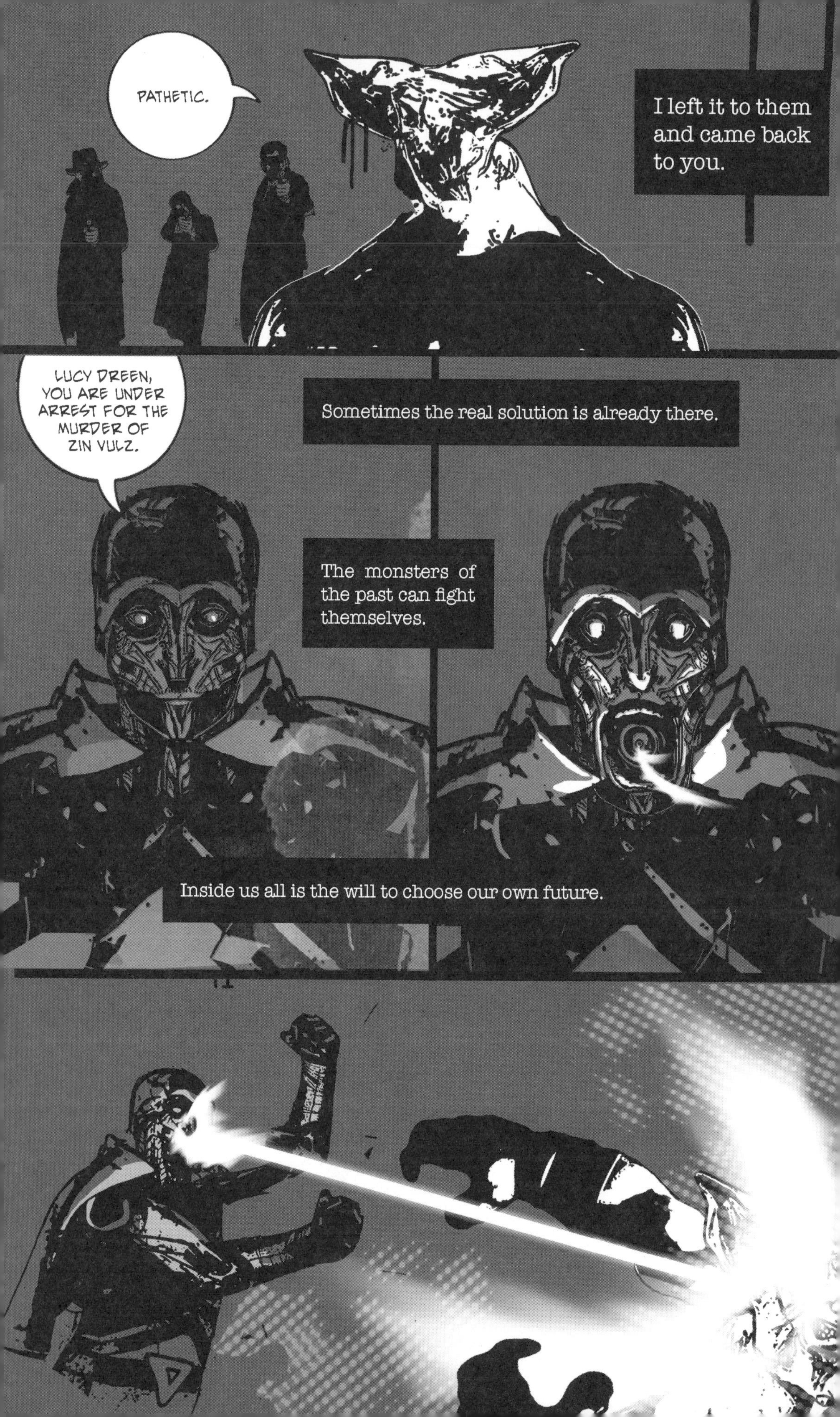
PATHETIC.
I left it to them and came back to you.
LUCY DREEN, YOU ARE UNDER ARREST FOR THE MURDER OF ZIN VULZ.
Sometimes the real solution is already there.
The monsters of the past can fight themselves.
Inside us all is the will to choose our own future.

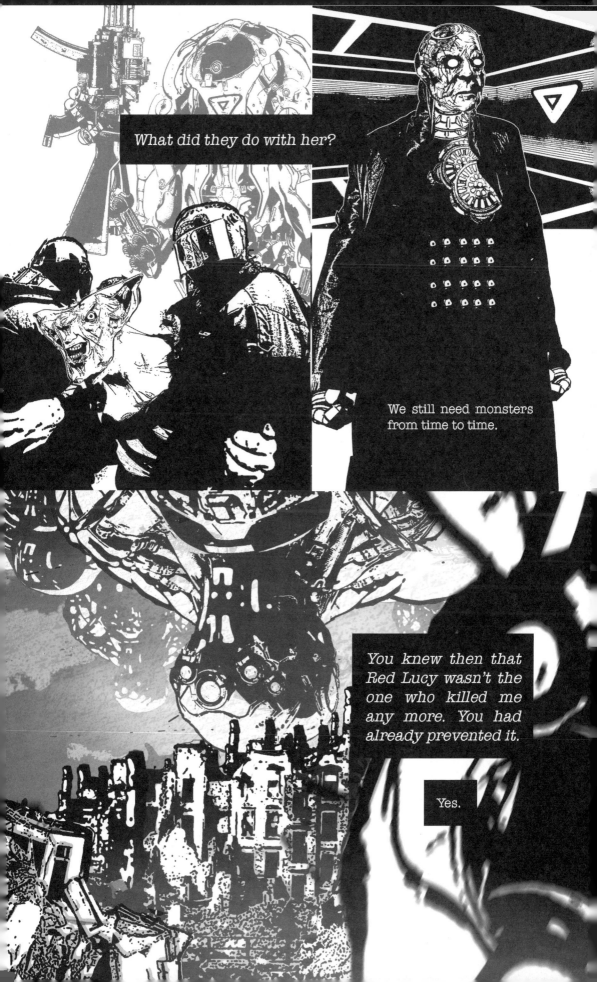

What did they do with her?

We still need monsters from time to time.

You knew then that Red Lucy wasn't the one who killed me any more. You had already prevented it.

Yes.

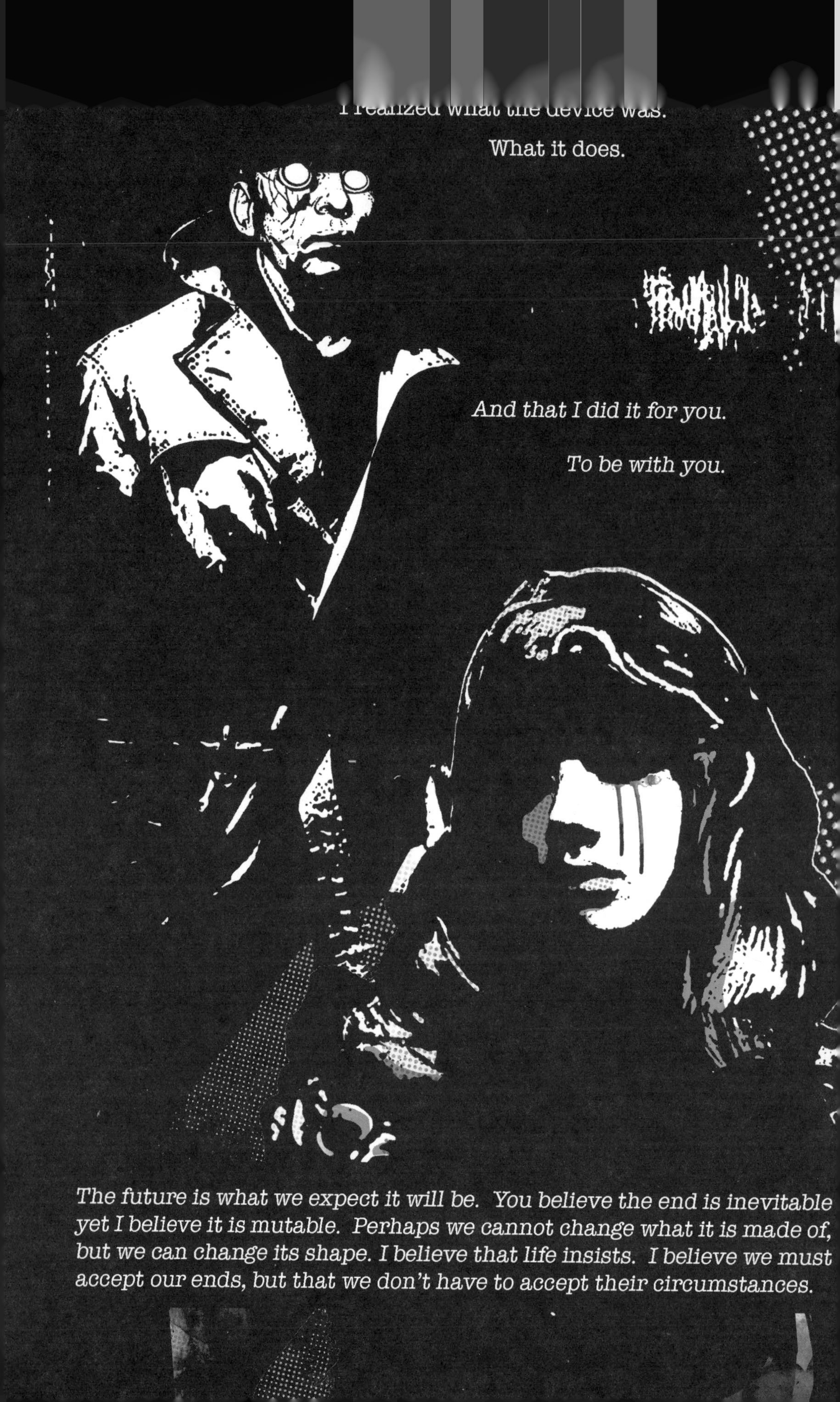
I realized what the device was.
What it does.
And that I did it for you.
To be with you.
The future is what we expect it will be. You believe the end is inevitable yet I believe it is mutable. Perhaps we cannot change what it is made of, but we can change its shape. I believe that life insists. I believe we must accept our ends, but that we don't have to accept their circumstances.

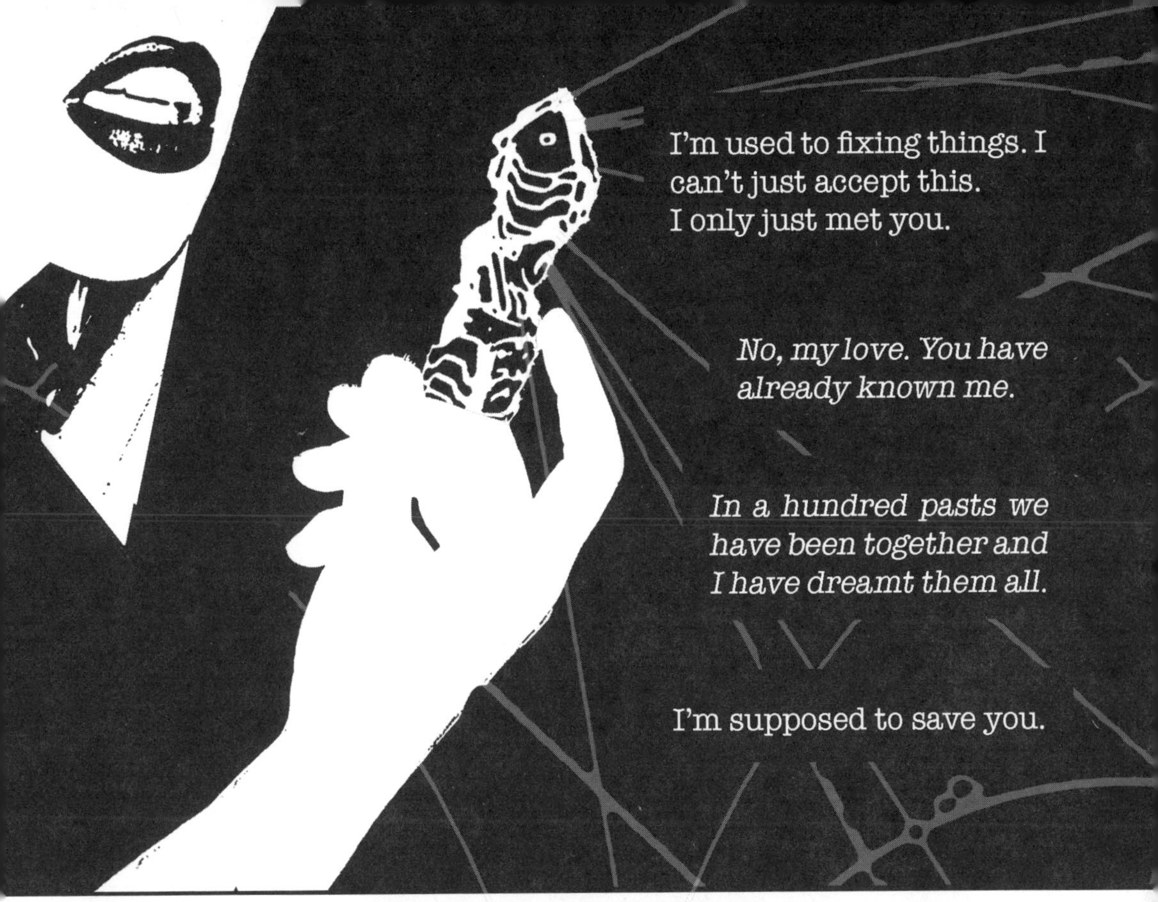
I'm used to fixing things. I can't just accept this. I only just met you.
No, my love. You have already known me.
In a hundred pasts we have been together and I have dreamt them all.
I'm supposed to save you.

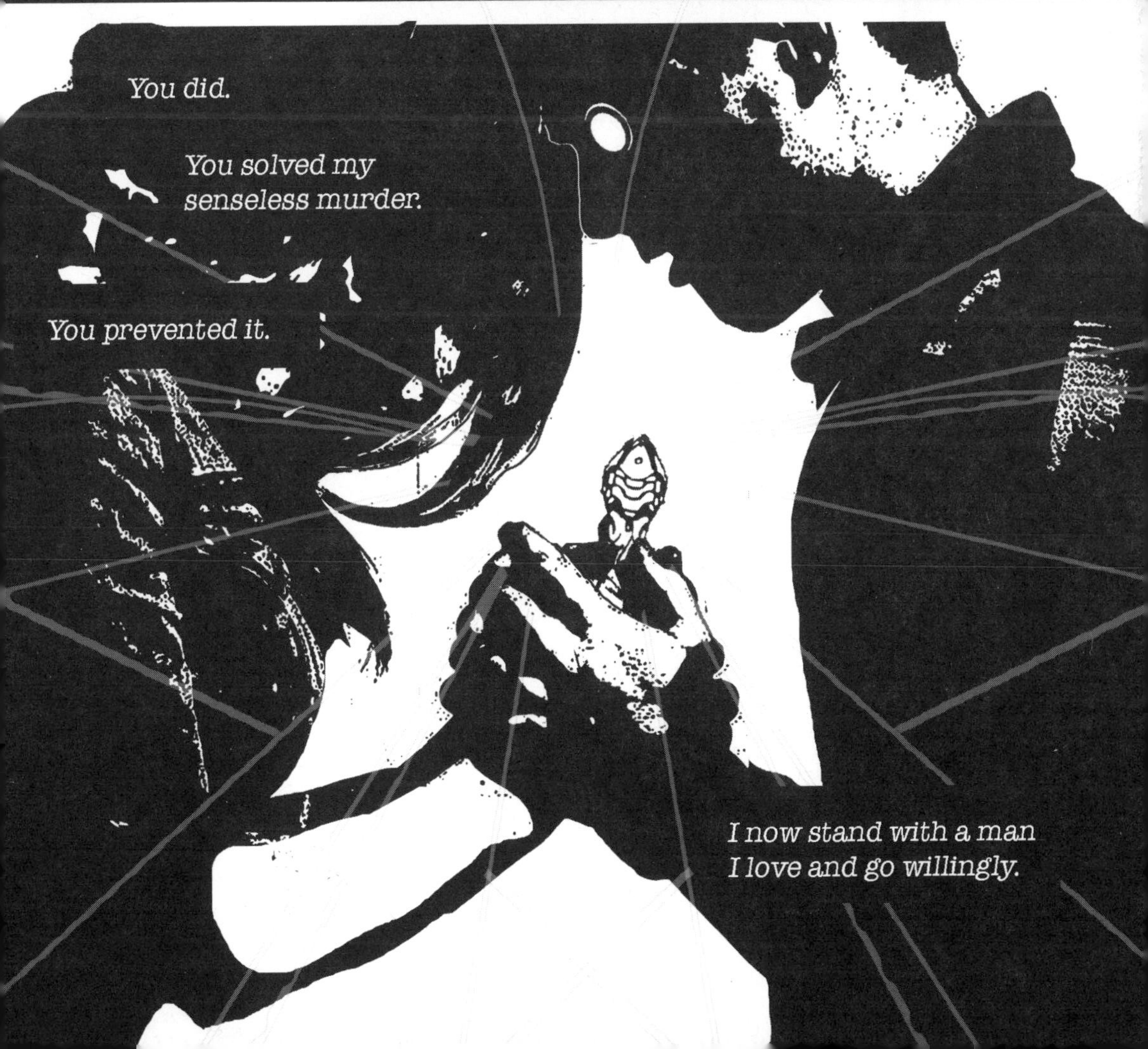
You did.
You solved my senseless murder.
You prevented it.
I now stand with a man I love and go willingly.

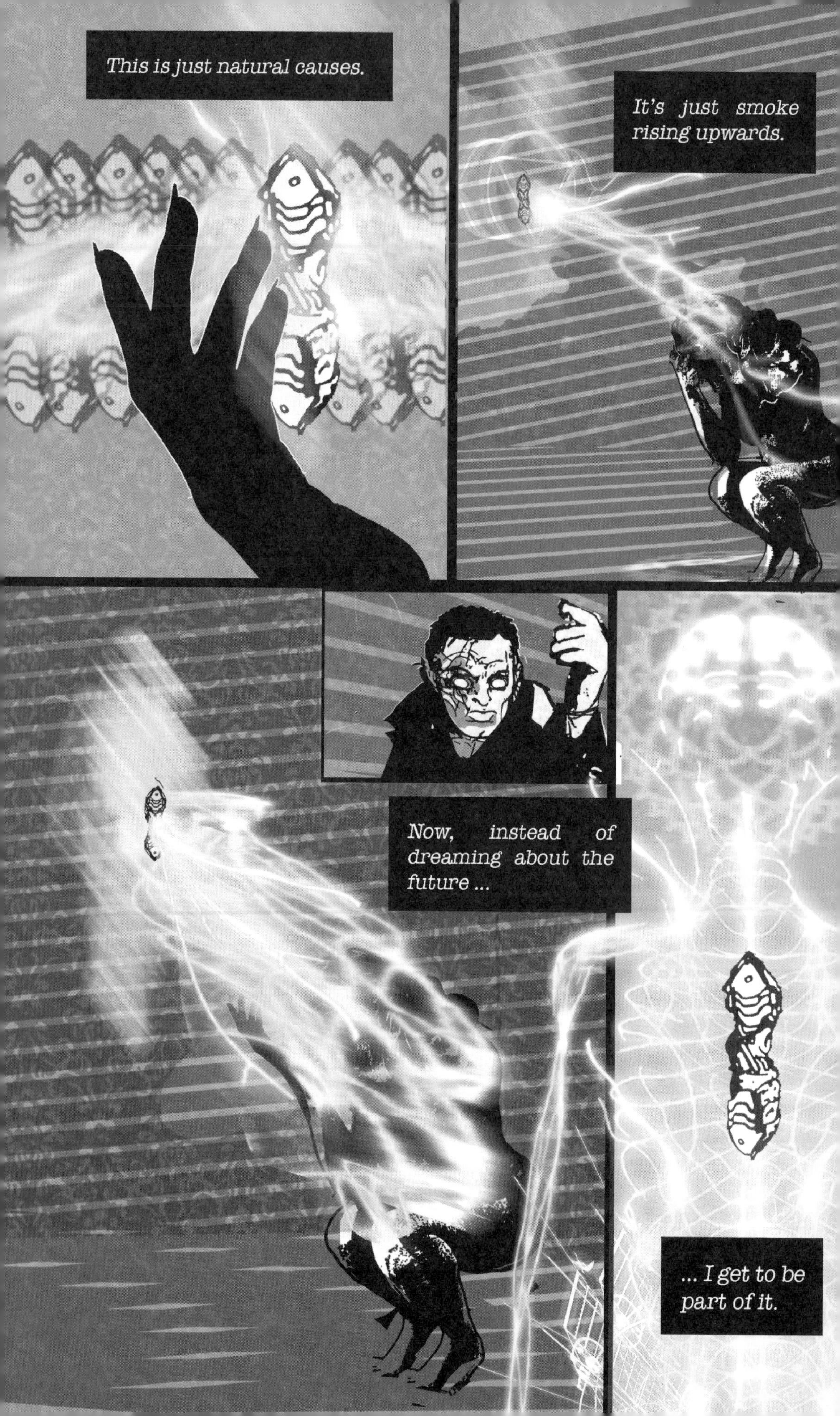
This is just natural causes.
It's just smoke rising upwards.
Now, instead of dreaming about the future ...
... I get to be part of it.

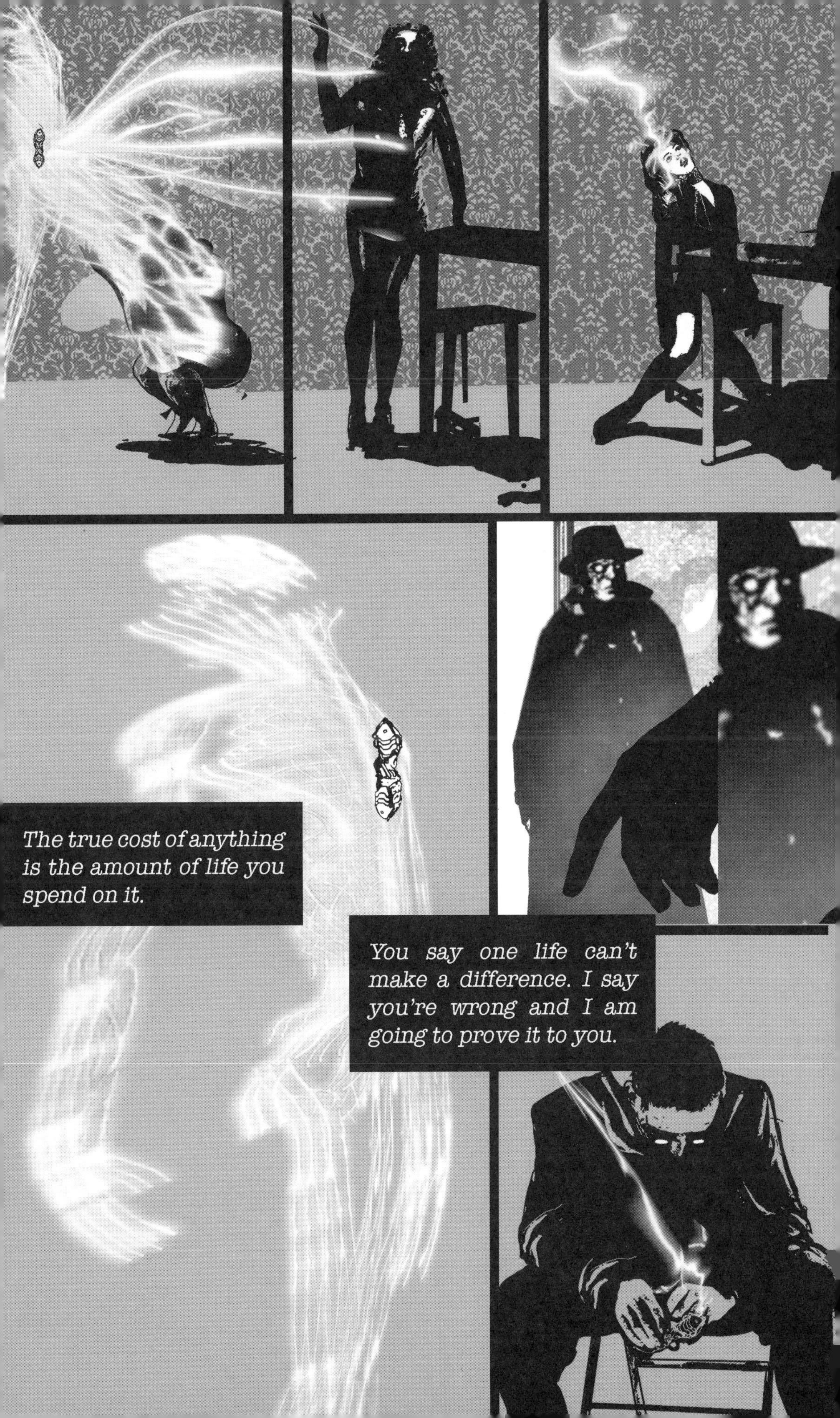
The true cost of anything is the amount of life you spend on it.
You say one life can't make a difference. I say you're wrong and I am going to prove it to you.

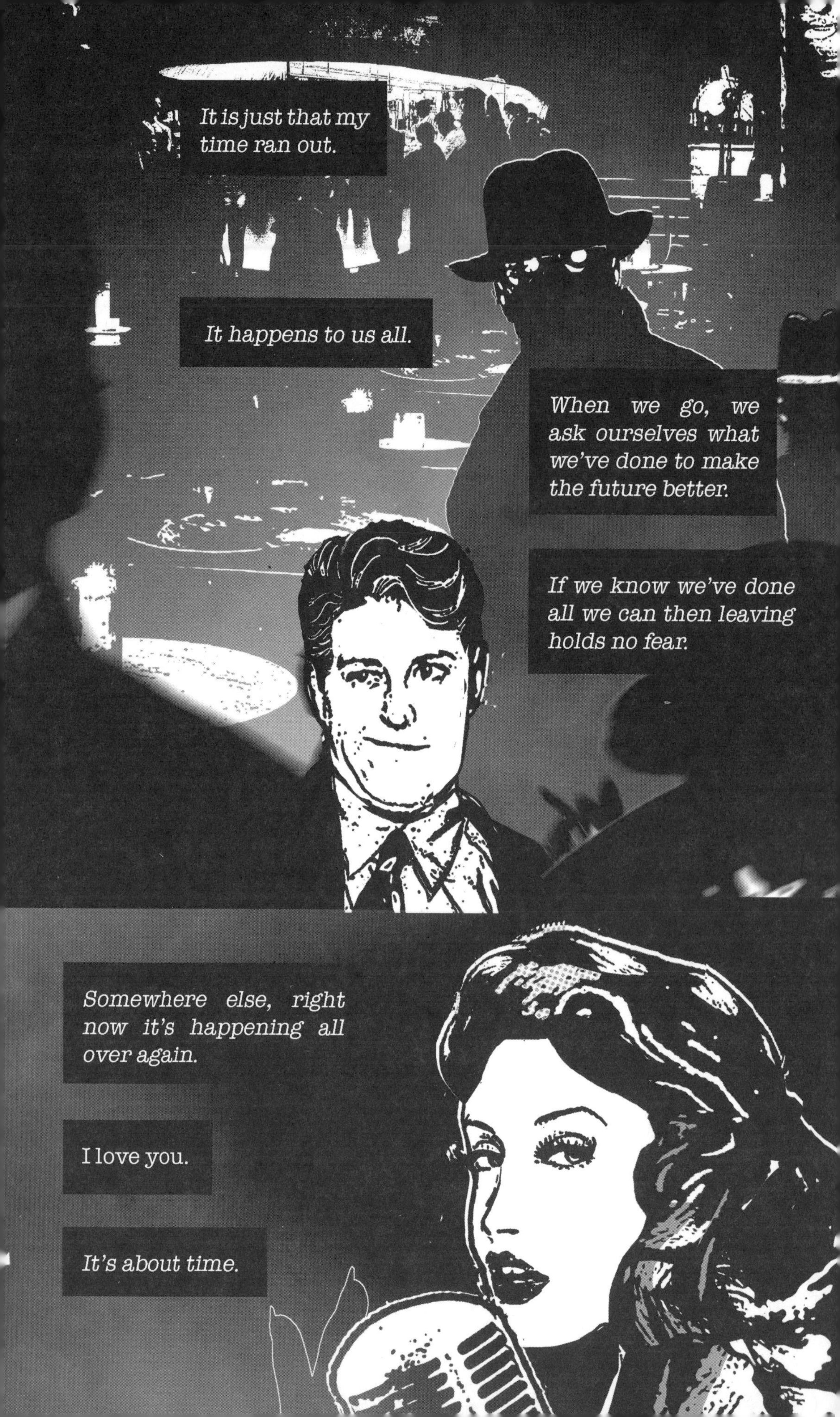

It is just that my time ran out.
It happens to us all.
When we go, we ask ourselves what we've done to make the future better.
If we know we've done all we can then leaving holds no fear.
Somewhere else, right now it's happening all over again.
I love you.
It's about time.

AFTERWORD.

My Mom was feeling stronger that day and had asked, rather uncharacteristically, to watch TV.

Everything modern that was on that night just wasn't right somehow. Too loud, too crass, too fast. Then there it was: *The Time Machine* starring Rod Taylor. We left it there. It was classic movie night suddenly, the family gathered around the TV. The pleasant decor, the good company, the conversation, all of it lent itself to a thin illusion. Except for the nurses, you could almost believe everything was normal.

Time travel stories are a unique form of wish-crafting. None of us said it, but we all knew what we'd use a time machine for if you had given anyone in that room a moment to clutch at the impossible.

Just as the Morlocks made themselves known Mom needed to escape. All of us wanted to take her up in our arms and take her anywhere but reality.

I, too, had a time travel story that I very much wanted to share with Mom. One I knew she'd like. It was her after all that had nurtured my love of genre. A story that went its twisty way round to the beginning. If things were as they should have been, I'd send it to her. I knew she'd get halfway through it and send me an e-mail with questions. I knew she'd send me one at the end and tell me what parts made her feel what ways. When I visited her, when her grand kids were asleep and there was fire going , she'd ask about the process of creating the story. She'd want details. Time was on my mind. She didn't have much left and she'd never see the story, because it wasn't finished.

Mom had been my first reader, as mothers tend to be, but she'd stayed on my first reader list well beyond those scratched-out kid stories. She understood the power of stories to take you places.

I lived at the hospital on and off for five weeks. People say that books can be an escape. In a way that's what the final draft of this one was for me. I worked in tiny sips, there was just too much happening, too much at stake in those strange days to let even a story I was making take me away very far.

I didn't want to risk missing a single word, a single conversation, a single held hand or promise between her longer and longer periods of sleep. I had a deadline. How I hated the very nature of that word. It was so empty compared to the real mortality I was a part of.

My father kept a near constant vigil. He searched out every possible solution. He used every resource. He is a man used to fixing things. This he couldn't fix. He offered to take her place in the way that only love can make you do. An impossible wish in an impossible situation.

I wrote the final words of the final draft of *Infinitum* only a few hours before Mom gave us her final wishes. She was so strong, possessed of a powerful will. She looked her future right in the eye and didn't blink. The determination of life, winning out against the futility of her own end. I was so proud of her.

Here then is *Infinitum*.

A world without a future.

A woman who chooses her own end and a man who wanted to fix things.

This one is for you, Mom.

I wish you could have read it.

G.M.B. Chomichuk
Just before midnight.